# Special Praise for *Who Stole My Child?*

"A straightforward road map for the bumpy journey from adolescence to adulthood. Of particular interest is the frank discussion on the five Cs of the last stage of adolescence (eighteen to twenty-three) where parents have the least input and control. I also found the section on what to do and what to watch for when signs of substance use begin to be extremely helpful. While most youth have been taught prevention tactics in school, for many the temptation and availability is hard to resist. Parents will learn the signals of a deeper problem and be able to intervene early."

**Gloria Souhami, Director**
Travis County Attorney's Underage
Drinking Prevention Program

"Masterfully wrapped with personal and clinical wisdom embedded in the relational aspect, Pickhardt does a phenomenal job in providing parents with both conceptual and practical understandings of the joy and angst of parenting adolescents. *Who Stole My Child* provides practicable ways to strengthen the crucial parent-child relationship. It's straightforward, relatable, and rooted in insight, equipping parents to navigate the adolescent years from a place of hope and confidence."

**Laura C. Edwards, EdD**
Educational Psychologist

"Dr. Pickhardt's insights into the components of adolescence, how it affects families, and his guidance on how to maneuver through this often-confusing time is essential reading for every family."

**Charles J. Sophy, DO, FACN**

Los Angeles Family Services

"An excellent, helpful book. For any parent navigating the bewildering, turbulent, and often uncharted territory of parenting a teenager, this book is like holding hands with a warm and reassuring friend who has been there, done that, and always knows exactly what to do next. Dr. Pickhardt gives practical guidelines to address the everyday situations parents encounter, as well as effective strategies for handling the really difficult situations that sometimes develop with older teens. With gentle, clear, and calming advice, Dr. Pickhardt helps parents understand the 'why' of adolescent behavior while also providing the words to use in real-life examples."

**Jane Guenther Parent**
Senior Editor
*Your Teen Magazine*


"Carl Pickhardt is a brilliant writer and thinker with so much to offer parents, families, educators, and professionals in a variety of fields. He speaks to and writes for those concerned with the well-being and health of emerging adolescents. Pickhardt has a way with reality and hopefulness that is needed in interactions that can feel tumultuous. His work became the cornerstone of a successful program, "All Behaviors Count," developed to help educators deal with social cruelty, described by Pickhardt as teasing, bullying, rumoring, ganging up, or exclusion from the group.

Putting caring ideas into the hands, minds, and hearts of those who work with young people is a gift that Carl Pickhardt shares widely and so well."

**Dr. Mary Lee Webeck**
Director of Education
Holocaust Museum Houston

# WHO STOLE MY CHILD?

# Who Stole My Child?

## PARENTING THROUGH THE FOUR STAGES OF ADOLESCENCE

### CARL PICKHARDT

CENTRAL RECOVERY PRESS

LAS VEGAS

**Central Recovery Press** (CRP) is committed to publishing exceptional materials addressing addiction treatment, recovery, and behavioral healthcare topics.

For more information, visit www.centralrecoverypress.com.

Publisher:   Central Recovery Press
             3321 N. Buffalo Drive
             Las Vegas, NV 89129

23 22 21 20 19 18      1 2 3 4 5


*Library of Congress Cataloging-in-Publication Data*
Names: Pickhardt, Carl E., 1939- author.
Title: Who stole my child? : parenting through the four stages of adolescence
   / Carl Pickhardt.
Description: Las Vegas, NV : Central Recovery Press, [2018]
Identifiers: LCCN 2018026177 (print) I LCCN 2018034933 (ebook) I
ISBN 9781942094845 (ebook) I ISBN 9781942094838 (pbk. : alk. paper)
Subjects: LCSH: Adolescent psychology. I Adolescence. I Parenting.
Classification: LCC BF724 (ebook) I LCC BF724 .P563 2018 (print) I DDC
   649/.125--dc23
LC record available at https://lccn.loc.gov/2018026177


Author photo by Irene Pickhardt. Used with permission.

Every attempt has been made to contact copyright holders. If copyright holders have not been properly acknowledged please contact us. Central Recovery Press will be happy to rectify the omission in future printings of this book.

**Publisher's Note:** This book contains general information about the stages of adolescence, family dynamics, and related matters. The information is not medical advice. This book is not an alternative to medical advice from your doctor or other professional healthcare provider.

Our books represent the experiences and opinions of their authors only. Every effort has been made to ensure that events, institutions, and statistics presented in our books as facts are accurate and up-to-date. To protect their privacy, the names of some of the people, places, and institutions in this book may have been changed.

*Cover by The Book Designers. Interior design by Sara Streifel, Think Creative Design.*

To my parents and stepparents,
under whose loving watch I took
my journey of growing up.

# "HANGING ON WHILE LETTING GO"

## Metaphor from a Parent

"I'll tell you what, parenting teenagers can be one wild ride! While you're hanging on so they don't get hurt, you're also letting go so they can find their way. Of course, there are times when they're determined to buck you off to show they don't need a rider anymore to reset their course or slow them down. So you can get thrown. But because you love them, even after feeling bruised and weary, you pick yourself up, climb back in the saddle, and ride them to the finish.

"'Independence' they call it. And despite little thanks for your efforts, it's a race worth running to the end, bumps and all. Because, you know, we each are only doing what both of us are meant to do."

# AUTHOR'S NOTE

The ideas and opinions about parenting adolescents contained in this book are drawn from many years of private counseling and public lecturing experience. Using personal observation and reflection, I try to conceptualize and illustrate how adolescence often changes the child, the parent in response, and the relationship between them.

I think of these changes more in terms of tendencies rather than certainties, since no one description of the adolescent passage can fit the great variety of them all. As for case examples and quotations used, these are fictional, created by me to illustrate key psychological points. Any resemblance to actual persons or life situations past or present is purely coincidental.

# TABLE OF CONTENTS

PART FOUR: Issues in Late Adolescence
(Ages Fifteen to Eighteen)

## Acting More Grown-Up

PART FIVE: Issues in Trial Independence
(Ages Eighteen to Twenty-Three)

## Stepping Off More on One's Own

PART SIX: Special Cases

## Factors That Can Intensify Adolescence

# ACKNOWLEDGMENTS

Thanks to the editors at *Psychology Today* for continuing to publish my weekly blog, *Surviving (Your Child's) Adolescence*. For many years they have given me a forum for developing, posting, and circulating my emerging notions about the endless challenges of parenting teenagers to a wide internet audience.

Thanks to my agent, Grace Freedson, for continuing to find publishers for my nonfiction books.

Thanks to my wife, Irene, who lovingly lives with a man who spends so much time happily playing in the world of his ideas.

And lastly (but most importantly) special thanks to the many dedicated parents and young people whose struggles, with themselves and each other, have taught me so much about the harder and more challenging half of child-rearing called growing up, coming of age, or adolescence. Onward!

# Why This Book?

"A few months ago I was living with this delightful little kid who was delighted with me; but now she's changed! Who stole my child?"

Why this book? The short answer is that I believe most parents aren't ready for how the relationship with their child changes when he or she enters adolescence. Consider three common examples: First, having been used to a physically affectionate child, parents can have some adjustment to do with an adolescent who doesn't want to be cuddled anymore and only reluctantly accepts a hug. Second, the child who once kept parents well informed now becomes the adolescent who tells them much less. Third, the parent who could do little wrong in the admiring eyes of his or her child finds he or she can't do many things right as far as the more critical adolescent is concerned. Who stole their child, indeed!

What's going on? As parenting began to feel different, one mother reflected, "It's so hard to accept that they are growing up when we still cherish and miss our sweet little child!" Or one father sadly invoked the famous phrase from *The Wizard of Oz* to describe his child's adolescent sudden change, "I tell you what, 'this isn't Kansas anymore!'"

Who disenchanted their child? But this "fall from favor" is mutual. As parents become less "in-love" with their less "adoring" adolescent, the adolescent becomes less captivated by less idealized parents. For both, the honeymoon of young childhood, that mutual entrancement society, is over. However, this is only a loss of infatuation; it is not a loss of abiding love.

For many who plan and picture having a family, the image they entertain is a shortsighted one: parenting a child. Yet starting around ages nine to thirteen, and ending around the early to mid-twenties, they will have an increasingly abrasive adolescent to contend with, one who is no longer just an endearing child to look after. There is so much to learn on both sides of the relationship that parenting an adolescent often seems like the shortsighted leading the blind. Most of what parents know is limited to what they have known; while the adolescent has never grown this way before. I believe that reducing ignorance can help.

Adolescence, the "harder half of parenting," comes last. In general, those parents with a low tolerance for change in relationships tend to have the hardest time adjusting to their child's adolescence, which is all about redefining on the way to growing up.

Whether starting a family early or late, this long-term parenting commitment is worth keeping in mind, as is having some general expectations of developmental changes through which the adolescent will likely pass. The best way for parents to keep up with adolescent changes is to have a set of realistic expectations that help them to stay ahead of the growth curve. "We don't like that there can be more social meanness in middle school, but at least we won't be taken by surprise should this possibility occur."

Parents may not only miss the loss of their adolescent's childhood; they can feel an ongoing loss as adolescent development continues the transformation. Growing up is not a single simple change from the past; it is also a sequence of changes going forward that requires constant adjustment. In the process, parents can feel like they are parenting a different child each stage of the way—whether it is adjusting to the more disenchanted early adolescent, to the more self-absorbed mid-adolescent, to the more risk-taking late adolescent, or to the more overwhelmed last-stage adolescent.

Knowing what developmental changes to anticipate can help. To that end, this book will descriptively and prescriptively orient parents to common adolescent changes and suggest ways to deal with them. As the Table of Contents suggests, this book is written for browsing and searching for specific ages and areas of interest and concern. It is topically organized as follows:

Part One describes How Adolescence Marks the End of Childhood (up to ages eight to nine), changing the child, the parent in response, and the relationship between them, often in unwelcome ways.

Part Two describes issues that commonly arise in Early Adolescence (ages nine to thirteen) and The Separation from Childhood.

Part Three describes issues that commonly arise in Mid-adolescence (ages thirteen to fifteen) and the complexity of Forming a Family of Friends.

Part Four describes issues that commonly arise in Late Adolescence (ages fifteen to eighteen) and the risks of Acting More Grown-Up.

Part Five describes issues that commonly arise in Trial Independence (ages eighteen to twenty-three) and the challenge of Stepping Off More on One's Own.

Part Six describes Special Cases, four common Factors that Can Intensify Adolescent Development: parental divorce, rate of growth, having a strong-willed adolescent, and having an adolescent only child.

An Epilogue forecasts a few general issues about parenting your young adult, because "once a parent always a parent"—in various ways—as this life-long job continues.

Because there is enormous variation from child to child, when I describe the general process of adolescence and the issues that commonly arise stage by stage, I am talking about *tendencies*, not *certainties*, and matters of degree. While some changes I suggest will fit many young people, none are likely to apply to all. Adolescence is infinitely varied this way. With multiple children, parents will experience adolescence somewhat differently with each child.

And just because I believe parenting an adolescent is usually more challenging than parenting a child, none of this complexity means parents are destined to go through agony with their adolescent. They are *not*.

The popular stereotype of "the terrible teenager" is largely mythical. Roughly speaking, I believe about a third of young people grow through adolescence without making much of a ripple in family life. I call them "easy adolescents."

Another third occasionally bump up against the family structure, creating collisions that are effectively resolved at the time. I call them "average adolescents."

There is a final third, those who encounter sufficient difficulty that the relationship with parents gets painfully stuck in a hard place for a while. I call them "challenging adolescents." These are the cases that tend to come into counseling for help in getting the relationship unstuck, and to put the young person and parents back on a more constructive course.

However, if you get one "easy adolescent" you are not likely to get another. To hang in there, parents have to learn to dance with adolescent changes by leading where they can and following where they must, holding on and letting go, all the while staying caringly and communicatively connected with their teenager as adolescence gradually grows them apart, as it is meant to do.

Sometimes, in their frustration, I have heard parents ask, "Is adolescence really necessary?" For the child's mental, physical, sexual, psychological, and social development into a young adult, I believe the answer is "Yes."

Additionally, consider this: As a society we sanction and shelter adolescence in multiple ways. We have compulsory K–12 education, which is also the major source of childcare for working parents. We have child labor laws that keep children out of the adult workplace. And we make a distinction in our assignment of legal responsibility and standing, whether the individual is treated as a child, a juvenile, or an adult. For all these societal reasons, I think adolescence is here to stay.

Parenting adolescents can be perplexing because decisions can be so hard to make. For example, "To allow or not to allow"—that is the question. And no parent gets these decisions right all the time. However, this uneven performance is par for the parenting course because the young person is going to turn out as a young adult partly because of and partly in spite of whatever parents choose to do. A mixed job is the best job most parents can make of this daunting task—a human mix of strength and frailty, wisdom and stupidity, sensitivity and selfishness, good decisions and bad.

Of course, parenting is only one influence that determines adolescent growth—a lesser one, in fact, when you consider the many powerful influences they don't control, such as inherited characteristics, societal change, chance exposures, peer companionship, and personal choices the young person elects to make. In most cases, when parents give their full faith effort, the adolescent graduates from their care mostly okay, although with some personal work yet to be accomplished because all parenting is incomplete. The young person has to deal with whatever unfinished business remains, as some always does, completing the job of growing up by parenting themselves. "I still have to learn how to live within a budget," for example.

There is no perfect parent, and that is probably a good thing. After all, to be a perfect parent one would have to have a perfect child; and what loving parents would want to place that kind of pressure on their growing adolescent? As for the trial-and-error decision-making of the adolescent, growth is often two steps forward and one step back, a halting path of progress and regress to journey's end. Mistake-based education is often how most adolescents learn. Helping the teenager encounter and profit from these missteps and misdeeds, parents need to maintain a healthy perspective.

At such times it is well to remember several operating realities. Good parents have good children who will sometimes make bad choices in the normal trial-and-error process of growing up. A bad choice doesn't mean the adolescent is bad or the parent or the parenting is bad. A bad adolescent choice simply presents parents with an opportunity to help the young person learn from the error of his or her ways.

Most important: do not confuse the *process* with the *person*.

Don't blame the young person for the developmental changes of growing up. Understand, for example, that the girl or boy contesting childhood limits is likely to become more oppositional during early adolescence (approximately ages nine to thirteen). However, do hold the daughter or son accountable for how that opposition is managed.

Thus, while more arguing is to be expected, it must be respectfully and safely conducted. Hold the young person responsible for the expressive choices made.

Accept your child's need for adolescence and enjoy the privilege of helping the next generation of human life grow through the magical change of little girl into young woman or little boy into young man. In doing so, be sure to honor your daily contributions that help get this complicated transformation accomplished. After all, just because the adolescent takes your efforts for granted doesn't mean you shouldn't take credit for all the important parenting work you do. You absolutely should!

Please know that I do not have final answers to offer—just ideas from working with parents and adolescents over many years. I am simply sharing an individual vision and version of the parent/adolescent relationship. Therefore, feel free to take what ideas you like, reject what ideas you don't like, and ignore what ideas seem of no particular use. My goal is not to tell you *how* to parent teenagers, but rather to offer you my perspective on the subject to *help* you sort out and clarify best practices of your own.

## ADOLESCENCE MARKS THE END OF CHILDHOOD (UP TO AGES EIGHT TO NINE)

# CHANGES UNDERWAY

In any ongoing relationship, when one party significantly alters his or her state of behaving or believing, the other party is affected, and to some degree adjusts accordingly as change begets change.

When a child enters adolescence, not only is the young person redefining him-or herself, but the parent is also redefining his or her parenting role to cope with this transformation. This interaction is formative for each of them because adolescence grows both of them up, each maturing in the process—evolving the teenager and seasoning the adult.

So it's important to understand the full power of adolescence. It not only changes the child and the parent in response to those changes, but the relationship between them as well.

CHAPTER ONE

# Changes in the Child

"Well, how would you like it if your devoted dog began acting like a disinterested cat?"

Within us and outside of us, change is the relentless process that keeps upsetting and resetting the terms of our existence throughout our lives. It continually takes us from an old to new, same to different, known to unknown circumstance, experience, or condition. Because adolescence is one such experience of change, parents have a number of challenges to manage: Resetting Expectations, Recognizing Signs of Adolescence, Understanding Basic Adolescent Changes, and Being Mindful of Self-esteem.

## Resetting Expectations

By expectations I mean those mental sets that people choose to hold that help them anticipate their way through life, through passing time and changing circumstance. Knowing what to realistically expect as life proceeds is a very powerful human need.

When raising an adolescent, parental expectations matter. Having realistic expectations about common adolescent changes helps keep parents from being blindsided when normal alterations, tensions, problems, and conflicts unfold. To appreciate the importance of realistic expectations, consider what can happen when they are not. Specifically, consider what can happen when three kinds of expectations—predictions, ambitions, and conditions—are unrealistic and don't fit adolescent growth and how parents can emotionally react.

Unmet predictions (what parents believe *will* happen) can lead to parental anxiety and worry. "What's wrong, my adolescent is not as interested in time with family as before?"

Unmet ambitions (what parents *want* to have happen) can lead to parents feeling disappointed and let down. "What's wrong, my adolescent isn't the same hardworking dedicated student as before?"

Unmet conditions (what parents believe *should* happen) can lead parents to feel angry and betrayed. "What's wrong, my adolescent is not giving us the same forthright communication as before!"

Realistic expectations might anticipate: more interest in companionship with peers over parents; academic performance becoming less of a personal priority; and more deceptive communication by omission and commission. Such expectations can help parents stay calm as they emotionally adjust and reasonably respond to some unwelcome developmental changes that commonly unfold.

Because proactive mental sets like expectations (be they predictions, ambitions, or conditions) can have unhappy emotional consequences when unmet, in each case of a violated expectation parents can be at-risk of losing their emotional sobriety. They can do so when allowing their feelings of anxiety or disappointment or anger, for example, to do their "thinking" for them and overreacting with inappropriate or impulsive words to everyone's cost.

"You used to be such a great family kid; what's happened to you?"

"You've become so lazy in your schoolwork!"

"You're not to be trusted!"

Of course, as in the common adolescent changes described above, "expect" does not mean, "accept" or "endorse." I believe healthy parents need to insist on continued family involvement, sustained academic effort, and truthful communication. But if they already expect that some "falling away" from childhood behavior might happen, they are far less likely to respond in impulsive, excessive, or counterproductive ways should such changes occur.

In fact, by expecting their child to act more adolescent, they can calmly, rationally, matter-of-factly, and correctively explain what is happening. "We understand that at this changing age you may start believing you don't need to hang out with us, you can let school work go, and you should tell us only what you consider convenient for us to know. These are normal attitude changes that often come with growing out of childhood and wanting to act older. We are not here to criticize or argue to change this thinking. However, simply because we anticipate some of this attitude change does *not* mean we intend to accept the behaviors that can come with it. So long as you are in our care, we will patrol your welfare. To that end, for example, you need to know that we will continue to expect that you stay involved in family, that you regularly and thoroughly complete all school work, and that you keep us adequately and accurately informed. We intend to consistently hold you to this responsible account."

So how will parents know when their child's adolescence has begun?

## Recognizing Signs of Adolescence

Actually, it's not hard to tell. What follows are about twenty-five abrasive behavior changes that commonly emerge between ages nine and thirteen, during late elementary or early middle school. Often unwelcome to parents, they can signal that adolescence has begun.

Why *abrasive*? The answer is because these changes and others like them help wear down the old definition of a child that parents are used to and that the young person is striving to alter in order to begin the process of individually and independently growing up.

If your daughter or son is demonstrating at least half of these, I suggest you don't act like something is "wrong" with the girl or boy, but declare childhood to be over, adolescence begun, and adjust your expectations accordingly. In no particular order, here is a non-exhaustive list of behavior markers to look for:

- The young person finds parents more socially embarrassing.

- The young person acts like parents understand and know less.

- The young person becomes more argumentative.

- The young person voices more complaints about parental unfairness.

- The young person more frequently delays responding to parental requests.

- The young person frequently tests established parental limits to see what can be gotten away with.

- The young person displays lowering academic motivation and desire to do schoolwork.

- The young person displays more distractibility and difficulty concentrating.

- The young person becomes more disorganized and forgetful.

- The young person lives in an increasingly messy room.

- The young person complains more about household chores and responsibilities.

- The young person becomes less openly communicative.

- The young person wants more personal privacy.

- The young person is more frequently bored.

- The young person is less receptive of physical affection.

- The young person is a more self-centered family member.

- The young person values time with peers over time with parents and family.

- The young person has an increasing preoccupation with personal appearance and dress.

- The young person pushes for more social freedom and experimental expression.

- The young person is more self-conscious and self-critical.

- The young person spends more time getting ready to go out in public.

- The young person is more vulnerable to parental teasing and criticism.

- The young person is more drawn to youthful media and entertainment icons.

- The young person is more moody, emotionally intense, and easily upset.

- The young person's relationships with peers are more complicated by "social meanness" (teasing, exclusion, bullying, rumoring, and ganging up).

- The young person, wanting to stay up later, becomes more nocturnal.

- The young person strives to act and appear more womanly or manly.

- The young person is more preoccupied with social media, texting, and internet entertainment.

- The young person takes parental efforts and services more for granted.

Just mark the changes that seem to apply. If you check 50 percent or more, you're probably parenting an adolescent. Congratulations! Now the harder half of parenting begins as you wrestle with when to hold on and when to let go, when to lead and when to follow, when to speak up and when to shut up, when to correct and when to accept, all the while remaining caringly connected with your son or daughter as adolescence begins to grow you apart, as it is meant to do.

It's important that parents do not get hung up by holding on to the childhood relationship after childhood has passed. That precious period with their best buddy and boon companion is now over, although they can still enjoy some continued good times together. However, by encouraging younger behaviors that they miss, making sad comparisons with how things used to be, and criticizing changes not to their liking, parents can make the detachment and differentiation of adolescence harder for the young person to accomplish. Adolescents sometimes say, "My parents hate to see me growing up!"

For parents, adolescence begins with the hard loss of childhood compounded by the new aggravations of adolescence since they are likely to find some of these changes in the above list unwelcome. Not only do they lose the endearing child; they can gain a more challenging adolescent who starts pushing against, pulling away from, and getting around them to get freedom to grow.

Adolescence is a time of more thankless parenting, when parents must continue to provide a family structure of responsible rules and expectations for the young person to operate within, often taking loyal stands for the adolescent's best interests against what he or she urgently wants, and enduring more disapproval and conflict in the process. At this stage, parenting is not a popularity contest. And, at this stage, positively noticing and appreciating what the adolescent is doing well becomes more important than ever, otherwise the parenting received will be experienced as complaint and criticism and correction only. "All my parents ever talk about is what I've done wrong!"

What works best for parents is to greet adolescent growth as magical as was childhood, only different. Now, seeing the girl grow into a young woman and the boy grow into a young man, parents are privileged to play an important part in this extraordinary coming-of-age transformation.

## Understanding Basic Adolescent Changes

Now consider six common ways that adolescence can *reset* childhood behavior with parents, and six ways that parents might want to adjust their expectations.

### From Command to Consent

While the child believed parents once had power of command to dictate what is done or not done, the adolescent now understands that parents can't make her, or stop her, without the young person's consent. Adolescents conclude, "Compliance with what my parents want is up to me!" Now parents must persuade and convince to get cooperation and consent, and now adolescents can argue their case in response, and frequently do. This realization is exciting for all the possibilities it creates. But it is also scary due to the vulnerabilities to worldly harms such liberation brings. Awareness of the dangers of excess freedom is why the young person gives much *consent* to parental rules and limits. Because of knowing she has more actual freedom than is good for her, the young adolescent also knows parental expectations and restraints have protective value, even when protesting that parents are being "overprotective."

In response, parents can simply explain their thankless task: "Our job is to structure, supervise, and support your freedom by making rules and responsibilities you can use to safely and constructively make your own choices as you grow."

## From Contributing to Complaining
While the child believed in contributing work to parents, often out of a need to please and to draw esteem from having something worth giving, the adolescent is less inclined to welcome doing work parents want and is more apt to pursue his own recreational wants. Thus where the child may have welcomed the privilege of contributing a chore because that felt grown-up to do, the adolescent can see a request to give household assistance as an imposition and be more inclined to respond with a complaint and objection. "Why do I have to? I'm busy now!"

Often it seems no time is a good time when the young person is more preoccupied with pleasing self rather than serving others in the family. So parents can take a contributory stand for mutuality with the young person. They state how they intend to live in a two-way contribution relationship with him where both his needs of them and their needs of him are to be served, not just his alone.

In response to any pushback from the young person, parents explain "Just as we do for you, we expect you to do for us, and sometimes that means doing for us before we do for you."

## From Confiding to Concealing
While the child believed that parents had the right (and might) to be completely and truthfully told about whatever they asked, and

so was comparatively confiding, the adolescent becomes less fully communicative. She realizes that parents have cast her in a very powerful role: they now depend on her to be their prime informant about events and intents in her life. Treating her as a reporter, they rely on her to disclose what *did*, what *is*, and what *will* be going on. In doing so, they have given her power of choice about what to reveal and what to conceal. And she knows that when it comes to personal freedom, how she discharges this vital role can have powerful consequences. "What I'm allowed to do partly depends on what I decide to tell."

So, sometimes, to protect and promote personal freedom, she reports the good stuff but not the bad. And thus, in service of more privacy, selectivity, secrecy, or dishonesty, the adolescent hides more than would the comparatively transparent child. Thus the youth begins leading more of a *double life*—the one that parents know about and the one they don't. From now on, parents are going to have to get by on less information than they ideally would like to know.

In response to less information, parents need to declare their need for adequate and accurate disclosure and explain why it matters. "There is no trust without truth, no intimacy without honesty, and no safety without sincerity in our relationship, which is why we expect reliable communication. Particularly when personal suffering, danger, or trouble is at stake; you telling us is vital. Keep secrets from us and you keep our help away."

## From Caring to Coolness

The child cordially welcomed the parent home with open arms and an eager embrace. It was a chance for them to spend time together. At a more self-centering age, however, sometimes it seems like the adolescent can barely afford a noticing glance at the returning adult, or even a return greeting, instead taking immediate refuge behind a closed bedroom door. This coolness is not a matter of lacking love; it is a matter of acting less sociable. Partly this is because acting more grown-up means creating more distance from parents, and partly this is because "parent as child friend" has been supplanted by "parent as adolescent keeper." As greater social effort is made to get along with friends than with family, it can be harder for parents to always retain the old warmth and closeness enjoyed with the child.

Adolescent lack of cordial caring and casual coolness with parents usually depends on degree of preoccupation with personal life. It does not connote any loss of lasting love.

In response, rather than act hurt and act cool themselves, parents can continually offer choices for communication and companionship for staying caringly connected. They can simply say: "We are happy you have friends, and we'd like to have some good time with you too."

## From Commending to Criticizing

While the child tended to look up to parents and see them in adoring and exalted terms, the adolescent has a need to see parents more realistically. After all, adolescents know they are now on the journey to adulthood, and the most powerful adult models with which to identify are parents. But how is the adolescent supposed to measure up to an ideal? She can't. Because attaining such perfection is beyond her reach, she needs to cut parents down to human size.

"You're not so great!"

"You don't understand!"

"You don't know it all!"

"You don't do everything right!"

"You mess up too!"

Recognizing parental frailties and failings and flaws, becoming more critical of their ways, is how this humanizing and downsizing of the adult role models is done. To accept her own imperfections, it helps for the adolescent to have imperfect parents.

In response, parents can understand this need to criticize, can humanize themselves by acknowledging their shortcomings, humorously and humbly put themselves down on occasion, apologize for any offenses or hurts given, and appreciate the adolescent's greater strengths. They can say, "We make mistakes too, you know; we're sorry when we cause suffering: and you do a lot of things better than we do."

## From Commonality to Contrast

While the child wanted to grow up and become just like her parents— sharing similarity to establish commonality as one way to bond with these primary adults—the adolescent wants to differentiate from them to become her own person. Because growing up requires giving up, some childhood losses have to do with the young person letting go of shared activities with parents in order to develop independent interests with more individual appeal. The parent sighs, "My teenager and I have lost our old way of enjoying being together and sharing the same view of life!" The adolescent admits, "I don't like doing kid play with my parents anymore, and I don't agree with their opinions as much." Seeking contrast from childhood and from parents, now the young person strives for similarity with peers and starts developing her own individual perspective.

"My parents don't get what me and my friends like to do, and they don't understand how I see things differently now."

In response, parents may let go of some old childhood enjoyments and treat growing differences in outlook as points of interest to better get to know what new tastes and beliefs matter to their more independent-minded adolescent. They can ask: "Can you help me better understand what you like about that so I can appreciate it too?"

In the case of all six general changes listed previously, adolescence tends to reset the childhood relationship with parents as the young person asserts more power of independence and individuality. If childhood is more the age of "up to you" (the parents), adolescence is more the age of "up to me" (the adolescent). Increasingly, however, the young person also knows how to practically influence the relationship so that parents feel good. "To get along with my parents, and to get what I want from my parents, it helps to act nice." To do so, for the moment the young person can push the reset button back to the "child setting" and reactivate the repertoire of old behaviors that still have the power to please. It's a time-honored adolescent tactic: "The best way to get what I want from my parents is to act nice to get them in a good mood first."

In many cases "nice" can mean some combination of complying with parents, contributing to parents, confiding in parents, acting as though caring with parents, commending parents, and sharing something in common with parents. And, if having an adolescent who is "nice" to live with matters to parents, they can take positive notice whenever any of these cordial behaviors occur. Most important, they should keep engaging in cordial behaviors themselves because being treated well by her or his parent still matters to that young person, even when she or he acts like it does not. One private and painful price of becoming an adolescent can be feeling less well liked by parents than as a child (hence teenage jealousy of younger child siblings who still have that old power to please).

"You love them more than me!"

Parents have to adjust their expectations to fit how the adolescent changes in relation to them—independence lessens dependence, as individuality lessens similarity, and as social distance lessens closeness. The reality is that when their child enters adolescence, parents have to start learning how to live more on the young person's terms. And by the end of adolescence, they must accept less traditional standing in the young adult's eyes—of authority, of knowledge, and of priority, as the young person assumes more self-governance. Most importantly, they must attend to changing challenges to the adolescent's self-esteem, and to their own.

## Being Mindful of Self-Esteem

A common question is: "Is the concept of 'self-esteem' a useful one?"

I don't know about the utility of that concept in research psychology, but in applied psychology (where I practice), with parents and adolescents, the concept can be serviceable indeed. A working definition, some examples of the power of self-esteem, and a caution for parents—all follow.

I define *self-esteem* by treating it as two words compounded into one. By separating them, the meaning of the larger term becomes clear. *Self* is a descriptive concept: by what specific characteristics do I identify who I am? *Esteem* is an evaluative concept: by what criteria do I judge the worth of who I am?

Self-esteem has to do with how a person describes and evaluates her or his definition of self.

In adolescence, self-esteem creates a very powerful mindset that not only can filter life experience ("How I perceive what is happening to me"), but can also motivate behavior ("What I want to do for myself"). As a filter, low or negative self-esteem can take the blame for mistreatment ("I deserve the bad I get!"), and as a motivator it can limit what one wants to achieve ("For someone like me, just getting by is good enough"). As a filter, high or positive self-esteem can reject mistreatment ("No one should be allowed to do that to me!"), and as a motivator can propose goals that actualize dreams ("I am worth doing the best I can!").

I believe a helpful objective for parents, when it comes to influencing the growth of adolescent self-esteem, is to encourage young people to define themselves broadly and evaluate themselves kindly.

A too-narrow definition can be costly when only one pillar of self-esteem has been meaningfully developed. The young athlete, for whom excelling in the sport totally self-defines that young person, becomes bereft when serious injury ends a promising athletic career. Now the adolescent has no other pillars of self-esteem to rely on and so feels at an incapacitating loss. Or consider the perfectionist adolescent who has no tolerance for mistakes and gets furious when one inevitably occurs. Ask the young person why they are treating themselves in this painful way, and they describe self-punishment as an obligation.

"I deserve to get down on myself for messing up. Maybe that will teach me to do better next time."

But I suggest that berating themselves only wastes energy, hurts feelings, and makes recovery longer to accomplish. Better to define one's self broadly and evaluate one's self kindly.

Of course, self-esteem is not a constant, but can rise and fall with the ups and downs of life, particularly during the transformative years of adolescence. For a young person to accomplish the twin goals of adolescence—acquiring a fitting identity and functional independence at journey's end—life changes and challenges to self-esteem must be faced each stage of the adolescent way. Adolescents must continually redefine who they are and constantly reevaluate how they are doing in the process. It's easy for a young person to get discouraged by a misunderstanding, mistake, or misdeed, pulling back into a more narrow definition, and getting down on him- or herself. This is a time to nourish self-esteem, not to diminish it.

Parents should continually monitor their adolescent's self-esteem. Is it sufficiently broadly based? Is it more positive than critical? Getting stuck in a narrow definition and hurtful evaluation can be dangerous. At worst, in cases of depression, addiction, self-harming, or victimization, self-definition can wither to inadequacy, and self-evaluation can be drained of positive worth. To promote growth of self-esteem, parents can say, "Find activities that matter to you and don't get down on yourself when things don't work out or momentarily go wrong."

Now consider some common self-esteem challenges as the adolescent must redefine ("What am I doing?") and reevaluate ("How am I doing?") stage by stage.

In Early Adolescence and the Separation from Childhood (ages nine to thirteen), the young person must give up his or her beloved-child definition and values to begin experimenting with acting older in a larger world of experience outside the family circle. At this stage, parents must be sensitive to this powerful loss and appreciate the courage it takes to leave the comfortable, sheltered world of childhood, and start the daunting journey of growing up.

Parents might say, "Missing being younger and bravely acting older are both parts of the hard growth you are beginning." Empathizing with loss and respecting the challenge, parents can support positive self-esteem at a fragile time.

In Mid-Adolescence and Forming a Family of Friends (ages thirteen to fifteen), the young person must contend with more social meanness as developmentally insecure peers vie for standing and belonging, sometimes not treating each other well in the process, particularly at school. At this stage, parents must declare that they know a harder social climate is the new norm, and they want to be told if any social cruelty (teasing, exclusion, bullying, rumoring, ganging-up) comes her or his way. They want to be able to give emotional support and perhaps some helpful coaching advice. Parents may say, "If you are teased or called names, don't treat that as anything wrong with you; it's really about the other person acting insensitively or wanting to act mean." Acknowledging the possibility of more social complexity with friends, they can help strengthen self-esteem during a harsher time by not taking ill treatment personally.

In Late Adolescence and Acting More Grown-Up (ages fifteen to eighteen), the young person sees older activities like dating, driving, partying, and drug use (like alcohol, marijuana, or cigarettes) as rites of passage to becoming older. These activities come with dangers but can be difficult to refuse and can be seriously damaging when risks are taken and harm occurs. At this stage parents must do their best to realistically inform the adolescent regarding choices they cannot control so the young person can benefit from their knowledge and experience. Parents may advise teens, "As growing older encourages acting older, life gets riskier. At these choice points it becomes more important not to act impulsively, but to stay clearheaded and take time to think before you act. Using substances can not only affect your mood, it can impair the sober judgment of your mind." Speaking matter-of-factly and practically about proceeding mindfully, parents can help strengthen self-esteem by providing preparation during a more hazardous time.

In Trial Independence and Stepping More Off on One's Own (ages eighteen to twenty-three), the young person finds him- or herself not fully prepared to effectively deal with all the self-management responsibilities that come with supporting a functional independence. So there is some slipping and sliding, breaking of commitments, lapses in self-discipline, and floundering for direction. Footing is sometimes lost. At this stage, parents must make themselves available, not as managers coming to intervene or rescue, but as adult mentors who can share the know-how of their longer life experience when the young person asks for help.

Parents may say, "We don't have all the answers, but we are happy to be your personal brain trust as you work out what to do, sharing from some hard life lessons we have learned along our way." Without censoring of any kind, parents can be an adult resource that strengthens the self-esteem of teens and young adults by providing invaluable education at a time when demands of responsibility can often feel overwhelming.

At each challenging stage of the adolescent journey, it's easy for a young person to get discouraged, narrow self-definition (diminish), and negatively self-evaluate (punish)—which make positive perception and resilience harder, not easier, to maintain.

Parents also need to beware of the self-esteem trap that is set for them. Parenting is a high-investment activity. They give an enormous amount of time, energy, resources, and care to support and nurture a child's growing-up years. It is often a self-sacrificial activity where parents set their needs and wants aside for the sake of a beloved child. With so much parental giving inevitably comes some expectation of return. For example, a child who becomes successful reflects well on the parents in a worldly way, so they may believe.

Here is where parents can attach personal self-esteem to how the child acts and performs. A parent may say, "I partly define myself as parent of my child and I partly judge myself by how my child grows." In certain high aspiration and socially competitive parenting subcultures there is a common and loaded question that parents can be asked: "How is your child doing?" "Compared to what and compared to who?" the parent might anxiously respond.

A parent whose self-esteem rests on the shoulders of his or her adolescent can really feel put on the spot. A parent may say, "The better or worse my teenager does when compared with peers, the better or worse I feel about myself." Try not to contaminate your parenting with social competition. Plus, it's best for the teenager not to feel he or she is pressured or obliged to "do well" to support fragile parental esteem—"I mustn't let my parents down!"

Appreciate the vulnerability of this parental position. If they see themselves too much as parent, at the expense of other personal definitions, that can present the problem of self-neglect. "Parenting is all I do and am, and sometimes that feels not enough!"

If they buy into the equation—parent = child—they can run into the problem of self-evaluation. This equation can be interpreted to suggest that the performance of the child is a measure of the performance of the adult. The parent may conclude, "How my child is doing shows how I am doing as a parent."

It can be best that parents don't declare, "We're proud of how you did," when the young person does well. Rather than imply congratulations to themselves in this way, they can place the credit where it belongs by simply saying, "Good for you!"

Of course, unlike little children, adolescents can be hard on parental self-esteem. Typically, children who are still at the age of looking up to their parents tend to be more supportive of parental self-esteem with expressions of honest admiration and appreciation. Contrast this to unmindful adolescents more inclined to look down on the job parents do with criticism and complaints.

"I don't get a lot of compliments from my teenager. Mostly I am taken for granted, so I guess I need to make do with that." My response usually is, "You know, if some appreciation from your teenager would feel welcome for all your hard parenting work, you could always ask for what you need."

To maintain healthy self-esteem, parents need to define themselves broadly and evaluate themselves kindly. Treating themselves well in these two ways not only leads them to being better positioned to support the adolescent when he or she is growing through inevitable hard times, but also helps them model how positive self-esteem can be maintained. They can even speak directly to how this can be done: "For me, it generally works better to credit effort more than outcome because the first is under my control, while the second is often not. So even though I can't always achieve what I want, I can always feel good about myself for continuing to try."

Finally, because parental approval and disapproval are so impactful (even on the teenager who declares, "I don't care what you think!"), any adult criticism must be handled carefully. Corrosive criticism attacks character ("That was a stupid thing to do!") and injures youthful self-esteem; constructive criticism instructs for improvement ("Here is what might be a more effective way") that can strengthen self-esteem. Parental wisdom observes the difference between the two. Better for parents to say, "This is just some of what I value about you," than to ask, "What is the matter with you?"

CHAPTER TWO

# Changes in the Parenting

"I liked how fast our child was acting older,
but with our teenager I want to slow this
growing down!"

From my perspective, there are two main developmental goals that a young person, over the course of adolescence, is striving to accomplish. One is to learn sufficient self-management responsibility to support a *functional independence* at the end.

"I can take care of myself."

A second goal is to acquire a sufficient self-defining individuality to claim a *fitting identity* at the end.

"I know who I am."

This is the adolescent challenge: to independently and individually become his or her own person. To enable this process is the parental job.

In what follows, I hope to simplify what is a complex transition from parenting a child to parenting an adolescent by considering multiple parts of this challenge.

## Attachment and Similarity to Parents

Start at the beginning. In childhood, two important interpersonal connections to parents need to be established to anchor the child in the family foundation—attachment to parents and similarity to parents. Attachment is developed through acts of closeness—comforting, caretaking, and communicating, for example—through which parents (or parent surrogates) help nurture within the child a basic trust in dependency on these loving adults. Similarity is developed through engaging in mutual imitation—copying, following, and sharing, for example—through which a sense of commonality creates a unifying sense of belonging with these primary adults. Tending for attachment and play for similarity have powerful bonding consequences at this early age.

It is with the onset of adolescence, usually around ages nine to thirteen, that both primal connections begin to be strained: the child starts separating and individuating from childhood and family, and the parents now set out on the journey of overseeing their child's growing up. So begins the slow developmental process of parent and adolescent letting each other go and accepting increased separation between them, a process that generally does not wind down until the early to mid-twenties. Let's consider how this growth of independence and growth of identity might proceed.

## Growth of Independence

To grow independent, the young person begins *detaching* from childhood and parents as life beyond the family circle arouses more curiosity and motivates more exploration. To gain the necessary room to grow, the young person starts letting go of some attachments to parents by pulling away from, pushing against, and getting around their authority. As the adolescent becomes more insistent on personal freedom and more resistant to their demands and limits, parents must sometimes exercise unpopular restraint: "You can't" and "You must."

The question for parents is how much and when to detach and let go. For example, how much freedom should be allowed the curious and adventurous adolescent to explore the offline and online worlds? Because the adult judgment calls are now more complex, parenting a detaching adolescent usually takes more thought and problem-solving than parenting an attached child.

Detachment can be scary for parents because in letting go they worry that they are losing some accustomed control and placing their daughter or son at risk.

"It's harder to look out for and protect our child now that she spends more time away from home and in the company of friends!"

Thus, for parents, detaching and letting go to permit more adolescent freedom can often be an act of courage, daring to allow more dangers into the teenager's life, particularly as the young person grows older.

"It's scary letting her go out on her first date!" "It's scary letting him take the car for his first licensed nighttime drive!"

Parents generally try to let go based on their assessment of the young person's readiness for more running room, which is a combination of capacity for mindfulness (thoughtful awareness), proven performance (practiced experience), and accountability (assumption of responsibility). Then there is eagerness of the teenager who believes that more freedom is the way to grow.

"Just because I've never done it before doesn't mean I shouldn't give it a try!"

For the adolescent, more freedom of action is the only way to grow.

## Growth of Identity

To grow identity, the young person starts *differentiating* from childhood and parents. In words and actions she seems to say, "I am different from how I was as a child, I am different from you my parents, and I am going to act differently than how you want me to be!" Now the young person experiments with forms of self-definition like dress and room decoration and entertainment. While adolescent girls can sometimes develop more interest in romance fiction and social networking, adolescent boys can sometimes develop more interest in pornography and computer gaming. Such expressions are not only new to the adolescent; they are often culturally questionable to the parents. How much diversity should they adjust to in response?

Differentiation can be scary for parents because it doesn't fit into what was traditionally familiar and acceptable in childhood.

Such differences are amplified when supported by the growing influence of the adolescent's second family—the group of peers who the young person hangs out with, who all want to become different the same way she does. Asserting individuality while conforming to belong, the young person now has the like-minded company of friends. So, one day their daughter comes home from middle school with her hair dyed Kool-Aid blue, courtesy of friends who helped her change hair color over lunch in the girl's bathroom. In consequence, parents can feel like outsiders to their adolescent's emerging beliefs, tastes, values, and worldly interests. Their teenager's differentiation requires some getting used to when it challenges their tolerance for the unfamiliar. For the adolescent, more individual expression is worth experimenting with.

Two practices that can help parents maintain connectivity with the detaching adolescent are Non-evaluative Correction and After-the-Fact Education. Two parenting practices that can help maintain connectivity with the differentiating adolescent are Bridging Differences with Interest and Working with Incompatible Differences. Descriptions of each set of parenting practices follow.

## Parenting Practices with the Detaching Adolescent

While the adolescent objective of detaching is to gain more freedom of operation, sometimes there is temptation to claim freedom that is not allowed, at which point the adolescent is more likely to run afoul of family rules and expectations. Words of correction are often required to encourage the young person to behave within the family structure that responsible parents provide. While it is easy for anxious, frustrated, or offended parents to censure the young person at these junctures, this is not wise. Particularly harmful is name-calling, because doing so attacks character, inflicts injury, and can alienate an already strained relationship.

Do not say, "What a thoughtless and irresponsible thing to do!"

Better to neutralize language and focus on choices made. Consider using the mantra of Non-evaluative Correction on these occasions: "We disagree with the choice you have made, this is why, this is what we need to have happen now, and this is what we hope you can learn from this experience." A specific statement addressing decisions made without any judgmental sting works best. Parental criticism not only can hurt youthful feelings, it can emotionally obscure the lesson being taught.

I may ask a young person, "Why are you grounded this weekend?"

"Because my parents are upset with me again, like always!"

Now the cause of punishment is totally missed in the emotion of the encounter. In this case it is restricting ordinary freedom for the moment because of sneaking out the weekend before. Using Non-evaluative Correction they might have simply explained, "We disagree with your choice to sneak out after lights out because not only are you breaking curfew but you leave us not knowing where you are; so we hope staying in next weekend will remind you to live within our family rules."

Adolescent detachment is also an opportunity for the young person to learn from After-the-Fact Education. It's important that the young person doesn't get so enamored by freedom that they lose sight of the baggage all freedom brings. For every "free" decision made and action taken, some outcome occurs, maybe intended, maybe not. While the attached child was taught a compass for "responsible" conduct by parents to guide early decision-making—what is safe and wise and right, for example—they must increasingly hold the detaching adolescent to an accountable standard of "responsibility" for freedom taken so she can learn from consequences of her choices. Sometimes the after-the-fact consequences can be affirming: "I did well on a test because I studied hard!" Sometimes the after-the-fact consequences can be sobering: "I didn't know hazing a freshman in high school could get me suspended!"

Because of responsibility that now comes with it, the adolescent can feel mixed about the reality of open choice. While they want their freedoms, and would rather not have to face the consequences, excuses can be offered.

"I didn't mean to!"

"I didn't understand!"

"It's not my fault."

"It was other people's idea!"

However, lack of intent, ignorance, denial of fault, and blaming someone else only offer escape from, not growth of, responsibility.

If a young person can't see the choice/consequence connection, or accept it, if they can't take responsibility for the choice/consequence connection, or if they can't learn what the choice/consequence connection has to teach, then without benefit of this after-the-fact education they are likely to repeat the errors of their ways. This is why one of the thankless parts of parenting a detaching adolescent is to hold the young person accountable for choices made.

"I'm sorry you got Saturday detention; maybe next time you'll think more carefully about cutting classes."

For the detaching adolescent, more freedom from restraint and for risk-taking will lead to some misguided choices; that's guaranteed. How should parents respond when misadventures, mistakes, or misdeeds occur? Harsh words of judgment can hurt feelings and obscure the lesson being taught, so instead of attacking character, use non-evaluative correction by simply addressing the choices made. Instead of saving an errant adolescent from encountering unhappy consequences of ill-advised choices, let unhappy consequences bite enough so that a hard life lesson can be learned.

Parents can instill the expectation for accountability by declaring and meaning that as the young person grows older, he has to live by the choice/consequence connection. By way of example, consider the single mother who could have interfered in her sons' choices, and the consequences that followed; who could have rescued them from the cost, but decided not to. She thought facing the consequence of an unwise choice was worth what an unhappy experience could teach that her words of warning apparently had not. She told her high school sons that the freedom to get themselves to school in the morning was now up to them. She would not check on them and hurry them up to leave on time because she had younger kids to attend to. That was fine for both sons, who welcomed more freedom from her supervision. So when they played around while getting ready, got to the school bus pick-up point late, and came back home asking what they could do, she didn't get mad, lecture, or criticize. She allowed choice and consequence do the teaching.

"I guess if I were you, I'd use your feet. You've got about twenty minutes to get there on time, so you might want to start running."

She later reported that they never missed the school bus again. For the detaching adolescents, after-the-fact education had done its instructional work.

Of course the adolescent often does not thank parents for allowing an outside consequence to happen or applying a promised one of their own, so taking these kinds of stands can feel very unrewarding.

"You don't care when I hurt!"

"You don't love me!"

It can be hard dealing with a detaching adolescent who is bent on "freedom at all costs" and who will make parents pay painfully for taking a firm stand for safety or a consequential stand for instruction.

In the extreme, with a very entitled or substance-abusing adolescent, these stands require parental courage and often benefit from parents getting some outside social support. Consider the substance-abusing child. In this drug-filled world, significant substance use can expand normal latitude of choice by offering freedom from sober self-restraints and freedom for impulsive behaviors. When the adolescent lies or denies use, makes false promises to quit, requests second chances, pleads, or charms for parental rescue from unhappy outcomes, parents need to consider that an abuse of freedom may be going on. Now, against what the young person wants, but for her or his best interests, the choice/consequence connection must be consistently enforced. When parents do not stand by this connection, but make exceptions or excuses, they enable the very substance use they wish would stop.

## Parenting Practices with the Differentiating Adolescent

Consider this parent question: "How can our daughter start changing so in middle school? She's acting like a different person than the one we've always known. What's going on?"

The answer is in the question. Adolescence is a transformative experience and is meant to be. "Acting like a different person" is part of what she's supposed to be doing. As a healthy adolescent, not only is she pushing for more freedom to grow to ultimately achieve responsible independence; she is also experimenting with expressing her individuality to ultimately create an authentic sense of identity. This process of differentiation means that parents will encounter more diversity in the adolescent than the child. For an extreme example, consider the rebellious teenager who is determined to liberate him- or herself from much-loved and traditionally dominant parents: "I'm not you; I don't want to be like you; and I won't be you!"

Adolescence is not simply about pushing for freedom; it is also about experimenting with the new and different. To this end, parents often encounter a lot of deliberate changes in the young person who begins testing a host of varied definitions. For example, there is experimenting with physical appearance, fashionable dress, friendships, social group belonging, social behavior, cultural affiliation, romantic attractions, dietary choice, gender expression, sexual orientation, popular tastes, activity interests, personal ambitions, even political or religious beliefs, just to name a few.

Rather than get worried or take offense at these differences, it helps if parents can understand that in most cases these are trial, not terminal differences, passing and not permanent. The young person tries a variety of expressions to see what they might offer and to see what might fit.

"I just thought it would be fun to try dressing that way for a while to see what it felt like."

A reason to work with some experimental differences is that they can create complications, even risks that parent and teenager should talk about.

"If you are determined to switch to a vegetarian diet, and want to eat at home and school this way, then let's talk about how to do so in a balanced and nutritionally healthy way."

It's fascinating to observe how many young people use the transition from middle school to high school to (experimentally) redefine themselves. Consider a few examples: I've seen a number of "shy-to-social conversions" where a lonely and reticent eighth grader decides to act more socially outgoing in high school and this experimental change creates a new and satisfying experience of community. Or a popular eighth grader who has been in a clique of close friends since the beginning of elementary school who decides to socially redefine by diversifying his friendships and enlarging his social world. Or another who has seriously practiced time-consuming dance since second grade who decides to give that accomplishment up so she can play a team sport and develop those capacities.

"I know I'd be sorry if I didn't do something athletically differently with myself in high school."

This can be a hard letting go for parents who have significantly either emotionally or financially invested in the young person's history of accomplishment. Experimenting with personal diversity, differentiating from how one was or for how one might want to be, is part of how most adolescents grow.

It often takes a lot of trial differences to sort out an older identity. Usually, some of these differences will be outside of the parents' familiarity and comfort zone. At these times, they can feel distant, even estranged, from a young person who now seems very hard to understand and relate to.

"He acts like a different person and lives in a different world!"

"We don't understand a lot of her new looks and likes."

It is easy for parents to dismiss or disapprove of the style of dress, cultural identification, or taste in popular entertainment that calls to the young person.

"How can you waste time on such a worthless activity?"

When parents react this way, they risk estranging the relationship. By discounting or rejecting trial differences, they can cause this diversity to further divide them.

"My parents don't want anything to do with what I enjoy."

Criticize trial differences in their adolescence and a parent can harden the generational division between them.

Parents can allow this passing difference to become a barrier to the relationship instead of one that can bring them together. How can a difference connect them? For differentiation to become unifying, parents have to Bridge Differences with Interest.

"The new music you like is really unfamiliar to me. Can you help me understand its appeal so I can appreciate it too?"

"Can you show me how to play your video game? I've never played one before."

With this educational request, the parent encourages a very powerful role reversal that is esteem-building for the adolescent. The younger person becomes the teaching authority, and the older person, the parent, becomes the student with a lot to learn.

Not all changes in their adolescent, however, can be successfully bridged with interest by a parent. Some are more intractable and can create significant incompatibilities between them. There are times when parents must work with incompatible differences, trying to remain connected as differentiation challenges the relationship across four powerful levels of adolescent change—in characteristics, in values, in habits, and in wants.

*Characteristic differences* are the most unchangeable because they are of the no-choice kind. They are vested in the young person's physical, temperamental, and personality makeup. Puberty, for example, creates the challenge of how to manage a sexually maturing body and the gender expectations that come with this transformation, all while anxiously wondering how one's older body is going to turn out and affect social relationships. As hormones trigger physical growth to sexual maturity, they increase self-consciousness, sexual interest, preoccupation with sex role development (womanliness and manliness), and do so with more intense emotions as well.

"She's so quick to take offense now!"

"He can be so moody!"

*Value differences* are very hard to change because they are founded in deeply held beliefs that are still embraced when the person runs out of reasons to defend them and are commonly expressed by personal dress, room decoration, and entertainment choices. As affiliation with peers becomes more important, so does subscribing to some identifying beliefs and tastes that define the lifestyle of that community. Sometimes countercultural differences depart from what parents grew up with and can feel foreign, unappealing, and even abrasive for them to live with.

"She's goth like her friends, listens to dark music, and dresses in black."

"He and his friends are skaters, looking like an urban outlaw is how it sometimes strikes us."

*Habit differences* can only be changed with a lot of effort because they are established patterns of behavior based on repeated practice over time. As adolescents act more grown-up by staying up later, they become more nocturnal. As they grow older they tend to stay up later for their electronic entertainment pleasure and communicating with friends, often shorting themselves on rest.

"School-day mornings it takes multiple wake-ups to get her ready in time."

"On weekends he sleeps 'til afternoon."

*Want differences* are most susceptible to change because they are a matter of what the young person would like or would not like to have happen. Differences in wants are consciously chosen at the time. So, for example, most desirable in adolescence is increased freedom in two forms—freedom from restraint (like parental supervision) and freedom for enjoyment (like parental permission), as the young person keeps pressing the family powers-that-be to get more room to grow.

"He takes forever to do what we want."

"Anything she wants she has to have right away!"

The adolescent has less in common and more in contrast to parents than did the child who strove for similarity to parents for closeness' sake. Experimenting with diverse expressions of individuality is how the adolescent develops an older identity. Coping with these emerging differences, and staying connected in the process, is a challenging part of the parenting job. Parental criticism doesn't help. On the first three levels (characteristics, values, and habits), an incompatibility can be pretty inflexible, so when parents demand an adolescent alter herself in some way, she is not empowered to change it. Parental lack of acceptance can result in feelings of rejection in the teenager, inflict hurt, and motivate resistance.

"Well, that's just how I am, so get used to it!"

Thus, in general, parents need to accept characteristic differences like puberty and the changes that brings. They need to tolerate value differences that set the parental and adolescent generations culturally apart. They need to adjust to habit differences that come with growing older like becoming more nocturnal and internet-active. And they need to negotiate differences in wants, particularly of the freedom and collaborative kinds. However, while honoring intractable incompatibilities, parents can often negotiate the expressions that these changes bring.

"I know you are feeling moody a lot, so let's talk about ways to manage those feelings to spend more time feeling better or feeling the way you want." (Parents shouldn't say, "Stop moping around!")

"I know you believe dressing to create a unique appearance is important, so let's talk about expressing your individuality in other ways you want." (Parents shouldn't say, "Stop parading around like some kind of misfit!")

"I know you are used to dragging out the time it takes to do what you don't want to do, so let's talk about getting to work sooner so you get more time to do what you want." (Parents shouldn't say, "Stop taking forever to get stuff done!")

Just as important as bridging new differences with parental interest is negotiating incompatible differences in characteristics, values, and habits by translating them into wants they dictate and where some mutual accommodation can often be made.

Come a child's adolescence, detachment and differentiation from childhood and family create more points of contention and contrast between parent and teenager. There are more differences to disagree about, to encompass, and over which to engage in conflict. For this reason, adolescence is a more abrasive time but also a rewarding one, as parents see the young person develop those powers of independence and identity that will carry her or him into young adulthood.

During this process of more independent and expressive development in the teenager, parents need to be more self-aware of changes in themselves that can be difficult for the adolescent.

## Changes in the Parent

It's important when discussing adolescent change for parents to remember that they are undergoing some powerful parental changes as well. In fact, one way in which the child can tell how adolescence has begun is from how parents are changing in response. Consider the young adolescent's point of view.

Years ago this mutuality of adolescent change was brought home to me when I asked a thirteen-year-old how he knew adolescence had begun. His response gave me pause.

"Because of how my parents have changed!"

When asked for more information, he immediately replied how they used to be fun loving, carefree, and relaxed when he was a child, but now they were more serious, worried, and tense. His response got me thinking.

The young man altered my view of adolescence. From then on I have tried to remember that adolescence is not simply about how a child changes on the way to young adulthood; it is also about how the parent changes in response, and how the parent/adolescent relationship alters as well.

So what follows, in no particular order, is an extended but non-exhaustive list of parental changes that can mark a child's entry into adolescence.

Parents can become more

- Irritable: "Will you stop doing that!"

- Critical: "As you grow older, we say what's wrong so you can know what's right!"

- Nagging: "We'll keep after you until you get it done!"

- Bossy: "Because we make the rules, that's why!"

- Suspicious: "Tell us why we should believe that's the truth!"

- Impatient: "When we ask for *now* we don't mean *later*!"

- Worried: "You need to think about the risks out there!"

- Sad: "We miss all the good times we used to have together!"

- Resentful: "The only person you think about is yourself!"

- Questioning: "We ask a lot because there's more we need to know!"

- Tense: "We can get wound up waiting up to see you make it safely home!"

- Serious: "Where you see fun we see possibility for harm!"

- Correcting: "We give consequences so you don't repeat misbehavior."

- Watchful: "We pay a lot of attention to how you're growing up."

- Unforgiving: "Apologies are no substitute for changing your actions."

- Uncommunicative: "We talk less because when we do talk we mostly disagree!"

- Unreceptive: "We listen less when we already know what you're going to say!"

- Emotional: "We get more easily frustrated because it's harder to get what we want from you!"

- Strict: "We limit freedom so we don't give more than you can handle."

- Protective: "We say No to keep you from getting hurt!"

- Distant: "We may be harder to talk to because there is less you want to say!"

- Ignorant: "Your world is not like the one we grew up in!"

- Argumentative: "We only argue more because you argue more with us!"

- Unfair: "We expect more of you than the other kids because you're older!"

- Embarrassing: "The more you change, the more socially different we become from you and for you."

- Complaining: "Focused on problems, we can forget to praise."

- Superior: "From longer experience we know more about life than you!"

- Demanding: "Our job is to keep adding responsibilities to build your independence."

I think it's useful to remember this list of unwelcome parental behaviors so the adults don't treat adjustment to the changing relationship as all one-sided, where the burden falls mostly on the adults. It does not. It is shared. When you are having a hard time getting used to your adolescent, so may your adolescent be having an equally hard time getting used to you. Adolescence changes the child and the parent in response, each now finding the other harder to live with.

In general, it's best not to make what can feel like hard adjustments worse by taking common adolescent changes personally, blaming the young person for deliberately offending you. In reality, adolescence is such a self-absorbing process that there can be diminishing attention paid to the sensitivities of others, like parents. While your daughter or son may act carelessly, it is unlikely that she or he is deliberately trying to get you upset. The young person may be more inconsiderate, but calculatingly so? Probably not.

When you would like basic consideration shown, be sure to explain what specific actions you need, and then follow through with proper supervision. For example, if a certain degree of household neatness is important to parents, they should keep after the more disorderly young person to pick up after him- or herself. This matters because one responsibility of parents is to socialize a teenager into a young person who is nice for them to live with, at least most of the time.

## Creating a Structure of Responsible Expectations

As the adolescent pushes for more independent action and individual expression, occasionally acting now like "anything goes," parents have to provide a structure of responsible expectations (family rules and restraints) for the young person to constructively live within. This is part of the thankless parenting that comes with raising an adolescent, as in: "Thanks a lot for not letting me go!"

Essentially, creating and maintaining this structure requires parents exercise four kinds of active influence:

1. They give constant Guidance, regularly communicating about what is working well and should be continued, and about what might be changed to beneficial effect. "We think the way you take good care of doing homework completely serves you well, but sometimes not turning it in on time and getting marked down does not."

2. They provide a set of Rules to create responsible demands and limits that define constructive conduct that they require the young person to operate within, expressing appreciation to the young person when she or he is in compliance, and correcting when needed. "Thank you for getting home by curfew, but it is not okay to lie to us about what you and your friends had been planning to do."

3. They provide loyal Supervision to see that what they require and request is complied with by following through with sufficient reminders, to see what was asked for is accomplished. "We know you find our nagging irritable, but it is honorable parental work; and even though neither of us enjoys it, it will continue until you deliver what was asked for."

4. They work the Exchange Points to communicate that for the teenager to get to do (or have) what she wants, she must also do what the parents want in fair exchange. "For you to get this permission, we need the following show of responsibility from you to make allowing this degree of freedom feel okay. We do for you, you do for us; that's how our relationship needs to work."

Parents who do not provide a structure of responsible expectations in which their adolescent can grow will encourage the young person to seek their frame of social reference from influential peers, often to the young person's cost. When it comes to Guidance: "Friends know best." When it comes to Rules: "Friends set my limits." When it comes to Supervision: "Follow my friends." When it comes to the Exchange Points: "I owe my friends." However, friends are not supposed to be parents, and parents are not supposed to just be friends.

Finally, parents must beware of two dangers. With adolescent detachment there is a risk of disconnection through losing parental closeness, and with adolescent differentiation there is the risk of rejection through losing parental acceptance. Taken to the extreme, these parental responses can leave the young person with feelings of isolation and alienation, which can motivate all manner of self-harm. So, when parenting an adolescent, staying connected and accepting can count for a lot.

CHAPTER THREE

# Changes in the Relationship

"We never thought our comfy childhood time
together wouldn't last!"

Adolescent change, and parental change in response, creates more emotional discomfort in the relationship, which is why the constructive management of emotion is so important for parents to model and teach with their teenager.

What follows is one simple approach to Understanding and Managing Emotion, and then a discussion of three factors that can unhappily intensify emotion: Growing Mutual Disaffection, Braving the Displeasure of Parents, and Parental Criticism.

## Understanding and Managing Emotion

It's a wonder in many human relationships that something as constant and fundamental as emotion can be so seldom discussed, or done so with such apparent reluctance or difficulty. Consider this interchange:

"How are you feeling?"

"I'm doing fine."

"Not how you're doing, but how you're *feeling*."

"And I told you, there's nothing the matter with me!"

Why this guardedness and avoidance? In spoken communication, simply talking about feelings can be complicated, whether in the workplace or at home. So at a meeting on the job, for example, where there's a lot of normal stress from daily organizational life, most of the talking is about what people are doing or thinking, but not about what people are actually feeling. In the protocol of occupational communication, exchanging information about actions and thoughts is the rule, but talking about feelings is the exception.

Of course, within the family, feelings are important: they color experience, arouse thoughts, and even drive behavior, while the mutual sharing of feelings creates empathy and intimacy in close and loving relationships. Feelings can create valuable understanding when shared and can cause significant misunderstanding when they are not.

"Until you explained your stony silence, I thought you were mad at me, not sad about something else!"

In this way, emotionally inexpressive adolescents or parents are frequently misunderstood.

Just as our vision and our hearing and our sense of touch sensitize us to our surroundings and ourselves, our emotions are informative too. I think of them as agents of our Affective Awareness System that direct attention to something significant happening in our internal or external world of experience. And they can be quite specific. On the "good feeling" side we may welcome news they bring. For example, Hope is about positive possibility, Love is about attraction, Curiosity is about interest, and Loyalty is about dedication. On the "bad feeling" side we may be less welcoming of what we are told. For example, Fear is about danger, Anger is about violation, Frustration is about blockage, and Grief is about loss.

With very young children who are just acquiring spoken language, parents spend a lot of time teaching "the feeling words" so the child can learn to transition from acting out emotion to talking out emotion. Thus, when the early-verbalizing child strikes out or throws something down or storms off, the parent helps attach a word to the emotional experience.

"Next time you are feeling like acting this way, tell me you are *angry* and then we can talk about what we can do."

Having a working emotional vocabulary is an extremely important acquisition in childhood, as is practicing the use of this spoken language to process feelings when they become intense. Coupled with this early childhood education in emotional literacy is learning to honor powerful feelings without letting them dictate immediate actions.

*Feelings can be very good informants, but very bad advisors.* Because child emotions can urge impulsive action (grabbing something from someone when feeling envious or striking out in retaliation when angry), it can be tempting for the girl or boy to let strong feelings dictate thinking about what to do. However, it is usually better to delay acting out to first consult one's judgment. As the child's mental development and brain matures, the parent may say, "I know what feels 'right' to you in the moment, but when you take a little time to think before you act, ask yourself what seems wise?" The same advice goes for the temper-prone adult as for the easily outraged child.

Sometimes, impulsive people are driven to "think" with their feelings: "I just popped off because I was upset!" And sometimes, insensitive people are those with limited emotional access, with an Affective Awareness System that is not well developed: "I don't know what I'm feeling!"

When people register an unhappy emotion, not only does the feeling direct their attention to some important aspect of their life experience, but it also mobilizes energy to make a variety of choices. For example, there is the Reflective choice: to simply acknowledge and ponder what is going on. There is the Expressive choice: to say something about what is going on. There is the Protective choice: to defend against what is going on. There is the Corrective choice: to change what is going on. Emotions are too important to avoid or ignore, and part of the parent's job is to educate their child or adolescent how to use them well; teaching by adult example, interaction, and instruction.

That said, in counseling with parents and couples, it often seems that the female is more comfortable and practiced talking about feelings than the male, who is more at ease conversing about thoughts or actions. So the woman complains: "You're so unfeeling!" And the man complains: "You're so emotional!" Maybe the caring sensitive female ethic and strong silent male ethic have contributed to this difference. In such cases it seems like revealing emotion can be treated as womanly for the woman but unmanly for the man. To the degree they can, it's usually best for parents to simply normalize talking about emotions so the adolescent can learn from this modeling to do the same.

In families, the closely attached little girl or boy who was so emotionally forthright can become less emotionally disclosing when the young person starts detaching and differentiating from childhood and parents into adolescence. Why?

"My feelings are nobody's business!"

"I don't like showing my soft side."

"I keep my feelings to myself."

In service of creating more room for growing up, young people can become more private about and protective of their emotions.

At the same time, they can also become more emotionally sensitive and intense, not only because of the hormonal influence of puberty and growing self-consciousness, but also because of the increasing complexity of their relationships with parents and with peers. Developmental change is physically and socially and emotionally upsetting and is resetting the adolescent's terms of operation. And now, with the secondary school years, there seem to be more emotional portals into unhappiness that young people experience than ever before. Consider just some that are likely to come a young person's way, such as boredom, sadness, disappointment, frustration, impatience, anger, confusion, uncertainty, resentment, hurt, rejection, exclusion, betrayal, failure, loss, loneliness, isolation, dissatisfaction, discontent, helplessness, hopelessness, regret, remorse, want, fatigue, neglect, envy, jealousy, injustice, unfairness, insecurity, anxiety, inadequacy, inferiority, self-pity, self-criticism, guilt, embarrassment, humiliation, shame, despondency, pressure, and stress.

With the onset of adolescence, the entries into unhappiness during adolescence tend to increase. The adolescent becomes "more sensitive" to live with, partly because she or he is becoming more emotionally complex. This is not a problem to be fixed, but rather a reality to be accepted and appreciated. Adolescents develop an increasing diversity of unhappy feelings they can identify, which is good for developing affective awareness, but also more challenging to manage.

Often when the teenager can only generally identify they are in a "bad mood," that means they can't yet locate specifically whatever is emotionally going on. Thus, emotional self-management, the processing of unhappiness through identifying and talking about unhappy feelings, is a skill parents want to model and encourage the teenager to practice. "Rather than retreat to your room after a hard day at school and escape into the internet, maybe you could take a few minutes to tell me about what happened. I promise to listen. At least this way you won't have to bear all that unhappiness alone. You might even start to feel better. When I've had a hard day, I usually tell you. And your caring enough to listen makes a positive difference for me. I think this is an important part of what families are for, to emotionally support each other when the going gets tough."

For the parents it is also a more emotional time because there is growing social distance with the teenager, less complete communication, and increased conflict with the young person over freedom of expression and action. Feeling less in charge than with a child, but as responsible as ever, parents experience more worry as they struggle to decide when and where to continue holding on and when and where to start letting go.

Through all these changes, it's easy to forget the importance of preserving emotional connectedness. To support talking about emotions openly, there are a few things parents can do.

They can routinely model the sharing of emotions from their own life. "Let me tell you about a good-feeling time and a hard-feeling time at my work today."

They can be appreciative when the young person shares strong feelings with them, whether those feelings are hurt or happy. "Thank you for letting us know about the hardship you are having with your friend. Is there any way we can help?"

They can forsake verbally attacking their adolescent, because such hostility undercuts emotional safety. "I don't tell my parents how I'm feeling because that just makes me easier to put down."

They can always put concern before correction. "Before we talk about what you did; we first need to know how you are feeling, if you are feeling okay."

Then there is a complicated distinction parents need to be able to make in their own verbal expression of emotion: the distinction between communicating about emotion and communicating emotionally.

Communicating about emotion, parents are striving for emotional intimacy by disclosing their own feelings in hopes of being better understood: "I felt injured (hurt/angry) that you didn't like my idea."

Communicating emotionally, parents may be using the expression of strong feelings to get their way: "I acted injured (hurt/angry) so you would change your mind." Between parent and teenager, the verbal expression of emotion is too important to be put to such manipulative use.

Of course, adolescence changes the child, and when those changes are hard to understand, accept, and keep up with, parents and adolescents can find themselves feeling estranged by the host of emerging differences. For example, Characteristics change, like from childhood to the onset of sexual maturity. Values change, like from family to the countercultural influence of peers. Habits change, like from compliance to more active and passive resistance to parental authority. Wants change, like from the young person's contentment to live within the family circle to pushing for personal freedom in the outside world with friends. Sometimes the increased human diversity between them can feel alienating.

"We have so many differences and so little in common anymore!"

However, one aspect of adolescence that doesn't change from childhood is sharing the same base of emotional experience. Thus, being able to talk about feelings is one powerful way to stay connected as more changeable factors grow them apart. "Since both of us feel more frustrated and unappreciated in our relationship right now, maybe we can talk about that!"

Despite the increasing diversity of characteristics, values, habits, and wants growing them apart, they have much emotionally in common. Through expressing empathy a parent can affirm this commonality: "I know how you are feeling because I've felt that way myself." Thus when a parent celebrates the happy adolescent for good times and successes great and small, and when the parent comforts the sad adolescent for hard times and hurts great and small, the adult emotionally responds on a human level that deeply connects them both.

This makes me mindful of what Muriel Rukeyser had to say about the separation and diversity in her poem "Islands":

> O for God's sake
> they are connected
> underneath . . .

Sometimes, when parent and adolescent are feeling most separated and estranged by growing differences between them, identifying mutual emotional experience can restore the sense of commonality they miss. "I guess we're both kind of frustrated and discouraged at the moment," says the parent. And when the adolescent agrees, by both recognizing this shared emotional experience, they start to feel "connected underneath."

## Growing Disaffection

Emotional discomfort from adolescent detachment and differentiation from childhood can lead to more times of mutual disaffection between parent and teenager. Disaffection, however, need not mean any lessening of love. It only means the parent/adolescent relationship must now tolerate more mutual dissatisfaction than before. While it was easy to feel in-love with the charming little child, to a degree it is easy to fall out of in-love with the more abrasive adolescent. By comparison, some of that old entrancement and infatuation with the younger child is usually lost with the adolescent. One sure test of loyally parenting an adolescent can be recommitting to lasting love when the object of that love has become harder to love because the adolescent is no longer an adorable and adoring little child. And the same goes for the adolescent who finds parents less wonderful and ideal than they used to be.

Common parental sources of disaffection might be found among the following:

"I miss how she used to be communicative and confiding in me, how we had so much companionship to enjoy together, how I was his favorite company, how she looked up to me, how he liked to work hard for school, how she was unselfish and thoughtful, how we rarely seriously disagreed, how he thought I was so cool and smart, how she loved to help and please, how he could focus on what needed doing, how she was positive most of the time, how he was good at following rules, how she kept her agreements, how he didn't need reminding, how I could take her at her word, how they liked to be kissed and hugged."

As for the adolescent, not only must childish enjoyments be given up for the sake of becoming older, but there is another more disaffecting change.

Common sources of adolescent disaffection might be found among the following:

"I don't like how my parents are more unfair than before, are harder to please than before, criticize me more than before, are less trusting than before, are more serious than before, worry more than before, ask more questions than before, set conditions for what I want more than before, refuse more than before, take away more than before, understand me less than before, listen less than before, lecture more than before, are tenser to talk with than before, are more boring than before, are more embarrassing than before, demand more chores than before, talk about grades more than before, or like my interests less than before."

Sometimes disaffection can momentarily degenerate into feelings of dislike when the adolescent feels parents are acting as an enemy to his interests ("Thanks a lot for keeping me in to do weekend chores!"), and when parents feel unappreciated for their efforts ("Thanks a lot for taking all we do for granted!")

Parents should stay alert to their feelings of dislike because this can be a danger point. Momentary feelings of dislike can cause parents to react to their adolescent in critically harmful ways. What parents find displeasing can be hard on the teenager. It can sometimes help parents on these occasions to remember that while causing them displeasure can be hard to take, for the adolescent it can also be hard to give.

## Braving the Displeasure of Parents

Sometimes, frustrated with their teenager "forgetting" yet one more time what she promised, again neglecting to pick up after himself, still doing what she was told *not* to do, continuing his active interest in trying the forbidden, or falling away from what matters most to parents, these adults will despair and remark, "The problem is, our adolescent just doesn't care about what we want anymore!"

Actually, from what I've seen, this is a false conclusion. Although youthful bravado can make it sound like their response is of no concern ("I don't care what you think!"), the little child's desire to shine in parental eyes is still alive and well in the teenager. In truth, such statements of bravado really mean: "I care too much to let you know how much I care."

This is why adolescence is often an act of courage. At times the young person must dare to displease parents—the most important adults in her or his world—in the process of pursuing the two major developmental goals of adolescence. Through experimentation with expression of individuality, the young person develops a uniquely fitting young adult identity: "I have tried out enough different images and experiences to become my own person and personality now." The other goal is to *detach* from childhood and parents. Through exercising increased latitude of choice, the young person can support a functional young adult independence. "I have learned enough responsibility for my actions to be self-reliant now."

It's best for parents to mind their responses as these normal changes unfold. The teenager is vulnerable to parental disapproval about failing to conform to parental wants, tastes, interests, and values. Their child's adolescence is a time when parents must encompass more human differences between them and their teenager. It is when adolescent acts of differentiation and detachment fail to meet significant expectations to "fit in" and follow what parents hold dear that they can express disappointment in the young person who is now burdened by the sense she or he has failed to measure up.

"They don't like how I'm turning out to be!"

Maintaining an authentic adolescent difference in the face of this displeasure can take courage. "I'm just not a social joiner and leader like my parents; that's just not the kind of person I am or want to be!"

I believe two things parents should never say to their adolescent are: "You have really disappointed us!" "You have really let us down!" I say this having seen teenagers get teary-eyed in counseling in response to these parental statements. I think the reason why is because they equate such statement of disappointment with a loss (perhaps irrecoverable) of loving standing in parental eyes. This is usually not what parents intended to communicate, but it is what the young person interprets their disappointment to mean. Parents can be positive and express their surprise by saying, "It's just that you caught us off guard; how you acted is not what we've come to expect from you." Since on the topic of what not to say, add one more: "You're just lazy!" Why does this hurt? Because by implication the young person can register what is meant but left out: "You are just a lazy *good for nothing.*" How hurtful is that?

As adolescence unfolds, opportunities for mutual disaffection increase. For example, becoming more resistant to their direction, pushing against and pulling away and getting around their authority for more autonomy, the young person actively, with argument, and passively, with delay, tries to see what opposition to requests and requirements can be gotten away with. These are tests of authority to see if parents mean what they say or will change their minds. The relationship hasn't become some kind of war zone, but there are increasing disagreements that create more times of tension in the relationship. According to the teenager, "I speak up to my parents when I don't agree with what they say." According to parents, "We live in a world where everything we want is subject to endless adolescent debate."

Taking on one's parents over a difference of opinion in the face of their displeasure can take a lot of courage.

"My parents don't understand that when I stand up to them, I'm standing up for myself!"

Treat disagreement as a sign that discussion may be needed, and as a chance for more communication. Sometimes having an adolescent who cannot bear displeasing very strict parents can signify how growth to full individuality and independence may be forestalled.

Occasionally, an incomplete adolescence occurs. At the appropriate growing up time, transformation and redefinition of individuality and independence was not adequately accomplished. Tyrannized by a desire for unwavering parental acceptance, driven by a need to earn total parental approval, can cost her or him developmentally.

"I didn't dare stand up to my parents, to question what they valued or oppose what they wanted."

When a young person does not dare these challenges at the adolescent time, they can be deferred, or so it seems. An example would be the adult who is in crisis over pleasing themselves some of the time as opposed to the tyranny of pleasing significant others all of the time. It's like she or he is in the emotional throws of trying to complete an unfinished adolescence.

"Whether other people or my parents understand me or not, at last I'm going to live on my own terms and become who I never allowed myself be!" Courage comes to the rescue at last, as well as costs to be paid.

## Parental Criticism

It is because parents possess so much power of affection, authority, and approval that good standing in their eyes can be so important to children and (despite what they may boast to the contrary) to adolescents too. Part of exercising adolescent independence is often pretending that one has grown beyond caring what parents think of them; but such indifference is only a posture.

Just as parental compliments can be very affirming, parental criticism can be painful when taken to heart. Does this mean parents should never criticize? Not at all, but it does mean parents should be sensitive to the hurt their criticism can cause. Use it for the good, not to inflict harm. It's a tricky issue. To navigate this complexity, consider two kinds of criticism—constructive criticism and corrosive criticism.

Constructive criticism is of the balanced kind, and is taken in a helpful way. It is instructive and can even be requested, as when the teenager wants his mother, who writes well, to look over his paper or application essay and make suggestions before he turns it in. Or it can be helpful when a young athlete wants her father, who is athletic himself, to give her feedback about the strengths and weaknesses of her performance in the game. Or it may not be requested by the adolescent, but offered by the parent, such as "Can I give you a suggestion for handling that situation with your friend differently the next time it arises? I think there may be a way that might work better for your relationship." Couching criticism in concern for the adolescent's welfare—and accompanying it with sincere compliments—can make it more welcomed to receive.

"You usually take care of so much business in your life so well; I'm just raising this particular concern because I think it might be getting in your way."

Corrosive criticism is usually hostile and given in anger, so the first piece of advice is never criticize in anger. Doing so when feeling injured or wronged, a parent can be at risk of giving deliberate injury in return. "You never learn! You can't do anything right! Why don't you try thinking for a change?" Sarcasm can be corrosive criticism at its most destructive: "Way to go, you just succeeded in screwing up again!" To put down, to humiliate, or to shame are acts of criticism that have lasting value of a very unhappy kind. And while an adult apologizing for hurtful words may be sincere, it can't take back what was said or undo the harm that was inflicted. The only parental apology that counts in such situations is committing to never repeat this kind of mistreatment.

The ultimate power of corrosive criticism is the poison of self-rejection, as the young person comes to believe he or she is inferior or inadequate. Corrosive parenting can wear down an adolescent's self-esteem. Repeatedly denigrated by parental authorities for not meeting their expectations, the young person can feel guilty as charged. Now the adolescent sees him- or herself in worthless terms. "My parents say I'm nothing but a problem, and I think they're right!" Obviously, I believe corrosive criticism has no good place in parenting.

Adolescence is harder to do than childhood, parenting an adolescent is harder to do than parenting a child, and the relationship between young person and parent becomes harder to manage for them both. From the beginning of adolescence to the entry into young adulthood there is so much developmental work for both young person and parents to do.

In the course of nurturing detachment to a functional independence and differentiation to an individually fitting identity, parents have to modify many of their old parenting ways. They have to let go of control to allow more freedom and they have to tolerate more diversity to accept more individuality. Rigidly controlling and absolutely intolerant parents tend to have the hardest time adjusting to and accepting these inevitable and essential adolescent changes.

## ISSUES IN EARLY ADOLESCENCE
## (AGES NINE TO THIRTEEN)

# THE SEPARATION
# FROM CHILDHOOD

Early adolescence begins with loss, with young people letting go many childish comforts, interests, and activities to create opportunity for acting older in a larger and more complicated world. In the process, missing the security of what is given up and facing the daunting unknown, they must brave more uncertainty and anxiety—some of the emotional costs for undertaking the journey of growing up.

So, as alluring and exciting as the new freedom of adolescence can be for a young person, it is not for the faint of heart. Particularly hard can be some "falling away" from parental approval as growing redefinition is expressed in changes—some of which, like more active and passive resistance to authority, are usually unwelcome in adult eyes. In this way, beginning adolescence can be an act of courage.

CHAPTER FOUR

# Disorganization and Distractibility

"If he keeps on losing track of things, one of these days he's going to forget his own name!"

Part of the child's task was to grow familiar, fit in, and become comfortable with her position in the family of origin into which she was born or adopted. For attachment and security's sake, to build a basic trust in dependency on parents, establishing this sense of conforming and belonging is all-important.

However, once the child begins to feel dissatisfied with being defined and treated as "just a child," and life beyond the family circle becomes more compelling than life within it, and time with peers feels more important than time with parents, then adolescence begins. And now this developmental change begins to overwhelm and overthrow the traditional order of childhood to which she had grown accustomed. Life starts getting more complicated in a hurry. There is suddenly much more to keep track of and attend to.

As the twin adolescent drives to detach for more independence and to differentiate for more individuality begin, as the larger world of life experience starts to reveal its vast variety, there is more to encompass, to keep track of, to process, and to attend to, than ever before. And now the self-management skills once adequate for coping with the simpler, sheltered, childhood years can prove no longer sufficient for the increasing *complexity* found in the young person's expanding arena of life. Coping with this magnitude of complexity becomes the demanding priority of early adolescence. Specifically, from this complexity two challenges grow—Coping with Disorganization of Order and Distractibility of Attention. On both counts the young person often struggles to maintain effective control.

## Disorganization of Order

Specifically and symbolically, an adolescent is no longer operating as a child. For example, for safety's sake the child was taught to reach out and hold the parent's hand and heed their advice while crossing the street. The adolescent, however, for responsibility's sake, is expected to watch out for him- or herself and cross the street unattached and self-directed. The comparative order of childhood in which a girl or boy is given rules and routines to count on and live within, to feel securely attached to family, starts to feel confining as the urge to detach for more independence and to differentiate for more individuality begins.

Adolescent growth is toward more complexity. As early adolescence gets underway there are more concerns to contend with. For example, physiologically (with puberty), psychologically (with emotional intensity), socially (with peer pressures), interpersonally (with parental dissatisfaction), sexually (with gender roles), educationally (with secondary school expectations), ability (with operating performance)—life keeps getting more demanding and challenging. As complexity grows, self-questioning increases, and for a while affirmative answers to these questions can be troublingly hard to find. "What's the matter with me!"

At the beginning of adolescence there is more information to process, more experience to understand, more questions that need answers, more decisions to make, more demands to keep up with, more expectations to meet, more work to do, more difficult relationships to manage, and more aspects of life to keep together as the young person struggles to cope with more change. Operationally, change encompasses everything that is starting, stopping, increasing, and decreasing in their surging young life. And as one tries to attend and respond to all that is happening, and to prioritize doing what matters most, some *slippage* usually occurs. Best not to treat this condition as a problem to be fixed ("Something is wrong with our son!"), but rather view it as a new reality with which the young person must contend, and with which parents can help ("Let's talk about some ways to manage the normal confusion you are experiencing.")

"The wheels have come off the truck!" was how one frustrated dad described this destabilization. With his eleven-year-old son, the man is contending with more forgetfulness, disorder, untidiness, impulsiveness, confusion, loss of belongings, inattention, and general disarray. What was going on?

The onset of adolescent change was proving to be a complicating factor in everybody's lives. For example:

The child who generally kept her personal space picked up becomes the adolescent who lives in a chaos of litter. "Don't even ask about her school backpack!"

The child who listened to what parents said becomes the young adolescent whose attention is very hard to hold. "I'm talking to him and his eyes start rolling as he tunes me out!"

The child who could be counted on to keep up with homework becomes the adolescent who loses track of assignments. "She says she knows she has them, just not where!"

In a world of increasing complexity, the young adolescent simply has a harder time keeping everything straight. "Mindful" can become "forgetful." "Careful" can become "careless." "Orderly" can become "scattered." "Attentive" can become "preoccupied." Because these behavior changes are often inconsistent with how they have trained their child, parents can be particularly unwelcoming of this developmental disorganization. What to do?

Sometimes parents respond to early adolescent disorganization by becoming irritated, critical, and even punitive. "Staying in this weekend will teach you not to forget your homework again!" "I thought I had it with my other stuff!" the young person explains, opening a backpack crammed full of who knows what. But punishment is not what the adolescent needs at this disorganized age.

Coaching and supervisory support are what the young person needs, help in creating and maintaining a new system of self-management to take care of the increasing variety of life demands and freedoms that growing older brings. This is one job of parents with a child entering adolescence—to teach and train increased self-management capacity and responsibility. In terms of parents seeking outside help at this point, occupational therapy or coaching with the emphasis on focused practice may be more helpful than some kind of psychological therapy with the emphasis on self-understanding.

Recognizing this need, some middle schools provide students with digital or paper planning calendars to keep track of their study obligations. At this juncture parents can helpfully share their systems for managing their busy lives. "We keep a written schedule so we don't forget; and you can do the same. From here on, your life will keep getting more complicated to manage, not less."

Through coaching, parents can help the disorganized young person develop the skills to simplify, systematize, structure, remember, account, and plan. Slippage into adolescent disorganization is emotionally expensive because, in addition to creating problems from what went undone, it can cause a measure of anxiety from feeling out of control of more demands than they have known before. "I hate it when I can't find anything!"

The antidote for disorganization is for parents to help the young person create a new self-management system that imposes some personal order in what feels like the increasing chaos of her or his daily life. Thus, although inclined by disorganization at this age to lapse into a messier room, that emblematic expression of early adolescent freedom, supervising a more orderly personal space can sometimes help a young person feel more in control. The parental message is: "In a highly changing time, it is still possible to live in a somewhat regulated way. And it is simpler and less stressful when you do." However, there is the other byproduct of more complexity—distractibility, which disorganization only makes worse.

## Distractibility of Attention

As the child ventures more outside the family circle and enters adolescence, a rich offering of older offline and online activities opens up in a bewildering profusion, threatening to scatter their attention in a host of exciting directions. With so much to take in, why wouldn't a healthy adolescent become more distracted? Why wouldn't it take more distractibility to attend to it all? With attention swiftly shifting from one competing stimulus and experience to another to keep up with this abundance, why wouldn't the young person be reluctant to focus on any one task for very long lest something more novel or compelling is missed? The media, the marketplace, and the internet all thrive on creating new and different and swiftly changing stimuli to compete for young consumer attention, so distractibility is culturally enabled. No wonder the temptation to escape boring offline demands for online entertainment is so tempting for young adolescents.

Because of age-related disorganization, early adolescence can be a very distractible time. To the good, distractibility enables the young person to take wide-ranging notice of many aspects of their expanding world. "Sometimes it seems like my teenager is trying to keep track of too much. He pays attention to everything that's going on but to nothing in particular for very long, unless something exciting grabs his notice for a short while." Distractibility can have a functional side—like in a highly dangerous situation by keeping one's attention constantly roving to track shifting human conditions in one's surroundings, such as with what is happening at a teenage party where there is alcohol in use. Or when parents train their young driver not to just concentrate attention on the car ahead in traffic, but to keep track of what is further up ahead, on either side, and to what is happening behind. Scanning keeps attention in constant motion.

However, paying attention to less interesting or less stimulating activity—like schoolwork, for example—can be hard to do.

"He isn't listening in class."

"Her mind is constantly wandering."

It takes self-discipline or high interest to concentrate attention when focus is required. High stimulation entertaining activity (like computer games and electronic communication) tends to hold an easily distracted adolescent's attention, while low stimulation or boring activity (like homework and chores) often does not. To cope with boring tasks, the young adolescent may falsely claim to parents that a project has been done, may put them off with delay, or when delay is no longer possible, rush through to get tasks quickly completed, unmindful of how well or thoroughly they are accomplished. "I just want to get the homework done!" The problem is, while rushing through work gives the adolescent more time, it creates a poor outcome for the task. But how can parents get the young person to slow down? One way is for parents, as thankless supervisors, to require repetition of a swiftly done incomplete and error-filled assignment, to get the quality of production back up. Now repetition makes adolescent rushing inefficient because of having to go through the work all over again.

"I would have been better off taking more time in the first place!"

Highly distractible adolescents can feel like they are spinning their wheels by trying to go everywhere at once, and getting nowhere fast. In addition, distractibility tends to be inclined to escape a dreary task, not engage with it. A counter to distractibility is parental supervision, helping the young person practice focus and paying attention. This is also part of thankless parenting, but it is worth doing. Just as the purpose of parental discipline is to teach the adolescent self-discipline, so is the purpose of parental supervision to teach self-supervision.

Practice doesn't make perfect; but it does help the young person strengthen power of engagement when the lures for social and online escape are ever-present.

At this more distractible age, there is a temptation for concerned parents to seek professional help that recommends psychoactive, stimulant medication for their child, to help restore focus and concentration, to reduce restlessness and inattention. There are plenty of helpers who believe a deficit of attention should be chemically moderated. In response to such a recommendation I believe that parents should make sure that they are not resorting to a prescriptive drug for some kind of "quick fix," which substitutes for the increased daily effort of parental coaching and practice supervision that is now required. Such medication without education is a wasted opportunity because no one is helping the young person learn daily, through regular practice, to self-manage attention more effectively; and who knows what long-lasting effects reliance on psychoactive (mood- and mind-altering) drugs at this young age may bring.

For early adolescent disorganization and distractibility, I think the best rule is to try education before medication. If deciding on medication, don't do so without accompanying self-management education. And since disorganization can increase distractibility, and since distractibility can increase disorganization, continual practice of keeping order and sustaining concentration is worth doing. Repeated practice can create positive habits.

CHAPTER FIVE

# Fear of Trying and Boredom

"How can a child so fascinated with everything become an adolescent so often at loose ends?"

Adolescence (usually starting late elementary to early middle school) begins with some psychological "emptying out." The young person forsakes the old comforts, purposes, and enjoyments from childhood years and experiments with new interests and seeks new experiences as he or she starts the process of growing up.

Maybe the simplest metaphor of early adolescent change is a reptilian one—the young person is starting to shed their childhood "skin" and growing another that fits an older and maturing self. Until the new cognitive "skin" starts growing in, and there is mental development required for this, the young person can feel exposed and awkward and vulnerable—so no criticism, joking about, putting down, or embarrassment, please. This is a very sensitive period of growth, so act accordingly. When at home, parents or siblings should refrain from ridicule or making criticism. Parents declare, "Home is a tease-free zone."

Detachment and differentiation challenge the young person to start redefining by acting older and becoming more worldly-wise. This letting go of childhood definitions can create two complicated losses—of confidence and of interest. Loss of traditional confidence can create a fear of trying ("I don't like doing what I'm not good at!") and loss of traditional interest can create boredom ("I hate having nothing I want to do!" "I hate what I have to do!")

Both states of mind warrant parental attention. Consider each of these losses individually.

## Loss of Confidence

For parents, this early adolescent loss of confidence can create perplexity. "Our daughter was so adventurous and bold about new experiences all the way through elementary school. That's how we've always known her—as a really confident child. But now she's suddenly become more cautious and hesitant. She often refuses to attempt activities that we know she'd like. It's so frustrating to see! Why is she now afraid of trying something new when she frequently complains about being bored with what is old?"

The answer often is that the young person feels caught between a rock and a hard place, both restless for and reluctant to change. Having to go forth and enter a less protected, more complex, and daunting older arena of life experience, the young person is going to encounter much ignorance and uncertainty. Confronting the first year of middle school, a young person is honorably anxious. "It's scary how much there is to know!" In addition, there is a new social constraint with peers. Friends who were simply playmates in childhood have become peers to fit in and keep up with in adolescence. Now more comparison and competition for standing, place, and belonging become urgent priorities. Fitting less into childhood, it's easier to feel more alone in the family and daunted out in the world, which is why friends start becoming more important for social companionship and sanctuary.

Early adolescence is truly a brave new world because it takes courage to cope with so much uncertainty and so many unknowns. Thus, most young people encounter some loss of confidence as adolescence gets underway. The child who was often more self-confident in the sheltered family world than the emerging adolescent now feels insecure more often in life outside of the comfortable family circle, sometimes feeling scared. This can manifest as a fear of trying. Consider some common fears of trying. There can be:

- fear of failing: of not performing well enough;

- fear of visibility: of public exposure;

- fear of judgment: of criticism;

- fear of embarrassment: of being laughed at;

- fear of rejection: of being refused;

- fear of disappointment: of being let down;

- fear of defeat: of losing;

- fear of injury: of getting hurt;

- fear of surprise: of the unexpected;

- fear of exclusion: of not socially belonging;

- fear of getting in trouble: of being corrected;

- fear of success: of ongoing achievement pressure.

Myriad are the fears of trying that can beset young people as the age of growing up begins. Myriad are the frustrations of parents observing a young person's reluctance to try what she or he has not done before or is not naturally good at. Seeing potential for growth of adolescent capacity and experience, parents can become exasperated when they see hesitation and timidity slow development down.

"He's holding himself hostage to his fears. If he'd just go to the middle school dance with his friends, we know he'd have a good time!"

"No way!" is the answer, basing this decision on social risks the young person does not yet feel ready to take.

Parents might want to treat early adolescence for what it often is: an act of courage in the face of many normal fears. For example, why would a second grader who waved an eager arm to answer a teacher's question become a middle school student who dreads being called on in class? For the child, classroom learning was exciting, but for the young adolescent it can be fraught with social risk. The companion trait to fear of trying is the urge to quit. It can really get to some parents. "Why keep trying if I might fail anyway?" Or for the parent who doesn't want to raise a "quitter" when the going gets dull or hard, this behavior flies in the face of their belief in stick-to-it-ness. At this juncture, firm but gentle encouragement to see an effort through works better than criticizing the discouraged young person for feeling like giving up. "It's brave to keep making an effort when trying becomes hard to do."

It may be easier to empathize if parents remember how trying something new requires learning, and that learning itself at this vulnerable age can be risky in at least five ways.

First, you may have to declare ignorance: "I'll show I don't know."

Second, you may have to make mistakes: "I might get it wrong."

Third, you may have to look foolish: "Other people can see me mess up."

Fourth, you may feel stupid: "I'll end up acting dumb!"

Fifth, you may get evaluated: "Suppose I fail?"

When it comes to daring the five risks of learning, the adolescent can have more to lose than the child.

Parents can support effort at this anxious early adolescent age by empathizing with fear and putting the risks of trying and learning in a positive context; particularly when the process feels painful or the outcome is unwanted. So a parent offers this perspective to a thirteen-year-old who just failed to make the starting cut. "I know this is disheartening after trying so hard. But maybe you could treat your disappointment not with sadness, but with respect. As far as I'm concerned, you should be proud of yourself. I believe that if a person doesn't fail *some* times that it just means he or she is not trying hard enough. Good for you for getting out there and giving it a go!" In early adolescence parental empathy, encouragement, and recognition of hard effort can count for a lot. "It's not easy to give something new a try, good for you!"

Parents can cast the risks of learning in a positive light.

They can affirm ignorance: "All learning starts with admitting we don't know."

They can value mistakes: "Getting it wrong is often how you learn to get it right."

They can be sensitive to feeling stupid: "You're not being slow; you're learning at your own rate."

They can be respectful of appearing foolish: "Letting others see you struggle to learn is brave to do."

They can be supportive in evaluation: "Now you know more than you did before."

It's usually when parents are feeling tired or irritable or stressed, like helping with homework or study or a project after a long day, that they do what they never should. They act in ways that increase the risks of learning.

They are intolerant of ignorance: "You don't know that?"

They are impatient with mistakes: "You got it wrong *again*!"

They criticize capacity: "What's the matter with you?"

They ridicule foolishness: "You really look slow!"

They harshly evaluate: "You'll never learn!"

As the primary teacher in the adolescent's life, the parent must treat adolescent learning as sacred and safe or else they will end up encouraging reluctance to learn by making it feel scary to do.

Comparing entering sixth graders with graduating eighth graders, what I have often found is because of growth from hard effort, and in spite of their fears, these acts of daring (or courage, if you will) have resulted in an amazing transformation. Comparatively speaking, some insecure sixth-graders, thanks to hard courageous effort, become eighth-graders who can seem downright arrogant. A developmental challenge has been accepted and met, so confidence has been boosted.

## Loss of Interest

The detaching and differentiating adolescent is often less interested than was the child for whom life was a source of constant curiosity and endless fascination. Having separated from childhood by letting go of attachments to many precious childish pastimes, a young person experiences more not knowing what to do and where attention can be meaningfully paid. Now, how to satisfy oneself, how to entertain oneself, how to direct oneself, and how to keep oneself good company are all challenges that boredom can create. As childhood enjoyments are cast aside, it takes time searching for new activities and interests to fill the void. Until then, feeling discontented, distracted, restless, disconnected, at loose ends, and disengaged is usually part of the uncomfortable transition of growing up.

An important goal for parents with a young person at this vulnerable age is to help him or her treat boredom not as an unhappy emotional state from which to escape, but as a challenge to engage with, as an opportunity to develop resourcefulness and create fresh interest to grow. I believe that to learn to do this at this early stage reduces the temptation for impulsive excitement seeking, compulsive internet escape, and even mood and mind-altering substance use when they encounter boredom as they grow older. Boredom can either serve as a staging area for a lot of adolescent trouble when seeking relief from the discomfort, or serve as an opportunity to engage with disinterest and treat it as an opportunity to develop resourcefulness and creativity that strengthens growth.

Where the child had much she wanted to do, the young adolescent can spend more time lying around complaining of life's dreariness. "I'm so bored!" "There's nothing to do!" "I hate what I have to do!" "I need something to do!" "I'm tired of doing this!" "I don't want to do that!" "I can't think of anything to do!" A mom once poetically described her eleven-year-old falling into a state of "developmental lumphood"—a term that I thought aptly captured the restless immobility of boredom about which the young person complained.

Boredom can also result from the young adolescent's new sense of liberation. What she discovers is that freedom is one birthplace of boredom. Now that she has more choice, what is she supposed to do with it? In many cases the early adolescent doesn't know. Parents can often see this dilemma at the end of a middle school year. The young person was so excited to have the free time of approaching vacation—a relief from the boredom that entrapment in compulsory education brings that he or she may remark, "Freedom from schoolwork at last!"

But within days comes the crash. "There's nothing to do! I'm so bored!"

The young person doesn't know how to fill up the emptiness inside: "I want to do something but I don't know what!"

When the adolescent complains how "boredom is a pain," he is telling the truth. What is hard to "stand" about boredom? It's no psychological accident that we use comparable linguistic images to describe the impact of two common feelings, boredom and fear. We routinely say that one can be bored or scared "silly," "stiff," "to tears," "out of my mind," or even "to death." Easily discounted by parents, boredom is not a psychological state to be treated lightly or casually dismissed by parents. It involves serious emotional discomfort that can lead a young person into self-defeating and even self-harming behaviors. I believe the core pain of boredom is loneliness. The young person may say, "I have no good-feeling way to connect with myself, other people, or the world." Absent is the young adolescent having any fulfilling purpose, meaning, or activity. Yet boredom is not so much the problem as is what behaviors young people, individually or collectively, engage in to cope with or quell the pain.

Boredom is like another emotion that parents often trivialize but that is actually very painful for young adolescents—embarrassment. Where embarrassment is one step from humiliation and two steps from shame (so don't tease), boredom is one step from aimlessness and two steps from desperation (so don't discount it).

When boredom builds, restlessness develops that can motivate impulsive acting out for diversion to escape the pain. "I only did that for something to do!" Or, consider what can happen when young people are hanging around at loose ends with each other. Now, what the bored teenager would not do individually, she or he may be willing to commit in the company of peers. So, when in a group, the teenager impulsively goes along with substance use, mischief making, vandalizing, truancy, dangerous risk-taking, illegal activity, or even random violence to relieve the monotonous pain of tedium. Afterward, a young person caught in an act of exciting law breaking explains to the arresting officer, "We were tired of having nothing to do! We were just bored!" Sometimes a bad choice feels like it beats the boredom of having no good choices at all. Boredom can be "the Devil's Playground," a staging area and trigger for a lot of adolescent trouble. It can be hard for an adolescent to resist the impulse to escape from boredom because it comes in a double dose as two types of boredom can arise.

There is Type One Boredom from Emptiness of Interest: "I can't stand having nothing to do!" Consider solitary boredom, not knowing what to do with one's self and feeling empty of purpose. An example would be a young person doing the forbidden at home because making mischief felt better than having to endure the misery of feeling aimless.

There is Type Two Boredom from Entrapment in Disinterest: "I can't stand what I have to do!" An example would be a young person acting out in class at school because continuing to fill out the worksheets feels mind-numbing.

The challenge of managing boredom is dealing with the dissatisfaction it brings. Boredom can be an opening for growth by generating interest in a new direction. However, what makes boredom hard to constructively manage is the discouraged feeling of being stuck with no good way out. Like fatigue, boredom creates a negative outlook on possibilities. Early adolescence is a good age to help the young person learn to manage boredom constructively because as she or he grows older, the worldly escape and excitement and entertainment options become more dangerous. Parents can be instrumental in this early education by empathizing with the hard feelings boredom brings and by helping the young person take positive initiative to work their way out. "Maybe you can find a new or different way to interest yourself." If possible, they want the young person to draw on personal initiative, resourcefulness, and creativity to fill the void.

It is important for parents to monitor the level of boredom that their adolescent is experiencing. Is it passing (occasional) or protracted (ongoing)? If it appears protracted, parents should definitely pay attention, because adolescents can find themselves in an increasingly hard emotional place in which urgent options for coping can lead to more self or social harm. "I just cut on myself because I was bored." "We went tagging buildings because we were bored."

Parents can help an early adolescent who gets mired in boredom. Ironically, they can do what is often likely to engender the young person's complaints. They can take unappreciated actions on the young person's behalf, keeping in mind that once the teenager has had his complaining say, he is likely to do what they say, and even enjoy what he said he never would. "I hate how you made me go, but I had a good time once I got there." Just because he lacks power of initiative to get him unstuck from boredom doesn't mean he won't piggyback onto what his parents push, while blaming them for getting him started. The age of thankless parenting has arrived.

So consider several possible helpful parental roles:

Parent as Door Opener: Knowing their son or daughter, they can scout out activities or interests they believe might fit. "I'm not asking you to make some lengthy commitment to this, only to give it a try."

Parent as Activity Director: Being a source of demand for service and assistance, parents can request all manner of household project and community service help. "I know this doesn't interest you but it interests me, and it will provide something to keep you busy."

Parent as Social Substitute: Offering recreational activity, parents offer themselves as social company. "I know being with us is not the same as being with friends, but we'll do something with you (going out to eat, going to a movie) that you find fun to do."

Not all early adolescents fall away into boredom. Some young people can carry over old childhood interests into adolescence, like practicing music or continuing athletics, but I believe most do not. They are truly at some degree of loss of interest for a while. For these young people, developmental boredom simply comes with the territory of early adolescence. So, should a young person get stuck in a protracted spell of feeling empty of interest or entrapped in disinterest, a parental hand may help them find and make their way. From what I've seen of adolescent boredom, I believe this. Never underestimate its power (particularly among a group of teenagers hanging around at loose ends with "nothing to do") because in collective desperation they are more at risk of seeking escape through excitement that can create mischief or cause trouble, or even do themselves or others harm.

An antidote for lack of confidence as well as boredom is challenge—committing energy to something new or hard to do and in the process growing stronger and increasing one's sense of capacity. Teachers most valued by bored students in secondary school are usually not the ones who ignore them and let them slide by, but instead challenge these young people to grow.

"Even though I complained, she kept after me and wouldn't let me *not* learn."

Both as boosters of confidence and interest builders, parents can support a wide array of challenges in a young person's life—for example, contributing to family activities, improving operating capacity, maintaining a healthy regimen, practicing a skill, creating imaginative expression, solving a tough problem, fixing what is broken, entering a competition, participating in teamwork, providing volunteer assistance, overcoming a fear, starting a neighborhood service, helping someone meet a need, joining a leadership group, or just giving some possible new interest a try. Many are the ways that parents can support and enable early adolescent challenges, and they should.

Hopefully, what a young adolescent can learn from treating boredom as a challenge to be met, and not as an unhappiness to be escaped, such as with internet entertainment or use of mind-altering substances, is that no activity, no matter how unrewarding or routine or repetitive, is inherently boring. Since it is possible to take human interest in anything, boredom is in the person, not the activity. In this sense, "boring" is name-calling, degrading, and dismissing an activity because it doesn't appeal to one's immediate interest. Learn to take creative responsibility during normal spells of boredom in early adolescence, and boredom is less likely to lead a young person impulsively astray during the riskier years ahead. The resourcefulness to overcome boredom can feel empowering.

"With nothing better to do, I tried reading a book. And, you know, it wasn't so bad."

The parent's job is to see that their young adolescent is continually challenged, understanding that they may get more complaints than credit for their efforts. The antidote to fear of trying from loss of confidence, and boredom from loss of interest is often the same: engage in some active challenges to grow.

CHAPTER SIX

# Resistance and Conflict

"After another argument with our teenager, we
feel exhausted; but he isn't even winded!"

It's not just that adolescent detachment and differentiation create
more personal disorganization and distractibility; they create
more disagreements with parents as well. Aspects of increased
disagreement to be discussed are: Testing Limits, Active Resistance
and Argument, Passive Resistance and Delay, Understanding Parent/
Adolescent Conflict, Managing Conflict, and Tolerance for Conflict.
There are many moving parts for managing this issue.

## Testing Limits

Motivated by no longer being content to be defined and treated as
just a child, the young adolescent tests parental limits and demands
that circumscribed childhood and being a child to see if they still
hold in the new adolescent stage of life. Thus parents usually have
to re-clarify expected terms of family conduct at the outset of
adolescence.

The young person naturally wonders about how growing
older will alter his or her permitted freedom. Another definition
of adolescence is "liberation." From what old terms of childhood
conduct will she or he now be freed? What new freedom of
independence and individuality will she or he be allowed? And what
traditional importance for acting in accord with founding principles

of family life still remains? Some of this testing is usually done illicitly by seeing what can be gotten away with, and some is done forthrightly by questioning old family rules and routines. Parents have to promptly confront testing of the illicit kind. "Sneaking by us by not telling the whole truth is not okay. As when you were younger, you have to keep us adequately and accurately informed." And parents need to answer questions about which old rules still apply: "Yes, you still have to do weekly chores, have a regular bedtime, and check with us that homework is adequately done." Testing old limits creates new tensions.

From now on, the relationship between child and parent tends to become increasingly contested and abrasive over the young person's freedom of action for independence and freedom of expression for individuality. So when the adolescent contests parental authority over some personal action they won't allow (going to a friend's home after school without asking them first) or contests for parental acceptance over some personal statement they won't tolerate (wearing torn clothes to school to be in style) the issue at disagreement becomes jointly contested and conflict ensues. "I should be able to lead my own social life!" or "I should be able to dress the way my friends do!"

The job of a healthy adolescent is to push for more social freedom and personal expression; and the job of healthy parents is to restrain this push within the interests of safety and responsibility. This conflict of interests unfolds over the course of adolescence. In the face of growing disagreement, parents have to keep taking stands that communicate the family frame of reference of limits, demands, expectations, and values against the contrariness of adolescents, the competing influence of peers, and the appeal of the popular (media) influences. And they must confront increased abrasion in the relationship with their adolescent in two common forms of resistance: active resistance in the form of argument and passive resistance in the form of delay.

## Active Resistance: Argument

Ask parents how they feel about their adolescent arguing with them and many will say they could get by with less or even be content with none. They can find adolescent arguments pointless, irritating, disrespectful, and exhausting. Parents encounter an endless parade of objections, commonly in the form of questions.

"Why should I?"

"Why does it matter?"

"Why right now?"

"Why not later?"

"Why can't I?"

"Tell me why?"

This is why adolescent argumentativeness has been given a bad name, at least by some parents.

But consider some positives about adolescent arguing, which parents might want to keep in mind.

*Arguing is speaking up.* Adolescents declare something about what they think or want when arguing. Declaring themselves, they become more publicly known and socially defined. They put themselves on record by the position they express. Contrast an adolescent who can speak up for themselves with an adolescent who can't, and which of the two is better equipped to make their way through an adult world where self-expression counts? An adolescent who has been brought up to be seen but not heard, who won't give parents an argument, can be an adolescent who is too used to shutting up, too inexpressive, too pleasing, too anxious, too unassertive, and too invisible for their own good.

*Arguing is informative.* When an adolescent argues with parents, she or he is telling parents something about themselves— what matters to them, how they perceive what is going on, how they differ from parents. Since the teenager is the best informant parents have about what is going on in the adolescent mind, why wouldn't parents encourage arguing for the self-disclosure it provides? Why, instead of telling them to stop arguing, wouldn't they try to draw the young person out: "Can you tell me more, can you help me better understand? I want to hear all you have to say." Parents should value being told. An adolescent who won't give parents an argument can be like having a mystery child, a child in hiding who never tells them when she or he really disagrees, one who keeps parents in a constant state of ignorance about what the teenager really thinks and wants and feels.

*Arguing is practice.* Parents are like safe sparring partners when it comes to arguing as the young person takes on parents verbally to develop debate skills they can use with others. What the adolescent chooses to argue about is up to the teenager, but how that practice is conducted is up to parents who teach how to speak and listen when one disagrees, and what kind of language is okay and what is not. Sometimes parents will ruefully joke how they have raised a trained litigator who has attorney-level skills when it comes to advancing and defending her or his position. To create a good argument takes explanation, refutation, and staying power. An adolescent who can't give parents an argument may not be very well prepared to verbally take up for themselves and make their case with adult authorities, or may be at a social disadvantage when it comes to standing up to more verbally expressive peers.

*Arguing is talking out.* Acting out to settle a disagreement, by physical aggression or angry yelling, for example, is not the same as using reasoned words to argue about differing opinions to reach an agreement. Acting out to get one's way risks more hurt from the interaction and makes a unified resolution harder to achieve. Parents need to appreciate when their adolescent chooses to use verbal argument (speaking up) over acting out—like throwing a tantrum, slamming a door, or storming off. An adolescent who won't talk out disagreements with parents, but only acts out to get her or his way, is ill-prepared for a world of relationships where arguing is how many disagreements must be confronted, discussed, and peacefully resolved.

*Arguing is respectful.* Sometimes parents consider adolescent arguing as "talking back" to adults and being disrespectful— questioning what elders say when silent submission is the approved way to go. Actually, arguing with parents is a sign of respect. Disrespect would be totally ignoring what parents have to say. By arguing, the adolescent acknowledges parental rights to take positions, set limits, and make demands. Arguing is exercising the adolescent right to challenge the family powers that be on the way to growing up. An adolescent who is disrespectful not only disregards what parents have to say and want to have happen, but also holds their authority in such complete disregard that she or he does not consider them worth arguing with at all.

*Arguing is thoughtful.* To argue one's case, the adolescent has to organize his or her ideas. Reasonable statements must be advanced, counter arguments must be created, and personal positions must be defended. Debate must be conducted. Arguing isn't easy, particularly with adults who have more life experience doing it than you do. Sometimes research is needed to find out information that will help your case. Then there's putting your argument in a form that is least likely to offend and most likely to convince. Through it all, you have to keep your composure so frustration with opposition doesn't cause you to get angry, upset, and you emotionally defeat your persuasive way. It takes a lot of mental discipline to argue well. An adolescent who can't keep their thoughts together during the back and forth of argument may become disorganized or lose emotional control in the process. In either case they undermine their own effectiveness.

*Arguing is courageous.* Parents are among the most psychologically powerful people in the child and adolescent's world. To the degree that parents feel intimidating, that displeasing them feels hard to do, that offending them, risking their disapproval is hardest of all, arguing with them as an adolescent, can feel daunting. It is because taking on parents can feel scary that arguing with them can be an act of courage. "Speaking truth to power" is never easy, particularly to authoritative parents. With this knowledge in mind, parents can make it safe to argue with them by listening respectfully, not putting the young person down in any way, such as with humor or sarcasm, or with a nervous smile because the adult is uncomfortable in conflict. For adolescents, arguing with parents is no joking matter. It is a serious business because they want what they have to say to be taken seriously and not discounted or dismissed by reason of younger age or less life experience. An adolescent who avoids arguments at home, fearful of a high-controlling, domineering, or overbearing parent, not only may lack openness in that relationship, but may also lack the courage to engage in honest disagreement with significant others later on in life.

*Arguing is problem-solving.* Arguing is not simply an oppositional or adversarial or competitive process; it is a communicative and collaborative and constructive one. It takes two parties working together (with and against each other) to make it happen. This is why argument has positive possibilities. For example, when the teenager wants one course of action and the parent wants another, sharing and hearing their respective arguments can create a larger picture of the disagreement between them. As argument increases understanding, there is more room for discussion, negotiation, and bargaining. In the process, both can prove smarter than one of them because each knows more than they did before, and together they can craft an alternative outcome that mutually works. An adolescent who is taught the collaborative and communicative value of argument can learn to treat it as a valuable tool for jointly working out human disagreements, for solving problems, and for creating better possibilities. "We started disagreeing over what you couldn't do and we ended up with a plan for what you can do."

Of course, by instruction, example, and interaction, parents need to teach their adolescent to argue "respectfully," which means that no one is threatened or hurt and everyone is heard. To know how to argue safely and effectively is an extremely valuable life skill that enables a young person to represent and advocate for self-interest, to collaborate with others, and to negotiate their way. If you are the parent of a high school age adolescent, don't graduate a son or daughter from your care without it. Argument is the dialogue of disagreement, and effectively conducting that dialogue is worth knowing how to do.

## Passive Resistance: Delay

Although parents can get tired of arguments, they can get exhausted by delay—having whatever they ask for put off until later. Dealing with this aggravation while keeping a sense of humor can really help. I don't mean making fun of the teenager. This is never a good idea because it can do harm to a young person who feels belittled or demeaned. Laughing at oneself as a parent, however, and at the quandaries parenting adolescents can create, is a good example of the helpful use of humor. It can provide a welcome perspective on the process, lighten the challenges involved, and keep undue seriousness at bay.

Consider two examples of how parental sense of humor can help ease the way with the frustration of adolescent delay—that seemingly eternal dance between the parent who asks for something done "now," and the adolescent who is determined to do it "later."

First, consider a dad who brought the saving grace of humor into play. With some alterations, the scenario he described ran like this.

The man, who had hoped for a continuation of his child's timely compliance with parental requests, increasingly encountered his adolescent son's persistent postponements as a contest of "now versus later." For the adolescent, the specific matter of doing as asked had become a symbolic issue about operating on his own independent terms; a cause for self-respect based on creating delay that the young man felt was now worth investing in.

To the dad, the adolescent strategy for reluctant cooperation seemed to run like this:

"My son's operating strategy is simple: You can tell me what, I'll tell you when, and when I get enough 'when,' I'll do what you ask, partly.' The main thing is for him to make me work for whatever I want him to do. So, he'll finally agree to do what I requested, but just not completely. That's how he keeps the upper hand when I am keeping after him."

Against this backdrop, to show his son that the man meant what he asked for, the dad found himself matching will and wits with what he smilingly called "the dragon of delay." According to him, he never slayed the monster, but could subdue it for the moment by backing up his words with relentless pursuit that finally overcame the teenager's resistance. In so many words, the following was an example of the exquisite aggravation that he frequently had to endure.

"My fifteen-year-old just took a shower and there they are, wet towels all over the bathroom floor, where he always leaves them. 'Would you please hang up the towels,' I ask? "'Sure,' he cheerfully replies. And I wait for what I know is coming next: 'In a minute.'

"I mean it's not like I haven't been through this torment before; like about a million times. So I wait an hour to check the bathroom, and everything's okay. No one has disturbed the towels. They're resting nicely and probably so is he. So I poke my head into his room and remind him: *The towels*! You said you'd pick up the towels!'

"He looks at me and shakes his head like he was the long-suffering parent and I was the troublesome child. 'I wish you'd make up your mind,' he says. 'I'm doing my homework. You're always after me to do my homework. Can I do my homework without being interrupted?'

"Don't ask me how he does it, but now I'm feeling on the defensive. 'After you finish your homework you'll pick them up?' He just shakes his head like I'm some kind of defective and he doesn't know how he puts up with me. 'Yes. Yes. Yes. Now can I get back to work?'

"I feel like I'm imposing, so I leave.

"Two hours later the towels (remember the towels?), are *still* where he dropped them and I find him watching TV. Now I have him dead to rights. This is indefensible, so I say: 'If you have time to watch TV, you have time to pick up the towels.' This is when he gives me this pained look. He says, 'Once a week, is that asking too much? Once a week, I get to see my favorite program. The only one I care to watch. I've done my homework like you wanted. Now, can I watch my program? As soon as it's over, I'll get the towels.'

"Well, he did get his homework done. 'Okay,' I say. 'But right after it's over, the towels. No more excuses.' He nods in agreement and impatiently dismisses me with a long-suffering wave of his hand.

"An hour and a half later I can't believe it. The towels haven't been touched. I storm off to his room. His light is out. 'The towels!' I yell into the dark. 'What? What's the matter?' a groggy voice asks as though I'd woken him up? But I stand my ground. 'The towels,' I repeat. Silence. 'You woke me up to talk about towels?' he asks, implying that if there is something wrong, it's certainly not with him. 'You're always after me to get in bed on time. To get enough rest. And now you wake me up for this? *For towels?* Can't I get them in the morning? I'm tired too.'

"'You promise?' I ask. 'I promise,' he says. 'Now can I get some sleep?'

"Next morning, there he is about to leave for school when I notice the towels from last night have been joined by more towels from today's shower. That's when I lose it. I feel betrayed: 'Your promise! What about your promise?'

"You should have seen the look of utter disbelief on his face. 'You want me to miss the bus? You want me to be late for school? For towels? Which is more important, towels or school?' Fortunately, for once in my life I made the right decision: 'School? The heck with school! FIRST, YOU PICK UP THOSE TOWELS!'"

So according to the long-suffering father described above, the young man did finally retrieve the towels, except for the sodden one apparently overlooked, left beneath the bathroom sink, perhaps as a reminder that the "game" was still on.

"Five out of six is not a bad average," the dad smilingly concluded. Then, feeling delayed but apparently not defeated, he laughed. "Back to work!"

In reflection, the man managed to keep his sense of humor and in doing so maintained a strategy of relentless insistence to wear adolescent resistance down. A sense of play allowed him to treat parenting his adolescent partly as an ongoing game: "Make me as you can." In this game, parenting was a process of move and countermove, win some and lose some, concession and compromise, but never giving up because he was playing for positive influence with his son, for the teenager's welfare.

Even when tired by the necessity of this pursuit, his sense of humor lightened up his frustration. He never used it to attack his son with sarcasm or insult, and so observed this family rule about the safe use of humor: laugh when it lightens somebody up; don't laugh when it puts anybody down. So the man told me a story about his adolescent that was really a story on himself—laughing at his predicament and his own reactions, grudgingly admiring his son's spirit of opposition. Not taking the problem personally, he used humor to create perspective and refresh resolve.

Or consider a mother, faced with the same aggravation of routine adolescent delay, who with resourcefulness and humor created her light and effective way for dealing with another uncooperative mid-adolescent whose immediate response to any household request was delay: "I'll do it in a little while."

Of course, what she discovered was that "in a little while," if not pursued, could last forever. Rather than get offended or irritated by being put off, with good humor she rose to the challenge. "Active waiting" she called it. "Active waiting," I asked, because I'd never heard that term. "Yes," she explained. "As soon as I ask, he promises 'later.' Then he retreats into his room and closes the door. So I wait a couple minutes and then walk in, and stand by where he's lying on the bed with his laptop. I silently look at him with a loving smile on my face. He looks up. 'Mom, what are you doing just standing there? Looking at me like that?' 'Just waiting for you to do what I asked,' I cheerfully reply. 'I said I'd do it later, and I will!' 'I know you will and that's fine,' I say. 'And I don't mind waiting wherever you are. I'll just follow you around until you keep your word.'" "And this works?" I asked. "Like a charm," she said. "And because I keep smiling while I keep after him, he shakes his head, usually gives a laugh, and ends up doing what I asked."

Although it's easy to get frustrated with adolescent delay, and tempting to punish on that account, supervision usually works best—relentless parental insistence at last wearing down stubborn resistance. The lesson for parents is that if a request is worth making, and if a rule is worth keeping, then always pursue the first to completion and patrol the second for compliance. In both cases follow-through can take some work, but when parents do, they show they mean what they say. When they do not, young adolescents can be tempted to exploit that inconsistency and doubt the firmness of parental resolve.

## Understanding Parent/Adolescent Conflict

As suggested at the outset of this chapter, the developmental forces of detachment and differentiation that drive adolescence typically result in more disagreements to experience and more diversity to encompass than was true between parent and child. This does *not* mean that parent and teenager enter some kind of "war zone" with each other. It simply means that now separation, experimentation, and opposition for freedom of action and expression's sake are going to create more points of contention. Conflict does not mean that something is "wrong" in their relationship. Conflicting interests are normal and verbal conflict is functional because it allows both parties to talk out (as opposed to act out) their disagreements. In a 2009 book I wrote about family conflict, *Stop the Screaming*, I reminded parents that if they lacked the tools for getting along and staying connected and in communication when significant differences arise, then something was amiss.

There can be an inequality in tolerance for conflict between parent and teenager. Sometimes it seems like the adolescent, used to more push-and-shove talk with peers, is often up for conflict with parents, which the parents would rather avoid. For parents it consumes energy and is a stressor but for the young person it is business as usual pressing for what is wanted, challenging what is not.

In general, both mothers and fathers need to beware the trap of *reactive parenting* where they develop a "tip-toe response" around their confrontational, intensely expressive, or explosive adolescent, by playing wait-and-see how she is feeling before asking for what they need. Through avoiding possible conflict, they have given the teenager active power of emotional initiative to drive their behavior with her moods. "The whole family revolves around not getting *her* upset!"

In this case, parents need to reclaim the active position. So when the front door slams to announce the teenager's arrival home after school, rather than stay out of her way, they get in her way, say they are glad to see her, and then initiate some request for what they need to have her do. Of course, she objects; but they persist. Now they have caused her to be more reactive because they have started setting terms of household engagement. This may not seem like a great choice, but it is better for the parents to make some demands so the teenager learns to operate in a healthy two-way give and take with them.

Verbal conflict is that essential process of spoken communication through which they can safely confront, discuss, and resolve inevitable human differences arising between them. Maintaining constructive dialogue when in active joint disagreement can be very hard to do.

## Managing Conflict

Safety is the most important rule for conducting family conflict. The parental model and message needs to be that when in conflict no one either threatens or inflicts any verbal, emotional, or physical harm on the other. This rule is not simple to comply with. In families, conflict can be an emotionally arousing experience, as members get frustrated and impatient when dealing with opposition. Impulse can take over and tempers can flare as people start "thinking" with their feelings (losing emotional sobriety) and increasingly resort to harsh tactics like yelling or threatening, and the use of negative labels about the other person, which is really name-calling.

"What a stupid idea! You're just too ignorant to understand!"

Thus, attacking language further inflames emotion, while vocal volume goes up. People who are in conflict yell to be heard, to get their way, and to relieve frustration. Yelling usually accomplishes none of these objectives; but it does intensify the interaction by raising the emotional stakes. Sometimes, yelling can be a tool of emotional extortion, like throwing a tantrum to get one's way. Instead of reasonably declaring what the person wants or doesn't want to have happen, she or he uses an expression of intense emotion like acting very mad or very sad, for example, to manipulate the other person into backing off, backing down, giving way, or giving in, to settle the upset person down.

"I'd rather give in to my parents when we disagree than to displease them. I can't stand it when they act unhappy with me!" Thus emotional extortion can inhibit honesty of spoken communication between parent and adolescent. And the reverse is just as common: parents who can't maintain firm stands against a teenager who knows how to act unhappy to persuasive effect. "We can't bear to disappoint her, and she knows it."

In general, it's best that parent and adolescent do not argue when either is feeling emotionally upset. There isn't a "thinking person home." Better to take a break to cool down before continuing with the discussion. In family conflict, it's better to let judgment, not emotion, rule.

Emotional arousal in conflict often causes the choice of words to become less specific and operational, more critical than objective, and more extreme and abstract. So the parent, tired of the teenager's dishes left unwashed once again, addresses the issue by attacking the young person's character, "You're so lazy and inconsiderate!" Feeling insulted, the teenager fires back, "Well, all you ever do is blame and complain!" Now they've managed to create a big emotional reaction to a small incident. Suppose, instead, that the parent had stuck to specifics and kept the conversation to "getting the dirty dishes picked up, washed, and put away." While it's easy to get upset and lose emotional sobriety in conflict, it's worth the effort to keep it.

In conflict with their teenager, parents must model the kind of verbal behavior they want in return. Imitating the parent's calm, the teenager can be encouraged to talk in more measured terms. Conflict can create resemblance this way. If the young person starts using hurtful language, the parent needs to declare a time out: "We need to stop discussing what we disagree about and talk instead about how to safely and respectfully conduct this communication. I don't name-call you, and I don't want you name-calling me. I feel hurt when you use language like that, and I want us to be able to debate a difference of opinion without either one of us giving or receiving harm. Let's separate for ten minutes, bring the emotions down, and then reengage when our cooler heads can prevail."

The first priority in managing any conflict between parent and adolescent is *not* resolving the issue at difference. That is secondary. Number one priority is keeping conflict *safe*, each party monitoring and taking responsibility for their emotional arousal, taking a short time out to restore reasonable control if needed, and in doing so setting a time when to take up the disagreement again. What the adolescent usually doesn't understand, but the parent *must* understand, is that the conduct of their conflict is formative. So the college student reflects, "I used to cut down my parents when we got into fights to get my way, and I'm doing it with my love partner now." Except there is this sad difference: where parents tolerated this mistreatment for the sake of love, the love partner may refuse to accept this mistreatment and simply exit the relationship. "I don't have to put up with that!" In general, sticks and stones may break more bones, but hostile words do most of the damage.

In the great curriculum of family life, much that is formative is taught—managing cooperation, communicating, coping with change, and conducting conflict amongst them. The primary teachers in an adolescent's life are parents. The adult example, interaction, and instruction they provide, is educational. So conflict is not something parents have with their adolescent, it is something they *do* with their adolescent. It is a performance act, and the adolescent is always watching and learning.

In most caring relationships, including those between parent and teenager, more disagreements are worked around by talking, tolerance, and adjustment than are worked through by confrontation and negotiation. A disagreement can only be turned into a conflict when both parties agree to mutually contest the issue at difference.

*Conflict is always cooperative.* It requires collaboration. It takes two to make conflict, and only one to stop it. If parents want to stop adolescent arguing, if they want that verbal exchange to cease, the way to do it is *not* arguing with the young person to stop arguing. Parents model and encourage the very behavior they wish to stop. The solution simply is to stop arguing back. For parents who always need to have the last word to feel in charge, this solution can seem impossible to do. However, when weary of the ongoing verbal conflict, and having stated all they have to contribute to the issue, ceasing their collaboration is usually the best option.

"I have nothing more to say, my mind is made up, but I will certainly hear all that you have to say." The adolescent can't have a "fight" with a parent who refuses to fight back.

Besides conflict between parent and teenager, there is growing conflict between adolescent siblings over issues of competition and dominance. Being close in age and of the same sex (except in the case of identical twins who can have a strong drive to share similarity) tends to create the most adolescent sibling conflict. Sibling conflict, from bickering to battling, can serve a number of purposes. It can contest a difference, test power, vent emotion, create companionship, and escape boredom because there is nothing better to do. Whatever the motivation, parents need to state the rule of safety. "While I will hold you both responsible for any quarrel between you, since it is cooperative, I will hold you separately accountable for how you each treat each other in the fight. Should either one of you engage in behavior that hurts the other person, the person doing the hurt will have some business to discuss with me about safe communication." Parents have to be willing to monitor and govern the conduct of conflict between siblings so it does not get out of hand, whether it's one teenager bullying or hurting the other, or both teens getting into damaging free-for-alls without restraint.

## Tolerance for Conflict

Come the child's adolescence, there can also be more conflict between parents about when and how to take a stand for regulation and opposition over what the teenager wants or doesn't want to do, or over who will take supervisory responsibility to keep after an adolescent to complete tasks or see a commitment has been kept.

From what I've observed in counseling, it is more common for mothers to be comfortable in conflict with their adolescent than for fathers who may want to avoid it or shut it down. So a mom may hang tough with an adolescent daughter while the dad stays uninvolved and complains about living with so much female discord.

"Why do you have to fight with our daughter so much?" the father asks.

"Because she needs that kind of attention from me right now," is the mother's reply.

"She has to push against me to get more separation from me, while fearing that if she pushes too hard she will push my love away. But I hang in there with her, going toe to toe, so she knows I'm there when the going gets tough and she can't drive my caring away. The conflict doesn't distance us; it keeps us close."

So why do more mothers seem comfortable doing conflict with their adolescent than dads? I think the explanation for this difference between mother and father may be rooted in how each was socialized in same-sex peer groups growing up. In girl groups there can be an emphasis on confiding for intimacy and a focus on relationship skills. Hence conflict may be treated as an act of communication to help better understand human differences. In boy groups there can be an emphasis on jockeying for position and a focus on competition skills. Hence conflict may be treated as a contest to defend or assert social dominance. In general, I believe the "female" model for dealing with conflict with adolescents works better than the "male" model. When in conflict with their teenager, it's better to treat the young person as an informant than an opponent. It's better for parents to normalize and appreciate the value of healthy conflict with their adolescent. Treat conflict as a challenge in interpersonal problem-solving, not as an exercise of power and parents will be teaching the young person to do the same. I wrote a 2007 book, *The Connected Father,* about how fathers often had a harder time parenting an adolescent, particularly when in conflict, than do mothers.

The "competition for dominance" approach to conflict can lead to power struggles, which are never a good idea because they tempt parents to "win at all costs" and thus risk damaging the relationship. As for the adolescent "loser" on that occasion, she or he may build resentment and increase resolve to prevail in the next encounter.

The parent declares, "I'll show you who's in charge!"

The teenager thinks, *Next time, I'll show you!*

When a parent engages in a power struggle with their teenager about who is dominant, that adult unwittingly creates an *isometric encounter*. Pushing hard against a tougher adult resistance, the adolescent is strengthened even when losing, and the adult is weakened in the long run, for now the young person will only be stronger in the next encounter. Parents can take a stand and remain firm for the adolescent's well-being. "When you don't agree with a stand I take for your best interests against what you want, please know this: I am not doing this against you; I am doing it for you. I am on your side. I do not enjoy frustrating or denying what you want. And just because I will not change my mind does not mean I do not want to hear all you have to say. I promise to be firm where I have to and give you reasons why, to be flexible where I can, and to always give a full hearing to whatever you have to say."

This last part is important, because a teenager who has been given a full hearing is more likely to grudgingly accept an unpopular parental stand than a young person who has not been allowed to have her or his say.

# CHAPTER SEVEN

# Reluctance to Work and to Study

*"I've got better things to do than schoolwork; it's good enough to just get by!"*

In a lot of ways, the concepts of adolescent and *work* don't fit together as easily as child and work did. To see this change of attitude in action, parents need look no further than the schoolroom. Doing so might help them understand that this altered attitude toward work is not from something amiss in their parenting so much as it is part of the impact of early adolescent change.

For example, the kindergarten teacher asks the children who wants to be on the "RCC," Room Clean-up Committee, this week (staying fifteen minutes after school on Fridays to help sweep the floor, straighten the shelves, clean the critter cages for the next week), and almost all the hands go up frantically waving, voices beseeching, "Me! Me! Me!" This is a high status job at age five, and virtually everyone wants to be selected. The opportunity for work is treated as a privilege, an empowering chance to participate in an activity grown-ups do and approve of, the child feeling more grown-up in the process.

Ask a class of seventh graders for comparable assistance, however, and the teacher is likely to find less volunteer spirit to draw on. What self-respecting middle school student wants to pull after-hours duty at school, and right before a weekend, not to mention looking like they're angling for "teacher's pet?" Now the opportunity for more work is considered additional drudgery. Something has happened to the reputation of work.

So, what is work, and what is the problem? For purposes of discussion, think of *work* as the process of will motivating effort to get some *task* accomplished. When work is for fun we call it play. But when work is not easy or freely chosen or enjoyable, it can become more unwanted and difficult to do. At such times, work ethic and self-discipline can come to the rescue. For the most part, these two self-management skills must be learned through practice which adults have had more time to do than young adolescents. In early adolescence, two work problems commonly arise: Reluctance to Work, and Reluctance to Study.

## Reluctance to Work

Because most parents find that it takes unending labor to live and make a living, accepting this hard fact of life they tend to feel frustrated when the early adolescent (around ages nine to thirteen) becomes more reluctant to do work compared to when he or she was a child. They naturally wonder, what happened to Mom's or Dad's willing and eager little helper? They fondly remember the child's delight in doing work assigned by parents. "Can I do it too?"

But what was an esteem-filling invitation for the little child can be treated as an aggravating imposition by the more self-centered adolescent, now preoccupied with an agenda of her own. "I'm busy!"

In the child's place parents see a larger, older, more capable young person who should be of even more help, but who turns out to be too otherwise occupied or too tired or too out of sorts or too disinclined to kick in the effort, at least without the parents making additional persuasive efforts. And when told that assistance is expected even when the young person feels disinclined, parental request can become a matter of debate: "Why do I have to?" An argument ensues or he can resort to delay:—"I'll do it later"—in the hopes that putting off the unpleasant task may make it go away. Here, parents often commit one of three common mistakes:

- they forget what they asked for,

- they get tired of repeatedly asking and let it go, or

- they give up and do it themselves.

These are big mistakes because on all three counts what is lost is the opportunity for the teenager to feel enrolled as a working part of the family, as an unpaid contributor to household functioning, and support. "You're a member of Team Family, and I expect you to join in when there's work to be done." The parental message needs to be that a working family takes a lot of shared, donated labor to support collective daily functioning. Everybody has some family contribution of value they are expected to kick in willingly and free of charge. To do none of the work and yet receive benefits can lead to an unhealthy adolescent sense of entitlement. "You should do for me; I don't have to do for you." Parents resent the inequitable situation and uncooperative attitude, often blaming the adolescent, when they are responsible for creating the inequity by allowing it.

One of my favorite lines about this early adolescent antipathy to work came from a parent at a public talk many years ago describing her middle school daughter's increasing reluctance to do chores.

"She's become allergic to work; it irritates her mood."

The early adolescent definition of work can be a demotivating one.

"Work is whatever older people make you do that you don't want to do or shouldn't have to do, or at least not right away."

Work demands are emblematic of adult authority and so, in token of emerging independence, early adolescents often feel they should resist requests from adult powers that be on that account. Subscribing to these beliefs about work, a youthful anti-work ethic may develop: to work as hard as you can, for as long as you can, to get out of doing as much work as you can, as often as you can.

So a parent complains, "I keep telling her if she'd just do it right away without arguing and putting it off, and then having to redo it because it wasn't done correctly the first time, she could get the whole job done in fifteen minutes instead of dragging it out for three exhausting hours, with the added aggravation of me chasing her down. But she insists on taking her time!" But I disagree: "No, she insists on taking *your* time, constantly putting what you want on hold until later, which is as late as she can make it. That's the point. You get *what* you want *when* she agrees to do it." That is a common early adolescent compromise.

So if the early adolescent is more developmentally disposed to not doing work for parents, should they just back off, save their energy, and let the young person have their more resistant way? The answer is absolutely not—both for the outcome now and later.

With relentless supervision, responsible parents need to keep after the completion of chores and homework assignments so that, with practice, a young person develops a strong work habit or ethic. He must learn to overcome his own resistance and accomplish what he doesn't always want to do.

What parents hope is that by the end of high school, the young person has forsaken his work-resistant ways and is able to take care of work demands in a timely and efficient way. When he has not, this developmentally acquired resistance can come back to bite him in the form of procrastination.

Type One Procrastination is when the young person waits until the last minute and then uses the sense of crisis to motivate emergency effort. Type Two Procrastination is when a young person waits too long and now it's too late to get the task done. Particularly when entering college, procrastination of both kinds (putting off work with all kinds of diversions, escapes, excuses, empty resolutions, and false promises) can contribute to the high rate of academic failure and flunking out among freshmen (on average, about 50 percent according to the *Journal of College Retention*). Now, this last-stage adolescent is no longer resisting work demands from parents, but from themselves: "I can't make myself get work done on time, and sometimes at all!"

So what might parents wish for their adolescent to learn when it comes to work? Here are a few thoughts:

- Be able to work to get what you want and to make your way.

- Be able to work when you don't feel like it, but there is work to do.

- Be able to work with and for others.

- Be able to get work done in a timely way.

- Be able to work to accomplish what you agreed to do.

- Be able to work hard at what matters to you.

- Be able to develop good work habits.

- Be able to find enjoy work you enjoy doing.

For many young people beginning adolescence, work is an acquired taste. Parents need to help encourage this acquisition. For some parents, there arises this motivational question: to what degree should parents monetize normal cooperation? For example, in the face of adolescent reluctance to do household work, should parents use the persuasive power of money—to give or withhold—to get chores accomplished?

One rationale for this payment can be to teach working to make money. "This is the way of the world," some parents explain. "This is why we have jobs and why we give you household jobs to do, so you can get used to working for money too." These parents teach chores as earning experiences.

Other parents might see a downside to paying for household help like chores because that gets in the way of household contribution requirements that everyone freely donates to help support the common good. This investment creates a sense of ownership in the family because everyone has a working part to play. Everyone has some valuable labor to offer to keep the family system up and running. These parents might explain, "For helping with the basics, nobody gets paid, but everybody benefits. Like it or not, life takes work, and that includes working to help maintain the family. You will need to do your share."

## Reluctance to Study

Early adolescence can be the enemy of academic performance. With many young people, there can be an Early Adolescent Achievement Drop as faltering effort results in falling grades. Parents need to understand why this can happen and what to do.

Early adolescence (around age nine to thirteen) can be the enemy of school achievement. No longer content to be defined and treated as just a "child," some early adolescents, asserting new independence and individuality, can rebelliously resist demands of formal education to their own expense. This self-defeating behavior can be supported by a kind of counter-cultural, anti-authority attitude mirrored in beliefs of the following kinds:

"It's dumb to ask questions."

"It's smart to act stupid."

"It's stupid to work hard."

"It's cool not to care."

"It's good to act bad."

"It's right to buck the system."

"It's good enough to just get by."

Entering adolescence, a child's priorities can change. While the child at school may have placed achievement number one, peer acceptance number two, and personal appearance number three; in early adolescence these priorities can be reversed. Now the young person puts personal appearance number one because it has so much bearing on priority number two, peer acceptance, and thus the importance of academic achievement comes in a distant third. This change in motivation can catch parents off guard when the conscientious child, who once took pride in doing well, becomes the apathetic adolescent who seems to not care about doing poorly. The old academic priority of working hard to do well can give way to a more urgent priority of fitting in with friends and being popular, and being internet-connected for entertainment and socializing's sake.

In most cases, this performance drop doesn't really mean the adolescent no longer values doing well academically, it just means he or she doesn't want to do the work to do well—such as classwork, homework, reports, projects, papers, and studying for tests.

So it is at this juncture that parents find themselves confronted by a number of anti-achievement behaviors. The most common ones are:

• Not bringing homework essentials home.

• "Forgetting" or lying about homework assignments.

• Not turning completed homework in.

• Not finishing class work.

• Not paying attention or being disruptive in class.

All these behaviors contribute to the early adolescent achievement drop. They are easily remedied by parents who are willing to take a stand for the adolescent's best interests against what he or she wants.

Two avenues *not* to take to address these behaviors include becoming emotionally upset or resorting to rewards or punishments to encourage different choices. Although both avenues can work with a young child who wants to please parents and values material incentives, they tend to be counterproductive with the adolescent who often courts parental disapproval and may resent a show of parental control over desirable resources.

Grades are too important to become emotionally upset about. Growth is just a gathering of power, from dependence to independence. The job of parents is to help their adolescent gather that power in appropriate ways. It is not appropriate for parents to give the adolescent power to get them upset over grades because the academic focus is lost and the young person wins influence over parental feelings. "I can really ramp my parents up by letting my grades go down." When parents act upset over grades, they often turn a performance problem into an emotional encounter with their adolescent that distracts effective attention from practically addressing the performance issues at hand.

Grades are too important to either reward or punish adolescents. Parents often mistakenly believe that offering an adolescent some significant payoff for good grades will be seen as a reward, when in fact it is not. Most adolescents will see it as a threat that they resent.

"If you say you're going to give me five dollars for an 'A,' that just means that if I don't get an 'A,' I don't get the five dollars!"

As for taking away some resource or freedom "until grades improve," that approach usually engenders more resistance than cooperation.

"I don't care what you take away; you can't make me do my work!"

And the young adolescent will go down in flames to prove to parents that such tactics are doomed to fail. When parents reward or punish for grades, they often turn a performance issue into a power struggle with their adolescent.

What then are parents supposed to do? Just stand by and watch their early adolescent fail by failing to work? Sometimes that's the advice middle school teachers give to parents.

"Don't be overprotective. Let your child fail and learn responsibility from the consequences."

However, in many cases this is bad advice. Unless the adolescent is unusually mature and manages to self-correct the downward spiral, he or she will only learn to adjust to lowered standards or failure, treating this adjustment as okay when it is not. He or she may say, "This is the best that I can do!" At worst, resigned parents will adjust their expectations downward by responding, "Well, all we ask is that at least you pass!"

What a terrible thing to say to a capable young person! What a betrayal of parental responsibility, which is to see that the early adolescent keeps performing up to operating capacity. "Well, how would we know what his operating capacity is?" the parents ask.

The answer is, find an academic benchmark. Take a look at how well he did in some fourth or fifth grade semester, for example, when he was performing all his classwork at school and completing all assignments sent home. Now, don't talk to the young person about "doing your best," "working your hardest," or "performing up to potential." These are just abstracts; and besides how many people ever achieve such ideals? Rather, specify the record. "Back in fifth grade, fall semester, you completed all your work and got a combination of A's and B's. So that is the minimal standard of performance we will hold you to now. And if for any reason you fall below that, we will give you our supervisory support so you can maintain the standard. Your report card counts." Why does it count?

The answer is that a report card is meant to act like a mirror, the adolescent seeing in that reflection an adequate picture of his or her capabilities. But suppose an early adolescent achievement drop occurs? If emotional upset, and rewards and punishments, tend to be ineffective with the early adolescent at this common juncture, then what can parents effectively do?

The answer is to give supervision. Remember that the early adolescent, unlike the child, does not want parents showing up in his or her world at school. Now social independence means keeping a public presence of parents as far away from his or her society of peers as possible. Now company of parents at school feels like a public embarrassment because he or she should be able to handle school without their interference. To which parents reply: "We have no desire to interfere at school so long as you are taking care of business. However, just to let you know, if you do not do school work and if you are acting inappropriately in class, we will extend our supervision into your school to help you make better choices." The operative word in the advice that follows is *together*.

So, if homework resources are not brought home, parents may want to say, "since you are having a hard time remembering to bring home materials to complete your assignments, *together* at the end of the day you and I will make the rounds of all your teachers to make sure you have what you need."

If parents are told there is no homework when it turns out there was, they may want to say, "Since you said you had no homework, but you did, we will meet *together* with your teacher. You will have the opportunity to explain why you said there was no homework when there was, how come you misrepresented what the teacher said, and what you will do differently the next time so we will be told the truth. And this weekend, before you get to do anything you want to do, you will have to complete the missed assignments, turning them in for zero credit because they are late."

If the adolescent does the homework, but chooses not to turn it in, parents may want to say, "Since you can't manage to turn in your homework, I will go up to school with you and *together* we will walk the halls and make the rounds of all your teachers to make sure your homework gets turned in."

If the adolescent is talking too much or acting out disruptively in class parents may want to say, "Although this is not something I want to do, I am willing to take time off from work and sit *together* with you in class to help you pay attention to what the teacher asks."

Usually, an early adolescent will not welcome any of these suggestions, considering them outrageously invasive, preferring to correct self-defeating conduct instead of suffering social discomfort. What parents are really saying in each case, however, is that so long as self-correction does not occur, they are committed to provide steadfast supervisory support because they know school performance that reflects actual ability will ultimately cause the adolescent to feel better about him or herself, now and in the years ahead. Offering to provide on-site supervision is something parents are not doing *to* the early adolescent but rather *for* the young person, for the sake of his or her well-being now and in the future. I believe what parents should not do is to leave falling or failing academic effort in the hands of an apathetic early adolescent who, discounting the importance of schoolwork, creates a record of substandard performance that will stand in the way of academic achievement and later opportunity.

One worthy goal for parents to have for their young adolescent by the end of middle school is this: "We want our daughter or son to graduate middle school in full self-management mode, able to complete all classwork and homework in a timely way without needing our support or our supervision to get it done."

## ISSUES IN MID-ADOLESCENCE
## (AGES THIRTEEN TO FIFTEEN)

# FORMING A FAMILY
# OF FRIENDS

Mid-adolescence challenges the young person
in two powerful ways.

First and foremost, most young people understand that
adolescence is no time to go it alone. On this journey of
redefinition, it's important to have the companionship
and support of peers who are also struggling to become
different in the same ways they are. However, because
everyone is struggling to fit in, group membership comes
with a degree of ongoing social *insecurity*.

Second, now that most young people are undergoing
puberty—sexual maturity changing their bodies in ways they
did not expect, do not control, and often may not like—there
is also the concern of one's expression of gender identity and
role—how to look and act more womanly or manly. Criticizing
themselves as compared with peers and media ideals they
can experience painful *self-consciousness*.

During this self-preoccupied stage of adolescent growth,
parents often find their teenager less considerate and more
difficult to engage with than before.

CHAPTER EIGHT

# Puberty and Vulnerability

"I don't like how my body is growing and
how it makes me feel!"

The physical, emotional, and hormonal changes of puberty can generate more discomfort for the adolescent. "She's become so preoccupied with her looks, acts like her image is everything, is pricklier to live with, and is extremely sensitive to other people's comments about her!" Puberty can be a challenge for a young person to manage, thus a challenging time for parents too. Consider four areas of vulnerability that the young person must manage: Changing Physical Appearance, Increased Self-consciousness, Rising Emotional Intensity, and Susceptibility to Embarrassment.

## Changing Physical Appearance

Puberty is a big deal. Usually beginning during early to mid-adolescence (around ages nine to fifteen), unfolding over a period of one to three years, puberty culminates in sexual maturity—the capacity to produce eggs for the female or sperm for the male. However, this hormonal process causes alterations in appearance as well. For example, growth spurts occur, endowing one now with a larger and older-looking body to manage. For girls, hips broaden, breasts swell, and menstruation begins. For boys, muscles enlarge, voices drop, and ejaculation begins. For both, there is more hair around sex organs, more bodily odor, and more active skin glands that can create blemishing. (See my book, *Surviving Your Child's Adolescence.*)

Now the young person feels anxiously at the mercy of bodily changes not in their control. There is concern about how their growing older body is turning out. There is an increased need for physical privacy. There is more time devoted to self-inspection and social preparation. There is more peer attention paid to personal appearance to the good (admiration) and to the bad (teasing). There is more awkward social association with the opposite sex after childhood years spent mostly with same-sex friends. There is an awakening of relationship fantasies and sexual interest as more girls sample romance fiction and more boys sample pornography. There are concerns about gender definition of womanliness or manliness and how to express them. There are early questions about one's sexuality. There's an increased preoccupation with managing one's looks because they can affect how one is identified, how one is treated, how one fits in, how one belongs.

Adolescence is a time of psychological and social change that grows a young person from childhood to young adult independence and identity; puberty is a biochemical and physiological change that leads to sexual maturity. Adolescent change often begins earlier than puberty; but when puberty coincides with the onset of adolescence, the adolescent process can become more intense.

While the child was comparatively unmindful of personal looks, with puberty and adolescence physical appearance becomes a primary concern. How best to look is the pressing question. Popular icons and models in the media and advertising marketplace now provide a compelling answer in the forms of idealized models of youthful femininity and masculinity, sexual attractiveness and beauty, which can turn out to have a lot of ugly consequences for young people who feel they do not measure up.

Since ideal is rarely real, very few young people can meet these physical standards of womanly and manly physical appearance, be it the gymnast or fashion model body type for females or the bodybuilder or jock body type for males. Thus, comparing themselves to these ideals and coming up wanting, they feel badly about their bodies more often than not. However, dissatisfaction with one's looks doesn't mean that efforts at changing appearance are not being made. At the extreme, girls, through diet and laxatives, can be driven to slim down and get thinner; while boys, at the extreme, through supplements and weight training, can be driven to bulk up to get stronger.

Now is when a lot of distorted thinking about body image develops: young women can't appear too slender, and young men can't appear too muscular. Having dressed wrong for school, the young adolescent might complain, "I've had a bad body day!" The problem, comparatively speaking, is one can't be physically attractive enough. Through the physical models used in advertising to the youthful icons entertainment celebrates, and through the narrow physical criteria of personal worth that are popularly encouraged, the media has a lot of adolescent unhappiness to answer for. To counter the media message, the repeated parental reminder might be: "The popularized physical ideal is a distortion because the human body comes in infinitely varied forms. That variety is what is real, each variation to be valued in its own way. We believe attending to your appearance is fine so long as you don't use it to judge the worth of the person you are."

Just because this message often seems to fall on deaf ears at this young age is no reason not to keep giving it. In addition, parents need to keep an ear out for critical thinking about body image, and they need to watch for emotional preoccupation with food in possibly harmful ways—to the extreme like fad dieting, bingeing, purging, or starving.

Dressing according to fashion becomes more important to keep up with and fit in with friends. Thus when the teenager complains they have nothing to wear, and the parent complains about a closet full of clothes that fit just fine, the adult doesn't understand that "fit" is not a physical issue, but a fashionable one. "I'd be laughed out of school if I showed up in that outfit. That's so last year!" Or consider the common case of the beloved blue jeans, which are treated as the adolescent's only pair. "What do you mean they're in the wash? Now I've got nothing to wear!" But when the parent suggests a lot of other available pants, the teenager rejects them out of hand. "This is the only pair that I look good in!" Dressing for a secure, comfortable, physical appearance counts for a lot.

## Increased Self-Consciousness

Puberty increases the severity of physical self-evaluation. Waking up in the morning it can take an act of courage to confront one's image in the mirror and behold the latest tragedy that has befallen their body over the night before.

"Where did this new zit come from?"

"Do I look fatter than yesterday?"

Now they have to take it to school for the whole world to see! Or maybe last night, in a fit of bored or desperate inspiration, the teenager took a pair of scissors to their hair, and while the new style looked great ten hours ago, in the light of a new day it feels horrifying. "I can't go to school looking like this!"

Or there are problems created by social expectations and treatment based on one's apparent physical maturity. If one is fourteen and appears to be twelve, looking so much younger can result in being discounted or pushed around. If one is fourteen and appears sixteen, looking so much older can result in pressure to act that way. It can be very hard for a mature-looking adolescent to resist the attention of older peers who invite her or him to act up to their age.

Peers and adults can make assumptions about what you know and want and have experienced based on your looks. So when you start looking sexually mature there can be a social expectation that you are inclined to act that way. And now you get a fast reputation you didn't earn. So the eighth grade boy, muscular and large and lightly bearded, becomes a sexual threat in the eyes of some parents who warn their daughters to stay away from the young man. His parents explain, "He's just a middle school kid in a young man's body, but they're treating him as a sexual predator!"

So what can parents do? To offset the ill effects of puberty and concerns about personal appearance, here are a few things parents might consider doing.

- They can explain common physical changes that can come with puberty so the young person knows what alterations to normally expect.

- They can respect increased importance that adolescents attach to looks and how appearance now socially matters more.

- They can understand the fashionable look the young person is adopting and what it signifies.

- They can give adequate privacy for the young person to have the time it takes to get used to their changing body and get ready to go out in public.

- They can never tease about looks because they are no laughing matter.

- They can never criticize appearance because that attacks self-esteem.

- They can tolerate varying looks because that is part of experimentation with individual expression.

- They can be watchful for product use to improve personal appearance (like using supplements for adding muscle or laxatives for losing weight) because damage can be done.

- They can nurture personal valuing that is separate and independent of looks, creating other—and often healthier—pillars of self-esteem.

- They can confront cruel self-depreciation based on looks because that devaluation constitutes mistreatment of self.

- They can encourage acceptance of physical imperfections because the ideal is not real.

- They can share their own history of issues with personal appearance growing up so the adolescent knows the parent struggled too.

- They can help their teenager understand the perils of equating personal worth with physical appearance, explaining that when appearance is given excessive importance, self-esteem tends to become more fragile.

- They can help the young person value her or his own company, interests, pleasurable activities, future goals, and relationships to appreciate themselves in more robust and varied ways.

- They can help the young person practice eating habits that are healthy and not potentially self-harming.

- They can explain how puberty can stimulate more fantasies about acting womanly and manly.

It's a challenge. Not only does puberty change adolescent appearance, it amplifies the importance of physical looks in adolescent eyes. In addition, on the emotional side there is usually more intensity to contend with.

## Rising Emotional Intensity

Adolescence often arouses more emotional intensity than childhood. Displays of strong feelings, like upset conveyed by a sullen mood or sudden outburst, tend to become more common with puberty and the onset of other adolescent changes. "Our teenager's emotions keep flaring up. And his moods can weigh him down. His feelings are so unpredictable now!"

Before accepting a "bipolar" explanation of the increased emotional intensity and mood swings, and for sure before resorting to some psychoactive medication to moderate what's going on, try some form of counseling first, or at least in conjunction with, whatever drug is prescribed. Medication has passing influence; but education from self-understanding and for emotional self-management can have lasting effect and growing value.

Because the onset of puberty during adolescence often creates a more emotionally charged passage, an important growth task of adolescence is learning to self-manage strong emotion. Consider a couple of simple approaches to teaching these skills that parents might use, first to help their teenager recover from an unhappy mood using the feeling/thought/behavior connection, and second to learn from an emotional overreaction.

A young person can get stuck in unhappy moods when painful emotion takes stubborn hold. Sometimes the emotional support provided by empathetic listening is enough to relieve an unhappy mood. However, if this is not comfortable or does not answer, parents can suggest: "To change how you feel, experiment with how you think or act."

Since feelings are usually accompanied by associated thoughts and actions, parents can suggest exploiting those connections to promote possible choices for change. Sometimes changing thinking or behaving can alter feeling.

So when it comes to mental sets, parents can ask: "If you were feeling happier, what kinds of thoughts might you have about your life? When the young person describes looking forward to something positive, parents can suggest trying that. So when it comes to current conduct, parents can ask, "If you were feeling happier, how would you choose to act?" When the young person describes some positive 'activities like exercising and socializing, parents can suggest trying those.

Sometimes a bad mood is triggered by an adolescent who makes a painful experience worse by berating him- or herself for what did or didn't happen. So, not making the middle school basketball team, the young man calls himself a "loser." Or the seventh grade girl labels herself a "reject" because the object of her crush treated it as a big joke and other guys laughed. In each case, adding punishing self-criticism to an unhappy event can amplify a bad experience into a generalized bad mood. Parents need to help their daughter or son not use negative self-talk to make a hard situation worse. "Beating up on yourself when you are down will only make getting back up harder to do. When you are feeling down, that is a time to be gentle with yourself, not harsh. And then find ways to start treating yourself well."

Sometimes the denial of a basic need can trigger an unhappy adolescent mood. For example, focused on what is socially wanted from peers that is not forthcoming and so feeling down, the young person neglects what she or he needs to do to boost her- or himself. So, it can be helpful for parents to encourage the adolescent to maintain themselves by getting enough sleep, cultivating personal interests, exercising, trying to perform well, eating regularly and moderately, or joining an extracurricular group, all can serve as bulwarks against the sensitivity and vulnerability to bad moods.

If, despite your adolescent's best efforts to the contrary (by sharing feelings or changing thinking or trying different behaviors) the troubling mood will not lift, sticks around, and deepens over time, take note. Such changes as protracted anxiety or anger or despondency justify getting counseling assistance because one key component of mood management is monitoring when passing unhappiness becomes significantly painful and protracted. Again, before resorting to mood-managing drugs, try counseling first. If medication is recommended, make sure some self-management or counseling education is part of the get-well program so resilience skills can be practiced.

There can be more frequent emotional overreactions, often unexpected and inexplicable for the sexually maturing adolescent. When a blow-up has occurred, in an incident of slamming doors or storming off or yelling for example, it is often in response to something apparently small. Rather than dismiss the outburst as an unfortunate episode best forgotten, it is usually better to take the time to understand what a little provocation may have to teach. So afterward, help the young person take the time to debrief the episode to reveal what may be emotionally the matter. Little things that set a young person off can really be big things in disguise. Consider five possibilities:

- Something *specific* has been said or done that hurt. "When you teased me it wasn't funny!"

- Something was *suppressed* and allowed to build up. "I couldn't take any more criticism after today!"

- Something *similar* to a painful past occurred. "This was just like when no one listened to me before!"

- Something *symbolic* occurred. "This just goes to show how you have never taken me seriously!"

- Something *surprising* happened. "I wasn't expecting this kind of response from you!"

Little provocations that arouse disproportionate emotional responses are worth attending to. When the response seems to be an overreaction, the cause not obviously apparent, it is usually worth discussing to find out what is really going on.

One reason why adolescents can be prone to overreactions is because self-consciousness and desire for privacy can feed a need to emotionally conceal what is going on. Showing one's felt side to others can feel too vulnerable for comfort. It may not fit the image of strength and well-being the more independent young person wants to show to the world. Such emotional self-disclosure may even be considered a sign of weakness. Parents might offer a different view: "Sharing unhappy feelings is not a sign of weakness, but a sign of strength." And they can model this behavior themselves.

## Susceptibility to Social Embarrassment

Puberty increases one's sense of social exposure and self-consciousness. Now venturing out in the world of one's peers does not feel the same as it did in childhood because taking a changing body, which feels unfamiliar to live in, out on public parade can be a daunting experience. If you are developing more slowly or faster than your peers, they are sure to notice. And notice of the worst kind is being teased about appearance because that can create embarrassment—that startled sense that you are caught in the headlights of unwanted public attention in some inferior or awkward or foolish way that makes other people laugh at you. At worst, embarrassment is a form of feeling frightened, a fear of having one's failings or frailties socially exposed to public ridicule. For the adolescent, this socially isolating moment can feel excruciating, threatening an abiding sense of personal disgrace. "I'll never live this down!"

The more self-conscious a person feels, the more painful embarrassment can be. Thus when a young person is growing through the intensely self-conscious hormonal changes of puberty, they can be maximally hurt by cruel middle school teasing about looks whether it be weight, shape, complexion, hair, lack of coordination in a larger body, lowering voice, or advanced or delayed physical maturity.

"You look weird!"

"You don't know that!"

"Look at what she's wearing!"

"See what he just did!"

It's when onlookers laugh that embarrassment gathers power. In the excruciating moment, the teenager can freeze, stammer, stutter, blush, or even break out in a sweat.

"I'll never be able to face anyone again!"

"I wish I could disappear!"

"I feel like I could die!"

Of course, people don't die of embarrassment; but in the painful moment they feel that they could. Even when such teasing does not come their way, they are sure to see it done to some other unfortunate and so know it could happen to them. Seeing a peer put down and laughed at, the insecure witness silently prays, *May that never happen to me!*

Make a misstep or mistake in middle school and peers can get after you. Now the opening for embarrassment occurs if the young person gives in to one or more of four common social fears:

- Fear of exposing oddity or inadequacy. "Nobody else looks this way!"

- Fear of being teased or ridiculed. "Everybody will laugh at me!"

- Fear of lasting damage to image or reputation. "This will always be remembered!"

- Fear of isolation for appearing unacceptably different. "I'll never fit in!"

Parents can explain how embarrassment is not inevitable, and these fears do not have to be empowered. They are susceptible to choice. Usually socially stimulated, embarrassment is always self-inflicted. Whether talking about peer-to-peer, teenager-to-parent, or parent-to-teenager, embarrassment is never something that another person can actually do to you. Blaming the other person for your embarrassment encourages you to believe that how they acted (in a way you don't like) has the power to make you feel scared. Blaming intensifies injury more often than it ever relieves.

Taking responsibility is the best antidote to embarrassment. For example, your adolescent can declare emotional independence and defuse the power of teasing. "It's about them wanting to protect their insecurities by being mean; it's not about something wrong with me." Your adolescent can choose to place the event in perspective. "I messed up in public; I just need to accept that, let it go, and move on."

I paint this harsh side of embarrassment so parents can appreciate how frightening and painful it can be, and can resolve *never* to knowingly embarrass their adolescent. It's easy for them to be blinded by their adult sense that being occasionally embarrassed is no big or lasting deal. Parents usually have a more confident and settled sense of self than in adolescence when personal uncertainty was the rule. Where the adult is comparatively fully formed, the adolescent is very much a work-in-process, insecure and prone to embarrassment, particularly around the age of puberty.

Forgetting what it was like to feel so vulnerable, adults can tease a teenager in honest fun, even affection, unmindful of the sensitivity they playfully attack. Then they can be surprised by the reaction they get in response as the young person storms off apparently angry, but actually hurt, smarting from the exposure: "It's *not* funny!" As for other adults, those few teachers or coaches in school for example, who employ embarrassment for classroom or team control, publicly demeaning one student or player as an example to intimidate the rest, such bullying by adult authorities may get obedience, but does so at the cost of respect. And they do a lot of damage. The same is true for parents in the home.

To the extent possible, I believe that homes should be tease-free zones for adolescents, and that parents should not knowingly embarrass their teenager by teasing. It's not "funny" or "cute" to see the young person avert their eyes, shrink back, or look alarmed. And for sure, never use sarcasm to cut the adolescent down. However, these provisos do not cover the unintended embarrassment parents can be caused when their son or daughter is foundering through early and mid-adolescence (around age nine to fifteen). Now the young person usually wants to conduct his world of friendships more separately from parents, the mere company of who can compromise and threaten the appearance of social independence that feels so important at this stage.

For many of these young people, to be seen with one's parents in public by friends can feel embarrassing. Thus the middle school student may not want parents to show up at school or attend school events as spectators of her or his performance. A lot of respectful deals are cut at this point, the parent offering, "We do want to see your game, but we are willing to make our presence as least intrusive and offensive as possible by not drawing attention to ourselves or to you, sitting quietly out of the way, and having you come to meet us at the car after the event, after goodbyes to friends are said." The lesson is to accept that once the journey to independence begins, parental company in public may be less comfortable and parental characteristics are going to be less acceptable than they used to be, both because of potential embarrassment's sake.

When parents are the agents of embarrassment because of what they intentionally or unintentionally do, don't do, or say, adolescents can feel betrayed and angry. For example, unintentionally, a dad causes his seventh grader enormous embarrassment by lapsing into a term of endearment the man had used in the boy's early childhood. "Snookie," calls the father to his son before the young man is about to leave with a group of male friends, "I need to ask you one more thing."

"*Snookie?*" laughs one of the friends, and then the other three take it up: "Hey, Snookie, let's go!" The boy blushes with pain to be baby-named in front of his teenage buddies, to be treated as younger than his age, to have his dad arm them with a nickname they're going to tease him with and maybe spread around for other guys to use, a name he wishes he'd never been called. How could his father be so insensitive and do this to him, to hurt him so? The lesson is that it's really important for parents to treat their teenager in age-appropriate ways in front of the young person's friends.

Or in jest the mom teases her son about just graduating from puberty.

"All the girls better watch out for you now!"

She was meaning to lovingly celebrate her son about his more grown-up appearance, but he took it as a sarcastic swipe at his sexual inexperience, about which he was already feeling insecure. "That's *not* funny, Mom!" The lesson is that if the teasing isn't fun or funny to your teenager, then it's not fun or funny, so cut it out.

Because adolescence, particularly around the age of puberty, is filled with enough embarrassing moments, young people don't need parents to provide any more. If your adolescent ever tells you that something about how you have acted felt embarrassing, tell the young person that you really need to know what you did that was discomforting so you do not do it again. And if your teenager ever talks about feeling embarrassed over something that happened at school, take it seriously. Empathetically listen, encouraging the young person to talk the painful episode out.

Finally, parents do need to beware an embarrassment trap that can be set by having a young child who prompted a lot of public compliments. They loved having a little girl or boy who reflected well on them and who provided a high positive return for all the parenting investment they made.

Detaching and differentiating from childhood in the normal course of adolescence, however, the daughter or son for an experimental time can become more abrasive, appear more alternative, and act more wayward in the public and parental eye. What happened to their star child? Now parents can feel embarrassed by the young person who may attract more negative public notice and sometimes fails to live up the parenting image to which they had become accustomed.

When parents feel the adolescent's behavior reflects on them poorly and feel less rewarded for their efforts than they used to be, then embarrassment and disappointment, even resentment, can follow. "He's making us look like bad parents!" Where is the old positive reflection and return? For such parents, it might be helpful to consider the following mantra:

o   o   o

We accept that our changing adolescent is no longer a young child and is not in this world to make us look good socially or to turn out in a way that necessarily rewards our parenting efforts. We do what we can; the adolescent does what she or he can; and we embrace the outcome. More important than any positive reflection and return is our ongoing caring connection and committed love.

CHAPTER NINE

# Peers and Popularity

"After being off with friends,
I want some time alone!"

Adolescence makes it harder to stay as closely and harmoniously in step with parents as one did in childhood, and everyone has times when they can wistfully remember the close connection they once shared. A parent may grieve the loss of the old tagalong buddy, and the adolescent may miss having the parent as a beloved companion with whom to hang out.

Now through words and actions the young person declares the changing condition of family membership. "I no longer want to be defined and treated as just a child!" Feeling more lonely and disconnected to home on this account, there is a natural desire to create a competing family of friends with whom one can belong, all of who are changing in the same detaching and differentiating adolescent way. Friends can now feel easier to fit in with than family.

Companionship is needed. The power of this peer group membership is amplified because the more one separates and distances from family, the more one needs social belonging with friends. When the young adolescent says, "My friends are everything!" that is a true statement of how he or she feels. Friends can feel desperately important. So, consider The Power of Peers, The Pursuit of Popularity, Parents and the Adolescent's Peer Group, and Parental Needs When Peers Matter More.

## The Power of Peers

The companionship of peers makes the adolescent passage more confident and less lonely. Fitting in less well at home, peers provide a social "home," a belonging place away from home. Similarity with peers has social value for the identity it confers. "I am like my friends; I have friends like me."

Because adolescence opens up interest, exposure, and experimentation in the larger world outside of family, excitement with fellow adventurers can help brave the growing curiosity, risks, and dangers. For example, what one would not dare to try alone, like yelling taunts at students from a rival school at an athletic competition, one is willing to try in the company of friends. Since parents have less understanding of what matters to the adolescent, as the generation gap grows between them, having peers who are confederates and confidantes and companions provides important support; friends with whom to share your interests, tastes, values, secrets, adventures, and who are in the know. Because parents are often opposed to some of what calls to the adolescent, and are uncomfortable or unwilling to discuss such topics, peers become prime informants about what is forbidden and what it is like. Since parents represent the rule of adult authority, peers can become a band of "outlaw" friends with whom one can sometimes conspire for illicit freedom and independence.

Most important, peer group membership does not come free. Joining a peer group, particularly a tight and exclusive group like a social circle, clique, or gang, is that membership can be costly. There are usually some fitting-in demands to socially conform. In so many words, these demands seem to say: "To be a member in good standing you need to be like us, believe like us, behave like us, appear like us, like us best, take sides with us, back us up, don't have important friends outside of us, don't do better than us, and don't betray us." When it comes to freedom for individuality and independence, peer groups may not tolerate a lot of personal freedom and expression of diversity. How to think, how to dress, how to act; one's group of friends are sometimes calling the shots.

Perhaps most important, this group of friends provides an invaluable training ground for practicing social skills such as speaking up and standing up for oneself, confronting and resolving conflicts, and maintaining individual integrity in the face of membership demands that a peer group creates. Then there is ever-present pursuit of popularity—the gold standard of social belonging.

## The Pursuit of Popularity

Come early and mid-adolescence, finding friends, and keeping friends, and staying friends is an enormous challenge because everyone is changing. Everyone is feeling more strained with family, is filled with self-doubt, is trapped in a changing body, and is feeling cast adrift into a world of acting older.

The developmental insecurity of early adolescence has been complicated by the social insecurity of mid-adolescence and the striving for belonging and place among peers. This preoccupation can become desperately important as social reputation can affect the social treatment one receives—from inclusion and respect to exclusion and disrespect. In the extreme, a "star" student with a reputation for being a winner is generally treated better than an "oddball" student with a reputation for not fitting in. One of the hardest lessons of early and mid-adolescence is that no one can control their own reputation in an offline and online world where whatever anybody has to say against you may have the power to socially stick.

One worst case example was the seventh grade girl who, for reasons she never knew, was first labeled by other girls, thinking they were being funny, as the "It" girl, with "It" being vaguely specified as something wrong with her that nobody wanted to catch by social association, and so they left her alone. This damaging tag on her reputation followed her all the way through high school. "I couldn't shake it and I never knew what 'it' was. I had a very lonely time. Somehow I knew the matter wasn't with me, but with them. So I buckled down, graduated a year early from high school, and socially started all over again at community college."

At this hard time, the reputation of popularity can be pretty persuasive: become popular and all your worries and problems about social belonging with peers will be solved! The more liked you are, the more you'll fit in, the more secure you will feel, and the less social meanness will come your way. Popularity secures a well-established social place among peers who want to be with you, with whom you have social standing, with whom you can hang out, and who can provide the companionship you need.

So at school, group affiliation is often signified by a certain gathering space, a physical place, like a hallway or courtyard at breaks or a table at lunch. If you have a place to hang out that means you have a gang of friends. Characteristics such as getting good grades, following rules, working hard, and being helpful can all create approval with teachers, but these traits are unlikely to engender popularity with peers who place more value on looks, confidence, outspokenness, possessions, dress, knowing what's "in," being athletic, and acting social.

The reputation you don't want is to be unpopular because then, unaffiliated and unprotected, you are left to make your way alone. Be labeled unpopular and peers may ignore or avoid you because they fear being known by the company they keep. Befriending an unpopular person can increase their risk of unpopularity that is often treated as a contagious social disease that can be caught through public association. So one girl explains why she no longer associates with a childhood companion at school who is growing through a socially awkward time: "I don't want the right people to get the wrong idea about me—that we're friends. But outside of school getting together is still okay."

It is here that parents might want to weigh in on what this restrictive definition of popularity can socially cost. They can talk to their young person about the larger society that she will be entering as an adult that will be filled with enormous human variation. In this more complex world, the capacity to get to know and get along with many different kinds of people will have a bearing on how well she makes her way. Then parents can explain how acting now is a preparation for how one acts later. If she "small sizes" her relationships as she grows up, by restricting them to a small safe social clique, she risks diminishing her adult capacity to get along in a much more diverse world.

Finally, parents might want to forewarn their son or daughter who is bent on popularity that to get to be popular and to stay popular, there can be a price to be paid. They can itemize common costs that can come with being very popular. Sometimes, it's not all it's reputed to be.

- Popularity requires pleasing: You must strive to be nice to people who you want to keep liking you.

- Popularity takes being current: You have to look cool, keep up with what's happening, and stay cutting edge.

- Popularity is precarious: People can vote you in and they can vote you out, and "elections" can be held at a moment's notice when you accidentally offend or someone "better" comes along.

- Popularity is partly unpopular: While some people admire you, others can envy you, can get jealous, and can want to bring you down.

- Popularity attracts imitators: People act like you so they can be liked by you, and liked by others by acting like you.

- Popularity breeds insincerity: You may often fake being nice to people, and people often fake being nice to you.

- Popularity is confusing: Sometimes you wonder if people want to be your friend because of who you are or because of how you're popular.

- Popularity attracts attention: You are noticed more, judged more, your flaws and failings are more closely observed, and you are more gossiped about.

- Popularity is competitive: Since so many people want to be popular, you have to perform your best against your rivals every day.

- Popularity can go to your head: Popular people can believe their own reviews and act special or entitled, injuring friendships they thought secure.

- Popularity can be limiting: The more you invest in popularity at school, the less you are likely to invest in creating a social life outside of school.

- Popularity can be demeaning: People who pursue popularity will sometimes accept mistreatment from more popular people just to be accepted.

Most important, popularity and friendship are not the same. *Popularity* is political; friendship is personal. *Popularity* is about rank; friendship is about relationship. *Popularity* is more casual; friendship is more caring. On all three grounds, good friendships tend to beat high popularity.

What can parents suggest to their adolescent about pursuing popularity? Maybe something like this: consider just being content with being friendly with people, having a few close friends you can trust, acquaintances that can be fun to be with, and having the capacity to enjoy the pleasure of your own company when you are alone—being a good friend to yourself. And consider taking occasional time with family. Family will still be with you long after most of these peers, who seem so important now, have grown up and gone their separate ways.

## Parents and Their Adolescent's Peer Group

As their young adolescent's peer group becomes more important, parents can feel that they and the family start to matter less. Part of parenting the detaching and differentiating adolescent is about letting go as the young person starts the process of becoming more independent by beginning to build her own social circle. Sometimes adjusting to this change can be difficult for parents. Those with an only child, for example, who have enjoyed the luxury of keeping the beloved child largely to him- or herself, may find it hard being preempted and having to share social importance with this growing community of teenage peers.

As their child's adolescence begins, they do indeed start "mattering less." And they should. This reminds me of writer Darrell Sifford's observation about how after they're grown up, children tend to matter more to parents than parents do to their adult children. "Mattering less" does not mean "loved less." It only means that at this age other social attachments are given a higher priority.

Nor does "mattering less" mean parents should discount and let go of family membership demands of the adolescent. After all, parents offer a constancy of love and caring concern with which peers cannot compete, while ongoing family membership provides an ongoing reference for what is allowed and not allowed, and what is expected, wise, right, and safe to do. In the greater scheme of things, friends are usually of more passing importance, while parents and family are likely to have more lasting value.

Parents can feel threatened by this second "family." There is the sense of being an outsider in their adolescent's life. There is a social allegiance that competes with family. There are contrasting values to those of family. There is insider knowledge about what is going on in the adolescent's life the parent lacks. And there is the dreaded "peer pressure," those social conformity demands that can lead the young person astray. "I only did it because everyone else was." Parents need to declare that such "group think" is no substitute for individual responsibility, and that following along to be accepted does not excuse wrong actions. They respect the adolescent's choice of friends so long as behavior in their company remains consistent with conduct that parents approve. Failing this, they may need to discuss placing some safe conditions on the association. "For a while, we feel more comfortable you doing overnights over here instead of at your friend's."

Real as it can be, peer pressure is not only negative. Peers also look after and warn each other away from unwise behavior—for example, preventing excessive substance use ("You've had enough!"), taking a dangerous dare ("It's not worth trying!"), or spoiling for a fight ("Back off!"). Peers also provide support—for example, being willing to listen to pain from parental divorce, or from a romantic breakup, or to cheer a buddy up after failing to make the team. Peers can even provide good information from their bad experience. "Sex that way won't keep you safe; at least it didn't protect me," or "Texting when you're angry can get you into a mess of trouble," or "I never would have acted that way if I hadn't been drunk."

It usually serves parents better when the adolescent's peer group is known and liked by them than when it is unknown and distrusted. Parents sometimes declare, "Don't bring those friends around here!"

to protect their home from youthful outsiders they fear. However, the social ignorance from lack of contact only makes this peer group scarier than it was before.

Parents can choose to treat their adolescent's peers with hospitality by creating a comfortable place to congregate. With peers who are close friends of their teenager, they can include them in the family circle with some explanation of house rules, treating them in friendly ways without insisting on friendship, and of course ever prepared to feed the troops when they happen to show up. After all, what is more hospitable the world over than a friendly smile, a place to relax, and the sacramental offering of food—emotional, situational, and provisional investments that usually more than justify the expense?

"Your parents are okay" is both a compliment to your adolescent and to you. This appreciation can give parents an influence connection when their teenager's friends treat these adults as surrogate parents. Viewing parents in a positive way, peers may recommend, "I think you ought to tell your parents about what's going on."

When it comes to your adolescent's peer group, it is better to understand than to be ignorant, to be interested than to be critical, to welcome rather than to exclude, to know rather than not to know, and to grow to like rather than to dislike. To the degree that you can accept and welcome your adolescent's friends, your child will feel more accepted and welcomed by you too. If you feel a friend is a "bad influence," rather than criticize the choice of friend to your teenager, specifically cite the behaviors of concern the friend is into that you expect your child to stay away from.

## Parental Needs when Peers Matter More

Finally, as your adolescent's need for peers grows, it helps parents to not feel discounted or neglected. They need to have some basic needs from the young person to continue to be met. Here are ten:

1. *Considerate Treatment.* Parents tend to experience acts of thoughtfulness and courtesy as evidence of sensitivity and caring. "When we're helped without having to ask, it really feels good."

2. *Constant Communication.* Parents tend to feel more secure when they are accurately and adequately informed. "We appreciate being kept in the loop of what is going on."

3. *Mutual Cooperation.* Parents tend to feel more equity in the relationship when there is an ongoing exchange of effort for each other. "We are happier to do for you when you also do for us."

4. *Rule Compliance.* Parents tend to worry less when family rules are mostly followed. "Respecting the demands and limits that we make for your well-being makes our job less anxiety provoking."

5. *Assumption of Responsibility.* Parents tend to feel confident when the teenager is able to learn from consequences of choices made. "When you can learn lessons from good and hard experience; that shows you can teach yourself."

6. *Family Assistance.* Parents tend to feel supported when the teenager not only contributes regular chores but is also on call for unexpected aid. "It's good to know we can count on your help when we need it."

7. *Safe Conflict.* Parents tend to feel more able to differ with their adolescent when they know disagreements will be conducted without risk of harm. "Our arguments with you are safe and constructive."

8. *Keeping Commitments.* Parents tend to trust their adolescent when they know agreements will be honored. "We really value that with you a promise made is a promise kept."

9. *Willingness to Listen.* Giving a full hearing in discussion makes a positive difference for parents when they get a full hearing in return. "We are usually able to talk everything out with you."

10. *Family Participation.* Parents tend to feel strongly unified with an adolescent who acts as part of the family. "We want you to have a community of friends, and we expect you to maintain valued membership in our family while you do."

# CHAPTER TEN

# Higher Intensity Friendships

"My friendships matter more than
my parents understand!"

Between more distance from parents and more unstable social relationships with peers, it's easy to feel unanchored during mid-adolescence and the middle school years. Now as connections to peers become more important, parents have to be mindful of Best Friendships, Dominance Relationships, and Crush Attractions, each bringing their own type of challenges.

## Best Friendships

Although most adolescents wish they could be so lucky, not everybody finds a best friend—a great gift when it occurs, but a source of significant pain when it is lost. What sets a best (usually same sex) friend apart from other friends is a special caring based on liking that person's company more than others, a special sense of knowing based on more confidential intimacy than with others, a special commitment based on willingness to self-sacrifice for each other, and a special compatibility based on shared fitness of personality and match of interests with each other. In addition, there is often a special "extra child" role each occupies in the other person's family home.

The attachment is very powerful, and it can be enabled by technology. Time spent together is what matters. Between girls there is usually more time spent communicating with each other and today there are many electronic ways to stay connected. Between boys there is usually more time spent engaging in activities with each other, and with today's technology there are many electronic ways to online game together.

In either case, a special bond is formed between best friends such that each person feels part of a shared identity, a part of each other. In some cases there is even an identical-twin-like sense of mutual knowing without having to be told what is in each other's mind and heart. Socially they are considered coupled—more committed to each other's company than to the company of anyone else. As best friends, they usually proceed on two powerful assumptions: best friendship is forever, and they will never find another friend as good as the best friend they have.

Like most gifts in life, these relationships are double-edged, the hardest side becoming apparent when the friendship comes to an end, and at least one party is truly bereft on two counts. First, best friendship proves not to be forever. And second, how will they ever find as good a friend again? Because young people are rapidly detaching and differentiating from childhood, it is very common for historical best friendships to grow apart during or shortly after the middle school years.

A parent described it this way. "They've been inseparable since early elementary school, and now in seventh grade, my husband and I think that the friendship has just run out of growing room, at least for our daughter's best friend. It's not that the girl has stopped liking our daughter, but she's acting as if their old relationship doesn't fit anymore and is holding her back from developing new interests and making new friends. She wants to spend more time apart, and our daughter is so sad. It isn't anybody's fault. Neither girl has done anything wrong, but both are feeling hurt. One feels guilty for leaving, and the other feels abandoned and left behind."

Particularly when the adolescents in question have been so closely identified with each other throughout childhood, losing a best friend feels like losing part of oneself, a loss made worse for the one who feels abandoned, blaming herself or himself for no longer being good enough, and feeling at a loss for not knowing how to fill the empty space in their life. At this juncture, parents can play a helpful role in a number of ways. They can explain about adolescent "growing apart," provide empathetic support, encourage other personal interests and social involvement, encourage investing in oneself to strengthen relationship to oneself, and provide transitional companionship until their son or daughter has had time to recover from loss and gather the energy to socially reengage.

## Dominance Relationships

Of concern to parents is when their mid-adolescent gets caught up not in a best friendship, but in one of comparable power: a dominance relationship. A journalist in Chile once asked the following, "How would you explain the willingness of one adolescent to be dominated by another?" The question suggested that adolescence poses similar challenges in many cultures. Why might an adolescent choose to be in a relationship with a friend who sets the terms, calls the shots, and is given commanding power? Why would a young person choose to socially shackle themselves to a dominating peer?

The answer often seems to be because the young person is sufficiently attached to childhood dependency and still wants to be directed, but not by parents except in a rebellious way. (Rebellion is not an act of independence, but of dependence dedicated to doing the opposite of what parents expect and demand.) In the early stages of adolescence, the need to still be directed can remain alive and well.

If you don't want to be directed by parents, but don't feel ready to independently direct yourself, there is an adolescent middle way: establish a transitional dependence on a dominating peer who will take the lead while you follow along. From what I've seen, the window for domination relationships tends be from early (ages nine to thirteen) through mid-adolescence (ages thirteen to fifteen). Beyond this developmental stage the young person has usually secured enough sense of individuality and independence to want to operate on their own terms. The tradeoffs no longer feel worthwhile.

What tradeoffs? For the sake of feeling socially connected (and not isolated), directed (and not aimless), and having an identity (and not be undefined), the young person agrees to follow a self-assured peer by acting similar (imitating the peer), by conforming (fitting into the peer's beliefs), and by giving compliance (going along with what the peer wants).

At an age when self-confidence can be hard to find, there's enormous security in following someone who will take the lead, show the way, someone who can be relied on to tell you what to do and not to do, how to be and not to be. In most cases I have seen, choosing to have a dominating friend in adolescence is really about needing a transitional relationship between depending on parents as a child and depending on oneself as one grows older.

What parents notice is how their young teenager seems so completely wed to the influence of this dominating male friend, for example using that person as a model for how to dress, act, believe, decide what's of value, and treating that person as most important to please, whose opinion seems to matter more that anyone else's.

There can be a wide variety of follower motivations in play. They are as follows:

- Social Standing. "I am empowered by the association."

- Social Safety. "I am protected by the association."

- Social Belonging. "I am connected by the association."

- Social Identity. "I am defined by the association."

- Social Acceptance. "I am valued by the association."

- Social Guidance. "I am directed by the association."

Witnessing their teenager enthralled with a dominating friend can be scary for parents because, by comparison, they seem to have lesser influence, but mostly because they wish their son or daughter didn't give so much self-definition, self-worth, and self-direction away. They fear their teenager will self-sacrifice, lose self-confidence, be exploited, and perhaps be led astray.

It's best for parents to befriend the dominating friend if they can, welcoming the relationship, to keep communication open and gain some influence in how it is conducted. If they ever object to some of what is going on with their child they can focus only on the behaviors of concern and not on the friendship itself. "We value the value of this friendship to you, but we need to have you enjoy it without becoming involved in activities that put you at risk or that we believe are not in your best interests. So we need to talk with you about your behavior."

It's usually best to keep the focus on their child's choices, not on the friend's influence, because by blaming the friend they reduce their teenager's responsibility. More importantly, they put her or him on the defensive. By criticizing the friend or the relationship, because of the dependence, parents will be criticizing their teenager.

There are a couple things parents can try to do to lessen the hold of the dominating friendship. First, at a relaxed time, being totally non-evaluative, they may be able to express misgivings not as criticism but as concern about what tradeoffs may be in play. "Sometimes we wonder for all you get in this relationship, what you may be giving up. You might want to consider what this exchange gives you, and what it costs." Second, they may be able to open up other social exposures and encourage other esteem-filling activities that are of interest to the adolescent.

Also, as breadth of social relationships increases, the power of this single most important one can lose its attraction and power.

## Crushes

Teenage crushes have a significant role to play in the journey of adolescence. Consider crushes of two kinds—identity crushes and romantic crushes. In both cases, the teenager feels smitten by a compelling person who captivates their attention for good and ill. (A third kind is the celebrity crush that shapes ideals and stirs fantasies, but there is usually no interpersonal contact to play them out. However, this is definitely where the market for celebrity posters comes in—used to decorate teenage bedroom walls.)

In all three cases, the young person projects onto another person idealized attributes the admirer highly values and wants to be associated with. The young person then attaches strong positive feelings to the perfectly wonderful image that has been created. Crushes have more to do with fantasy than with reality, and they tell much more about the admirer than the admired. It's because they usually prove unrealistic in a relatively short time that they soon wear off. But it is because of the idealization that crushes have such momentary power. This is why parents need to respect an adolescent crush and not dismiss or put it down. After all, it is an early approximation of love. While it lasts it is seriously held, so it should be seriously treated.

Identity crushes are formed by finding someone they admire, want to be like, and treat as a leader or role model they are eager to imitate and follow. Unlike dominance relationships that are mediated by insecurity, identity crushes are mediated by admiration. Romantic crushes are formed by finding someone powerfully attractive to them, who they feel excited to be around, and with whom they want to spend a lot of time. In both cases, the person with the crush gives enormous power of approval to the object of their affection—wanting to be liked by them and wanting to be like them, willing to do a lot to get in the other person's good graces. They go out of their way to be around the attachment.

There is a great outbreak of and gossip about romantic crushes in middle school ("Guess who likes who?"). By this time, early adolescence and the separation from childhood has caused young people to want to act more grown-up, and sexual maturity from puberty has motivated them to act in more young manly and young womanly ways. Girls usually enter puberty before boys; they are more likely to experience the wave of crushes first, are more drawn to boys than boys are to them, and take romantic feelings seriously— feelings that boys are more apt to treat lightly or even laughably. However, the time for same-age boys to become romantically smitten is not far off. When it arrives, a crush proves to be no laughing matter when they too become smitten.

Because a romantic crush is a potent mix of idealization and infatuation, it doesn't require knowing another person well. In some cases, a superficial impression can be provocation enough. "I like how she's so quiet and watchful and keeps to herself." "I like how what others think doesn't matter to him." Crushes are very revealing. "My son is always getting crushes on young women who seem the opposite of him, as fun-loving as he is serious." Crushes are not only the stuff that dreams are made of; they signify a lot about the dreamer.

Of course, romantic crushes can have a risky side. You don't want a teenage crush to become a fixation, in which a young person is unable to stop daydreaming and fantasizing all the time about this person. You don't want the young person to act out under the influence of a crush in self-endangering ways, soliciting or expressing inappropriate interest. And you don't want the crush to be exploited by the object of the crush, such as an older adolescent taking advantage of a romantically besotted younger adolescent.

Because a romantic crush is so intensely felt, parents must not take it lightly or make fun of it. An awakening of romantic feelings, it provokes a lot of anxiety because there are many problematic questions for the young person to answer. These questions include "What am I supposed to do with these feelings? Should they just be kept secret, increasing the power of my preoccupation? What if I tell close friends? Suppose I get talked about and teased, increasing the risk of embarrassment? What if I have to be around the other person who doesn't know how I feel?" Feeling nervous, there is more risk of doing or saying something awkward. "What do I tell this person about my crush?" To declare the crush to the person creates the risks of exposure and rejection. It's not easy managing a crush.

One way to manage it is by telling the object of the crush. The language used, however, is important. The temptation, because the romanticized feelings are so intense, is to express the feelings with the "love" word. However, it's best to talk about these feelings in "liking" terms because that reduces the pressure on everyone. "I *like* talking with you." "I like hanging out with you." Enough said, and leave it at that.

Most romantic crushes don't last very long because once the object of the crush becomes better known, their magic wears off and the ideal falls away. "I can't believe I felt he was so great! What was I thinking?" However, this kind of crush does have one lasting value; having experienced an awakening of infatuated feelings, the adolescent has opened themselves up to the pleasure and possibility of romantic love.

Identity crushes often last longer because the adolescent is focused not so much on pleasing the other person as on altering themselves, using the leader whom they admire as a model to shape their own womanly or manly growth. So a shy seventh-grade girl gets a crush on a popular female classmate and wants to become highly social like her, hoping the association will rub off as she learns to become more outgoing. It's an unstated bargain. She gets to make friends with the friends of the popular girl and gets to be looked up to in that same admiring way. Sometimes sexual feelings are aroused in an identity crush, even acted on to express liking, but that does not usually mean a homosexual orientation has become established, only that the identity crush can have a sexual component.

Of course, the risk associated with following an admired leader is that the young person with the identity crush may be led astray, which is what some parents fear. "Our son worships a classmate who rides his skateboard to school, stashes it in his locker, dresses like an outlaw, all in leather and black and chains, and has this angry attitude toward authority. But if we say anything against him, our son gets really angry, defending his hero and criticizing us. What are we supposed to do?"

Parents need to respect the friendship, get to know the friend, and if there are behaviors the friend is into that parents don't want for their son, they need to talk to him about not doing those things. Sometimes parents discover that beneath the appearance they find alarming is a person they get to like.

Teenage crushes can be of the attraction (romantic) kind and of the admiration (identity) kind. When a crush combines both components, a very high intensity relationship is created. In most cases, growth is usually advanced by this influential experience, most often for the good, but sometimes not. This is why parents need to pay attention, not just leave it to their son or daughter and look the other way.

# CHAPTER ELEVEN

# Social Cruelty at School

"Why can nice kids treat each other so badly?"

I wrote the 2010 book, *Why Good Kids Act Cruel,* to help parents better understand how social meanness among peers tends to increase with the mid-adolescent age, and how to help a daughter or son cope should this mistreatment come their way. I also wanted to give middle school staff some strategies for reducing incidents of social cruelty at school, where it is most likely to occur. What follows deals with what socially cruel behaviors are, why social cruelty can increase in middle school, and how parents can respond to social cruelty.

## What Is Social Cruelty

Operationally, I define social cruelty as five kinds of deliberately hurtful interpersonal behaviors—teasing, exclusion, bullying, rumoring, and ganging up—which inflict emotional injury and endanger social safety. How does social cruelty harm developing adolescents? Each of the five tactics of social cruelty plays on a different young adolescent vulnerability and fear.

- *Teasing*. To humiliate with insults. Teasing plays on the fear of being inferior: "There is something wrong with me!"

- *Exclusion*. To shun with rejection. Exclusion plays on the fear of isolation: "I have no friends!"

- *Bullying.* To intimidate with threatened or actual harm. Bullying plays on the fear of weakness: "I won't be able to stand up for myself!"

- *Rumoring.* To slander by broadcasting smears and lies. Rumoring plays on the fear of defamation: "I can't control my reputation!"

- *Ganging-Up.* To pit the group against the individual. Ganging-up plays on the fear of persecution: "They're all against me!"

In whatever form it takes, social cruelty is usually the enemy of school performance. The reason why is that social cruelty reduces the academic focus of student targets or victims who now become primarily concerned about their own social survival. There is simply no way you can have students attending to instructional content and performing classroom tasks up to potential if the school setting is one in which they have daily cause to act guarded and feel afraid. The safer the school, the better students are likely to learn and the more likely they are to perform up to actual operating capacity.

## Social Cruelty in Middle School

Why does social cruelty increase in middle school? By the middle school years virtually all students have been destabilized by early adolescent change that typically begins around ages nine to thirteen. For three causes, young people can become more developmentally insecure and socially vulnerable.

First, as the adolescent begins to detach from the shelter of childhood and is no longer content to be defined and treated as just a child any longer, family membership becomes less compatible and comfortable than it was before, and socially belonging to another "family" of friends matters more than before.

Second, as the adolescent begins to differentiate from the old child identity by experimenting with new images and expressions, becoming "different" can not only test parental tolerances, but can also make fitting in with peers harder to do when it fails to conform to the accepted norm.

Third, as the adolescent undergoes puberty, with all the physical and hormonal alterations that come from gaining sexual maturity, it's easy to feel self-conscious and out of control of one's body, over involuntary changes that they must bring to school for all the world to see and notice.

Of course, most parents understand that with the entry into adolescence comes the young person's push for more social independence. However, what they usually do not comprehend is how this sense of independence causes the young person to cut himself off from them at a time when their understanding and support could help him face these new social challenges. In this world of peers, the adolescent believes that acting more grown-up means managing things on her own without parental awareness or interference. It's almost like a sign is posted on their social world to keep parents out: "No Adults Allowed." Plus, the code of the schoolyard forbids snitching on peers.

Thus at a time when adolescents could benefit from some parental support and coaching, to deal with the rising incidence of social meanness, the more independent-minded young person forgoes such assistance. Along with this decision are beliefs that at home and at school adults don't really know what's going on, don't really care about what's going on, and can't really do anything about what's going on. So what are parents to do?

I believe parents need to declare that they are in the know, that they care, and that if the situation warrants, with the young person's permission, they will act. "We know at the middle school age there can be more push and shove in student relationships than in elementary school. Specifically, there can be more teasing, exclusion, bullying, rumoring, and ganging-up as people struggle to establish social standing. Not only do we wish that you will not participate in these behaviors, but we hope that should any come your way you will let us know so we can give you support, provide possible coaching, and even intervene if you believe that is advisable. The most important thing to remember is that should school relationships get hard in any of these ways, you need not feel alone. Please know that you have us on your side, ready to listen and to help."

In this self-conscious, developmentally insecure age, young people need to know that parents understand how a friend today may not speak to you tomorrow, how a public put-down can unexpectedly embarrass, how a bigger and stronger student can prey on a smaller and weaker one, how people can take sides as the many torment the one, and how malicious rumors can attack reputations.

Does every student this age receive this mistreatment? No, but I believe they all witness it. Thus a single act of social cruelty poisons the well for all who know that what happened to someone else could also happen to them. So they better watch out and stay on guard. Does every student participate in this mistreatment? No, but they all see slight or severe examples of it, and when they choose not to intervene (so it is not directed at them) they only enable its continuation.

At its worst, severe social cruelty can be formative. For example, the bullied student can grow up to become submissive in relationships and the bully can grow up to become coercive. Habits of social behavior, learned in middle school and unquestioned in high school, can carry forward into adulthood. Parental testimony about the lasting harm social cruelty can do is sad to hear. "In the small community where we live, our daughter was chosen to be picked on and pushed around in middle school and that mistreatment followed her into high school. No one we talked to, not the teachers nor the principal, would do anything about it. Finally, come the end of sophomore year, our daughter decided she had had enough and dropped out. She got a job and then her General Equivalency Diploma (GED). Now at eighteen she's recovered enough confidence, after the damage that was done, to pursue some further education. But it's a pretty hard climb from here because she paid a pretty heavy price."

Social cruelty to their son or daughter of any significant duration (not limited to isolated incidents) should be a matter of serious concern to parents because the young person's attitude toward self, others, and school can be adversely affected.

## Parental Response to Social Cruelty

So, how might parents act when their child reports receiving some of this mistreatment at school? First, consider what not to do. Don't disbelieve it because "that kind of thing really doesn't go on," don't discount it as oversensitivity to or exaggeration of normal "kids will be kids" behavior, and don't assume that the child somehow brought it on him- or herself. Further, don't take this mistreatment of your child personally, feeling victimized as though it were directed at you. If you do that, you shift the focus off your child's hurt and onto injury you feel on her or his behalf. And don't impulsively rush to the school "to fix" the situation. Intervention should be the last resort after helping the child determine if he or she can mobilize sufficient personal resources to quell the situation, and only with the young person's permission, because any actions taken will affect the social world of school in which the young person must continue to live.

More specifically, what can parents do? Here are five steps to consider:

1. *Listen.* It is not easy for a young adolescent to tell parents about being meanly treated by peers. In the process, she sacrifices some pride in social independence, admits to some degree of unpopularity, violates normal privacy about her world of peers by going "public" with parents about it, violates the code of the schoolyard by telling on a peer, and worries that the mistreatment reflects badly on her. By listening, parents provide understanding and acceptance. Now the young person is not alone.

2. *Empathize.* To be on the receiving end of social cruelty can cause a host of unhappy feelings. There can be hurt feelings from being attacked. There can be anger at mean treatment. There can be helplessness from not knowing what to do. There can be fear for safety. There can be embarrassment from enduring mistreatment in public view. There can be self-loathing from believing the cruelty is somehow deserved. There can be shame from feeling something is "wrong" with themselves. By empathizing, parents express concern and let the young person know they feel for and care about how he or she is suffering. Now the young person feels emotionally supported.

3. *Specify.* Sense of injury caused by social cruelty can cause the young person to emotionally exaggerate the painful situation and lose sight of what is objectively

going on. "It's all the time!" "It was everyone!" "They all hate me!" "I have no friends!" By specifying what is happening, parents can help restore a realistic perspective. They can help sort out what is actually happening, who specifically was involved, when precisely it occurred, where the incident took place, and exactly how often this mistreatment has been going on. By specifying, parents anchor the incident or incidents to reality and prevent emotional overreaction from distorting perspective for the worse. Now the young person has an accurate picture of the problem. A specific few people were acting mean in an identifiable way at a given time.

4. *Strategize*. Better for a young person to feel like he or she is the target of social cruelty than a victim. To feel targeted can cause the boy or girl to consider choices that may ease being picked on, things they may do to actively discourage social "shots" from being taken. To feel victimized can create a sense of helplessness because, as a victim, he or she identifies no power of choice to challenge or change the mistreatment. To specify current choices and where choices might be changed, parents can help the adolescent identify what she or he was doing before, during, and after a mean event, and what she or he might do differently. "I didn't say anything at the time and just looked away and backed away. I guess I could speak up about not liking how I was being called names and tell them to their faces how I would like to be treated differently."

Since targets have more power of choice to respond to social cruelty than do victims, parents need to help the young person stay in target mode. Then they need to coach their son or daughter in new and different ways, before, during, and after the event, to deal with tormentors to discourage the mistreatment. Now the young person goes to school empowered with a plan of fresh choices for dealing with the problem should it arise again.

5. *Assess.* Parents need to assess complicity and power. Is the young person doing anything that is unintentionally inviting or provoking mistreatment that he or she could helpfully stop? As for power, not all acts of social cruelty can be discouraged through the efforts of the targeted child. Sometimes the young person's social safety is sufficiently compromised, psychological well-being is sufficiently injured, or the young person simply lacks the resources to stop mistreatment, and parents must consult with the adolescent about intervening on her behalf at school. They need to meet with the administration, counselors, or teachers to stop what is going on. Now the young person has on-site adult advocates on her side.

The "poster child" behavior for social cruelty (the one that gets all the public attention) in middle school is *bullying*. Because it can result in physical violence to the victim or cause the victim, in despair, to harm himself, bullying is the form of social cruelty that most often gets the most headlines. A news story may pick an event when a bullied student becomes physically hurt or self-harms, or resorts to violence in retaliation. This coverage is unfortunate because it obscures more than it informs. By sensationalizing the extreme—when social cruelty turns to social violence—it focuses attention on the tip of the iceberg at the expense of noticing the day-to-day lesser damage being done, leaving the other four forms of social cruelty unaddressed. What never makes the news are the vast majority of acts of social cruelty that school staff and parents tend to miss because the damage is less frequently reported by students and is also harder for adults to acknowledge and to see.

As for bullying, it satisfies the need for dominance in exploitive adolescents who are striving to assert social power by pushing other students around. It preys on the weaknesses and vulnerabilities of others, particularly through fear, in order for the bully to feel strong. Bullies are usually not looking for a fight, but for an easy win. They are looking for someone who will give in, give way, and back down. This is why there is no such thing as a self-made bully. Bullies are made by other people who, when pushed around or threatened, are willing to act intimidated. This is also why, if socially possible, parents may want to empower their son or daughter to assert him or herself when being accosted by a bully. It takes courage and builds self-esteem to stand up to a bully; it erodes self-esteem, even induces shame, when one cannot.

So the job of parents is to coach their son or daughter about how to counter this aggression when it comes his or her way. Coaching may prove helpful as you try to strengthen your child to meet the challenge at hand. Five suggestions follow:

1. Accept fear. Let the young person know that there is nothing wrong with experiencing fear. Fear is a functional emotion, not a weakness. It alerts people to the possible danger of getting hurt. However, fear can feel hard to talk about, so appreciate your son or daughter expressing it to you. Then explain that while feeling afraid of a bully is okay, acting afraid may not be okay since it often encourages the bully to carry on. Bullies feel strong when the person bullied acts afraid. So how should the target of the bullying act? First, consider actions to avoid before, during, and after the event.

2. Identify how NOT to act. Ask your son or daughter how he or she could behave to show the bully that he or she was afraid. For example, the young person might identify running away, shutting up, crying, backing down, giving money, or pleading to be left alone. Praise the young person for knowing some things not to do—actions that could make the bullying worse or encourage it to continue. Next, consider possible actions to take.

3. Identify how TO act. Ask your son or daughter how he or she would deal with the bully if he or she was NOT feeling afraid, if he or she simply didn't like being treated that way and wanted it to stop. For example, the young person might identify things to say such as, "Cut it out!" "Go pick on somebody else!" "I can push and shove too!" Or the young person might identify things to do: stepping closer, making eye contact, acting mad. Praise the young

person for knowing some things to do. Next, consider doing the unexpected.

4. Violate predictions. Ask your son or daughter how the bully predicts he or she will respond to the bullying. For example, the young person might think the bully is predicting how he or she is going to give over the lunch money, not tell any adult at school about it, and act like this mistreatment is okay. Then ask your son or daughter "What could you do to violate those predictions and not give the bully what he or she is expecting from you?" Your child may say, "Not give the money, tell my counselor what is going on, and say I don't want to be asked for my lunch money again." When bullies don't get what they predict they often decide to go after someone else. Next, consider how to treat the bully after standing up to that person is accomplished.

5. Normalize the relationship. Ask your son or daughter how he or she relates to someone who is a social acquaintance at school, but not really a good friend. When the young person replies, "I greet them, call them by name, and usually smile," you can suggest that is how to treat the bully after the bullying over. "You don't have to interact beyond that, just engage enough for the bully to know that he or she is not being avoided by you but is now being treated as just another acquaintance in your social world."

As parents, how to tell when your child (from needing to appear independent and in charge or from fearing to tell on peers) is the target of significant social cruelty when he or she will not directly tell you? Six signs to look for are:

1. Observable drop in self-esteem by talking badly about themselves: "There's something wrong with me! I hate how I am, just like other people do!" This can be a sign of taking social cruelty personally by believing mean treatment is deserved.

2.  Unexplained anxiety about attending school, harder to get ready, or repeatedly making up excuses not to go: "I feel sick today." But nothing physically the matter can be found.

3.  Before and after school there are observable changes in normal behaviors—acting sadder, anxious, socially withdrawn, less communicative, or angry.

4.  Response to electronic communication (phones messages, texting, and online postings) is secretive and dispiriting.

5.  Evidence of being physically harassed or hurt, unexplained bruises on body, torn clothes, possessions damaged or missing or "lost."

6.  Drop in grades as fears for social safety cause a loss of academic focus.

Social Cruelty violates a student's right to a safe education. If we believe in safe homes for our children, why wouldn't we believe in safe "second" homes for our children—the schools in which so much of their lifetimes are spent growing up?

Consider how a middle school teacher might impact how students treat each other by explaining at the outset of the semester something like this: "As your teacher, I intend to have a safe classroom. This means that there are five kinds of behaviors that are not welcome here.

*No Teasing:* Don't use names or labels that hurt people's feelings.

*No Exclusion:* Don't socially isolate and deliberately keep anyone out.

*No Bullying:* Don't threaten or push anyone around to get your way.

*No Rumoring:* Don't create or pass along mean gossip.

*No Ganging Up:* Don't join in with others to pick on anyone.

How I expect you to treat each other here is very simple, call it the Golden Rule: treat others the way you want them to treat you."

**(4)**

# ACTING MORE GROWN-UP

Late Adolescence is an exciting and scary time. Now there are more opportunities and invitations and pressures to engage in such dangerous activities as driving, dating, romance, substance use, sexual activity, part-time employment, and social partying. These behaviors can feel like a rite of passage into more grown-up standing, rockets to independence that motivate a lot of acting older adventures. And now the age of eighteen fast approaches, which will increasingly emancipate young people to act more adult and be held to adult account.

Offline and online, as the desire for adult freedoms grows, each freedom requires more reliable information and responsible self-management to safely function. Now parents must help the young person find out, sort out, and figure out how to safely manage more risky decision-making of a more worldly kind.

# CHAPTER TWELVE

# Risk-Taking and Readiness

"I'm old enough to act older now!"

During high school, in addition to helping their adolescent keep academic focus, parents have two important educational jobs to do that the school will not. There is Preparation for Older Risk-Taking, and there is Readiness Training for Functional Independence soon to come. Start by considering the first of these two hard parenting jobs.

## Preparation for Older Risk-Taking

Adolescence increases the desire for freedom of worldly experience from which to grow, a push that continues what the separation from childhood first began. Thus in early adolescence (ages nine to thirteen), young people become more impatient with traditional parental demands and restraints, expressing that frustration through more disagreement and arguing with parents about what must and must not be done. In mid-adolescence (ages thirteen to fifteen) the family of friends offers a competing influence with family at home as peer groups provide collective motivation and support for more risk-taking in life. Now the young person experiments in the company of others with what she or he would not be inclined to do or dare to do alone.

Come the high school years that roughly encompass late adolescence (ages fifteen to eighteen), the magnitude and seriousness of freedom's call becomes even more compelling as acting-older experiences of a seriously risky nature are tried—like driving, dating, part-time employment, sexual activity, partying, and social substance use. In high school, the stakes of risk-taking appreciably rise. For this reason, parents need to be on higher alert and speak to moderating risks that are more likely to be taken.

Entering high school, one is at the bottom of older classes of more worldly students who are approaching the threshold of actual independence. By age eighteen, a host of grown-up rights become legally allowed. From owning access to one's educational and health records, to enlisting in the military and getting other jobs, to voting in political elections, to something as symbolically important as getting a tattoo or body piercing without parental permission (marking "legal age" on the form), one is now treated as an adult instead of a juvenile in the eyes of the law.

In counseling practice, I've seen a fair number of youthful casualties of high school risk-taking over the years. Some of the determining factors have been electing to be in the wrong place at the wrong time, rushing so fast there was no time to think, ignoring danger in order to act or appear brave, feeling despondent and not caring what happens, feeling too scared to refuse a dangerous risk, feeling too angry to restrain temper, allowing substance use to dictate decision-making, trusting others to determine what risks you take, remaining in denial and feeling immune to harm, feeling so bored anything feels worth trying for relief, seeking thrills for excitement's sake, taking a challenge for reputation's sake, or going along with the peer group in order to belong.

A great adolescent incentive in high school is to act more "grown-up." While both parent and teenager are usually in agreement on this objective, their interpretations of the term can be quite different. Parents think about adolescents assuming more grown-up responsibility, while the adolescent thinks about experiencing more grown-up adventures. Adolescents can be inveterate gamblers. Eager to give something more grown-up a daring try, they gamble with freedom. Adolescents cannot grow without taking risks, experimenting with the unknown, and throwing themselves on the mercy of chance. Adolescents are often amazingly fortunate, at least according to the stories they tell of near misses, narrow escapes, and miraculous survivals that I hear in counseling. When it comes to adolescent adventures, surely luck is the greatest guardian of them all, and unhappily their greatest victimizer as well. Given the reality of more dangerous risk-taking, what are some ways adolescents might increase the odds of chance in their favor? Consider a few strategies parents might want to speak to as they encourage mindful decision-making.

- Parents can tell their adolescent about playing *The Great Lottery of Life.* "Every choice you make in life is a gamble because all outcomes are determined by many factors beyond our knowing. You make your choices, acting and reacting as you think best. You take your chances, never knowing for sure what the result is going to be. You face your consequences to the bad and good. You assume what responsibility you can for what happened. You learn from what went wrong, and what went right. And then you ready yourself to choose again, because the gambler's chain of choice and chance and consequence binds us all our lives."

- Parents can talk about *Positive Worry.* "Don't worry" is not good parental advice during the high school years. Better advice is: "Use worry to stay vigilant for possible problems. Use it to take predictive responsibility for your actions and plans by thinking ahead and asking yourself the two basic worry questions, 'What if?' and 'Just suppose?' Perhaps engage in some contingency planning just in case: 'If things started to go wrong, this is what I could do.'"

- Parents can recommend *Worry as a Guardian* worth posting. "Worry is warning; it foresees dangers. Worry is proactive; it thinks ahead about possible consequences. Worry is cautious; it slows down decision-making. Worry is preventative: it takes precautions. Worry is protective; it prompts preparation. Although worrying is not fun to do, in high school it's worth keeping your 'worry wits' about you. Well-focused worry can prevent a lot of problems."

- Parents can talk about *Resisting Group Think*. They can explain how collective action can cause suspension of individual responsibility when members get caught up in and go along with risky ventures they would never undertake alone. Social momentum of the moment and pressure to conform can both be hard to resist. Thinking by one's self and for one's self at such moments, refusing to go along for better judgment's sake, is often an act of courage greater than what it takes to accept the adventurous dare. Parents can say: "Majority motivation among friends is not always wise or right."

- Parents can also talk about *Resisting the Tyranny of Now*. They can encourage keeping larger life objectives in mind that immediate interest can obscure. "Don't live for the moment and behave in short-sighted ways that put at risk existing investments and important plans. Future goals help prioritize and direct present choices. Behaving now at the expense of later can be costly. "Don't sacrifice your future by satisfying present temptation."

- Parents can encourage *Routine Risk Assessments*. They can suggest, when confronted by a socially supported but perhaps unwise course of action, taking a moment to consider possible outcomes. Knowing that all choices come with consequences, the young person can take less than a minute before automatically going along with some exciting idea by asking and answering for themselves four questions:

"Why would I want to do this?"

"What are the dangers?"

"Are the benefits worth the risks?

"If I go ahead, what is my plan if things go wrong?"

- Parents can talk about *What the Adolescent Knows That Isn't So*. Prevalent adolescent myths, advanced by their peers, often sanction unwise and illicit activities. Consider a few. "You can't get drunk on beer." "You can't get pregnant if the guy pulls out in time." "You can't get addicted to pot." "If you only sniff it and don't swallow it, you can't be hurt." "If you're still in high school, police will just let you off with a warning." A good question to ask their teenager about any high-risk topic is: "About this activity, what did your friends have to say, what have you heard or been told?" With this information on the table, parents can respond with older and more accurate understanding of their own. "True, you probably won't be sentenced to prison for first-time shoplifting; but you can definitely be taken to court and given a warning."

When they raise the issue of risks, parents can be troubled by the adolescent's response. "Oh, you worry too much. I know how to take care of myself. I know all about it. Nothing bad is going to happen to me!" Now denial of risks appears to stare with blind eyes and listen with deaf ears to parental warnings, and speaks with perfect confidence. However, what parents are hearing is not confidence, in most cases, but bravado. Scared of all the freedom in this brave new world, but too proud to admit it, the young person wouldn't dare try a lot of the risk-taking required for growth if he or she didn't deny the likelihood of danger.

Risk-taking = impetuosity + denial of danger. That's one formula for adolescent growth. This is why parents should not argue with denial, but accept it, and then proceed to talk about their cautions and concerns. Their job now is less to control the young person's choices than to inform them. "We are not trying to change your mind; what you choose to think is always up to you. We are only adding another point of view for you to consider." Since some young people seem to be more drawn to the impetuosity and denial of danger than others, parents have a lot of talking to do with these naturally adventurous teenagers.

So, perhaps a parent says something like this: "I know you don't see any cause for concern or anxiety, but I do. And as your parent, part of my job is to help you consider possibilities to be on the lookout for, and have plans for coping just in case. I am not distrusting you; but I am distrusting all that can harmfully happen in an unpredictable world. Therefore, safety and normal precautions and thinking ahead are going to be part of our regular conversation from here on out as new and different opportunities for you arise."

As with children, so with adolescents, parents still have a duty to warn. That's not "scaring kids straight" or "helicopter parenting," "adult terrorizing" or "hovering," that is meant to frighten or interfere with adolescent growth. This is responsible parenting, lending the adolescent a more seasoned pair of eyes and ears to help the young person become more fully aware of possibilities. "Think of us as another head on your shoulders to help you evaluate and think twice about what you may want to do, and if so, how to do it relatively safely."

The age of the adolescent can make a difference in the capacity for responsible risk-taking because mental capacity matures with physical growth. To risk-take responsibly requires delaying gratification long enough to take time to think ahead, to assess danger, and to plan sensibly. Thus the high-school-age teenager is more developmentally capable of this than the more impulsive middle school student, the college-age adolescent even more so. For whatever reason, some young people seem to mature faster or slower than their peers. With the more slowly maturing adolescent, parents usually have to extend their supervision and direction a little longer. Of course, all bets are off when the young person is operating under the influence of substances, because in that case, mature self-regulatory power is usually diminished, and impulsive immature decision-making is enabled.

Since all adolescents lead double lives (the one that parents know about and the other they do not) dangerous risk-taking is in the category of behaviors where parents are often kept out of the loop. So parents can explain: "The more we are told about what you are doing, the more readily available we are should you have need for help." Of course, parental desires can be mixed when it comes to late adolescent risk-taking. They want to be told and yet want to be worry-free. It takes courage to be privy to what one would rather not know. "Although we may wish you were not sexually active at this age, since you have told us that you are, let's talk about how you can manage this high-risk activity as physically and emotionally safely as possible."

## Readiness Training for Functional Independence

The best advice I've heard for parenting a student during the high school years was from a middle school counselor who had labored in the field of adolescence for many years. "When a teenager enters high school, parents have a lot of work to do," he told me. "They have just forty-eight short months to get the adolescent ready to manage more responsibility than ever before." I agree with that statement. Four years is not a lot of time to prepare a young person for the increased freedom and self-reliance after senior year. So a worthy parental goal for high school is to graduate a young person with sufficient self-management responsibility to create the shortest possible next step to independence.

Whether living at home in a more self-sustaining fashion, starting a job and supporting an apartment with a friend, or attending college and sharing dormitory space with a roommate, after high school or graduation age the young person starts operating more on their own. I call this last stage of adolescence "Trial Independence" (ages eighteen to twenty-three) and I believe it is the most challenging adolescent stage of all. Adequate readiness training from the high school years can make an enormous difference.

Consider four ways for parents to foster next-step readiness in their high school student: responsible goal setting, transferring parental responsibilities, practicing exit responsibilities, and taking choice/consequence responsibility.

### Responsible Goal Setting

Parents can help their high school teenager think about what she or he might want to be doing after high school—like pursuing an interest, internship, occupation, or education. They can set up in-person and in-place contacts to make those possibilities feel real so that the young person actually sees what that interest, occupation, or education is actually like.

With this next-step possibility in place, the young person has created an "anchor to the future" that can have a steadying influence on adolescent growth. It can provide a sense of direction and priority. "I don't want to do anything now that might endanger what I want to do next." In addition, future goals can motivate present effort. "I'm working hard so I can get where I want to go."

## Transferring Parental Responsibilities

To help the adolescent gather more self-management responsibility, parents can inventory all the routine services they provide for the young person that she or he could learn to do for themselves, and then start turning them over. They could ask themselves: "What are we routinely doing for our teenager that she could responsibly do for herself?" Make a list of these services, no matter how small—from getting the young person up in the morning to reminding them about school deadlines to doing laundry, for example—and let the young person start practicing these self-management tasks, including dealing with what happens when a responsibility is dropped. When the young person says, "You didn't remind me!" an appropriate response may be, "That's right, as we said, remembering is *your* job now."

## Practicing Exit Responsibilities

As soon as high school begins, the parental curriculum needs to kick in. Parents need to think ahead and ask themselves: "When our teenager graduates, what basic knowledge, skills, and responsibilities need to be in place so he can successfully manage more independence?" They need to specify these competencies and then ask themselves: "When and how during the last four years in our care are we going to teach our teenager what they will need to manage?" For example, consider the topic of money management. "Since he is going to have to earn, save, budget, bank, and bill pay on his own, when during the high school years are we going to have him start practicing those financial responsibilities while still at home?" From what I've seen, young people who have learned really good money management skills in high school benefit from knowing how to produce, plan, delay gratification, prioritize, and discharge obligations in a timely manner after they leave home.

## Taking Choice/Consequence Responsibility

Much capacity for responsibility in adolescence is acquired the hard way—by confronting and coping with the consequences of unwise choices, through mistake-based education, and through learning from the errors of one's ways. The temptation for parents of an older adolescent, on the cusp of independence, is to rescue the young person prematurely so hard lessons can be avoided and not burden the path ahead: "He's really a good kid, and we don't want to see him hurt. Besides, he promised not to do it again." The problem is that while promises are easy to make, they can be easily forgotten. Payment of responsibility is expensive, but can be hard to forget. Parents have to decide if suffering the consequence of a bad choice in high school is worth the young person gaining a lesson of lasting value.

A common oversight when parenting a high school student is becoming so preoccupied with maintaining grades and applying for jobs or further education (both worthy of adult attention) that readiness training for independence gets slighted. "Forty-eight short months," the counselor warned. That's the timeframe parents have to get the young person ready to self-manage more freedom and responsibility and master more basic living skills than ever before.

CHAPTER THIRTEEN

# Dating and Romance

"Dating just one person is socially simpler,
but it's more complicated too."

People are by nature coupling creatures, inclined to find a love partner with whom to take the journey through adulthood, often creating a family in which to birth and raise the next generation. Although most adolescents do not seek an immediate life partner or to have children in late adolescence, they do try more serious social connecting. They start to date. So what follows in this chapter addresses, Why Dating, Safe Dating, Romantic Dating, Healthy Dating, Dating Variations, and Falling in Love.

## Why Dating

While not everyone dates in high school, during high school is when most adolescent dating begins. Dating happens when one person summons the courage to ask another person to go out and spend some special time together. Because it can take courage to ask someone out (fear of rejection), and to take the invitation (fear of acceptance), early dating can carry some anxiety. "What will I wear?" "What will I say?" "What will we do?" "Will it be fun?" It's most relaxing to date someone you know well, although sometimes dating a "friend" can make a good friendship uncomfortable by implying feelings of a romantic kind that are not necessarily shared.

Dating is a big development. It's a social step up to step out in public as a member of a dating couple. It is an act of social independence and affirmation of social attractiveness. It declares some readiness for an older relationship and the acting-older feelings and activities to which it can lead. It signifies a new level of socializing by choosing to "go out" with someone you may not know very well in contrast to just "hanging out" with a friend. Dating is social selecting, takes a certain daring, and thus requires confidence and effort to make it work.

## Safe Dating

Most parents alert to adolescent dating by confronting a new set of worries about safety, substance using, and sexual acting out. How far and fast is this "older-acting relationship" going to go? It is definitely a time for parents to weigh in with their concerns and expectations, and most do. If the adolescent is going to act socially older, then they usually feel the need to talk about older risks and responsibilities— particularly *risks* for the woman and responsibilities for the man because in worst-case situations the woman is more physically vulnerable; and for same-sex couples there can be exposure to social intolerance and even physical harm.

Young people will sometimes report what parents had to say or how they acted when the teenager's dating began. For example, a teenage son summarizes what his straightforward single-parent mother had to say this way: "You are responsible for treating any woman you date as a guest in the relationship. This means you treat her with the same respect and care you would want any dating man to treat me or treat your sister. Is that understood?" Apparently it was.

Or, looking back, a young woman in her twenties describes her father's response to her dating. "My dad was a strange combination. He pushed me to push myself to try new things and get ahead, but he also watched over me while I did. All the way through growing up he had his eyes on me and mostly this was okay, except when it came to my dating in high school—when it definitely wasn't, at least not to me. It was embarrassing, even humiliating what he put me through when I was going out with a guy. I used to get so mad at him. 'Daddy,' I'd complain, 'nobody else, not one of my friends, has to go through what you put me through when I date! I hate it!' And he'd just smile and agree. 'Little darling, I know you do, but this is just what a father has to do.' And what he put me though was this. I came to call it 'taking my date into the kitchen.' It went this way. First, he had to meet anyone I was going out with, even if I'd gone out with them before. He was always welcoming of the guy, always shook his hand. Then after some small talk, and discussing plans for the evening, he'd say, 'Join me in the kitchen for a moment, will you?' And of course the guy always did. I soon discovered from my dates what my dad had to say because it was always the same thing. 'I appreciate you're taking our daughter out tonight. I want you to know she is very precious to us, and that we are entrusting her to your care. We expect to have her back on time in as good shape as when she left. If you run into anything unexpected, or need any help, please give us a call. We are always here, and we will be waiting up for her return. Understood? Thank you. Now I hope you both have a good, responsible time.' So you can figure it didn't take long for me to prep my dates for my dad, not that it caused him to act any different. And I resented him all the while. But later, after I'd been out on my own a few years, something about what he'd done changed for me. Maybe I grew old enough to appreciate what I'd been given, and it was this. I had friends who had bad dating experiences in high school, some pretty serious. But never me, never once. All through high school, going out with a lot of guys, and safe dating all the way, partly thanks to my dad."

In no particular order, here are some safety strategies to consider when a son or daughter is dating:

- Dating someone you already know is probably safer than blind dating.

- Dating done among a bunch of other dating friends is probably safer than dating as a lone couple with no social company around.

- Dating someone closer to the same age is probably safer than dating someone who is significantly older and more experienced.

- Dating structured around a planned activity is probably safer than dating with nothing planned and everything yet to be decided.

- Dating knowing parents who are only a phone call away is probably safer than dating without that ready access, should it be needed.

- Dating substance-free is probably safer than when one or both are substance-using.

- Dating with a curfew set no later than midnight is probably safer than extending it into the early morning hours when vigilance can become more lax.

- Attending to what friends have told you about the person you are dating can be safer than ignoring what they have to say.

- Trusting your dating instincts when feeling doubt, distrust, or danger is probably safer than denying your discomfort.

## Romantic Dating

What complicates female/male dating is that each is practicing a more grown-up gender role—how to act "womanly" or "manly" with each other—that they have not tried before. Many young people have had very limited meaningful social contact with the opposite sex through elementary and even middle school, primarily spending time with same-sex friends from whom they may learn what the other sex is stereotypically, or generally like.

"Boys are all hormones."

"Girls are all teases."

"Boys are unfeeling."

"Girls are emotional."

"Boys don't talk much."

"Girls talk too much."

Or suppose the first date is to the high school football game, a local pageant that can be very symbolically instructive when it comes to parading desirable manly and womanly definitions and contrasting differences between the two. Now young people get to see extreme sex role and appearance differences celebrated before an enthusiastic crowd. Tough boys are bulked up like gladiators to competitively play social aggressor in a collision sport, and pretty girls are thinned down in form-fitting costumes to play social attractor and dance and cheer the male players on with their support. Then of course the advertising and popular media relentlessly presents physically idealized young women and men effortlessly having a good time with each other, images that deny the dating awkwardness that many young people feel. What early dating does accomplish for many young people, however, is allowing them to start keeping older-acting social company than ever before, and to become more socially confident as a result.

Of course, the dating relationship changes when caring develops. It can start with interest ("Her smile caught my eye"), then attraction ("He has a nice laugh"), then enjoyment ("We had a good time together"), then affection ("I liked how we held hands"), then infatuation ("I can't think of anyone else"), then romance ("I dream about us getting together), then blossom into love ("We have a special caring for each other.")

The more caring is invested and returned in the dating relationship, the more powerful and complex it becomes. Parents have to monitor the relationship if it enters the infatuation/romantic/ love stage because the temptation for sexual activity becomes stronger. They should be weighing in on how they feel about that likelihood in terms of sex as a response causing arousal and leading to intimacy, and sex as a responsibility leading to physical, emotional, and relational consequences. And even though parents may declare they are opposed to the relationship becoming sexually active at this young age, thus playing for delay, they still need to address the issue of eventual sexual involvement that increases with growing older, and then they need to discuss safety measures for managing that eventuality. They can do this within the context of discussing a healthy caring relationship and how to evaluate what healthy conduct of a caring nature is.

It's when infatuated, romantic, and loving feelings for and from another person motivate the desire to continue and deepen this attachment that it can become increasingly challenging and confusing to navigate. So much feels at stake emotionally. The more caring the relationship grows, the more complicated it becomes to manage, because intimacy is demanding in two ways. One path to intimacy is through sharing human similarities for commonality and companionship; this is the easier way. The second path to intimacy is through sharing and resolving human differences through creating compatibility and conducting conflict; this is the harder way. Being able to relate both ways bonds caring relationships. The inability to do so is what grows the young couple apart with estrangement and incompatibility. And because infatuation, romance, and love are such dominant emotions, it is easy to lose perspective on what is happening and to lose judgment about what to do.

## Healthy Dating

When a young person is feeling frustrated, uncertain, confused, injured, or ambivalent about a developing relationship, parents of the empathetic and nonjudgmental kind can be of supportive help. They can give the young person some framework for considering the nature and conduct of a healthy loving relationship to help inform understanding and guide decision-making. To that end, consider several aspects of such relationships to which parents might want to speak: Treatment, Sharing, and Mutuality.

## Treatment

In a significant caring relationship, how the young people involved act toward each other and toward themselves matters. The more caring the relationship, the more there is emotionally at stake, the more carefully they have to monitor their own and each other's conduct. To that end, they need to be able to affirmatively answer four treatment questions for the relationship to be okay.

"Do I like how I treat myself in the relationship?"

"Do I like how I treat the other person in the relationship?"

"Do I like how the other person treats me in the relationship?"

"Do I like how the other person treats themselves in the relationship?"

For example, if I treat myself as a person of equal standing in the relationship, if I treat the other person in the relationship as worth listening to, if the other person treats me with empathy when

I feel down, if the other person takes a fair share of responsibility when we don't get along, then the relationship sounds like it is going okay.

However, if, for example, I treat myself as inferior in the relationship, if I automatically defer to the other person, if the other person becomes hostile when we disagree, if the other person acts as entitled to get their way, then there may be work to do in the relationship.

Caring or love is never a good excuse to treat the other person, be treated by the other person, or treat oneself badly. Because treatment behaviors determine the quality of the relationship, it is the responsibility of the teenager to monitor the four treatment questions to make sure it is proceeding on a constructive course.

## Sharing

One definition of a caring relationship is anytime two young people actively share a positive emotional connection to each other that they want to continue. The outcome is complicated because now they have to manage three competing interests in their two-party relationship—of *Me*, of *You*, and of *Us*. For the relationship to go well, the needs of all three interests must be met, and there are times when this is hard to do. When the sharing is not working well for one party, any of four sharing complaints can be expressed.

"This relationship is all *You!*" Here one partner feels like they are living too much on the other person's terms, that the other person is making all the important decisions. "I do and we do whatever you want to do!"

"This relationship is all *Me!*" Here one partner feels they have too much responsibility for directing and maintaining the relationship. "Whatever I do or you do or we do is always left up to me!"

"This relationship is all *Us!*" Here one partner fees like they have no individual freedom in the relationship for a life apart. "We do everything together; we spend all our time together; I need to have a separate life too!"

"There is no *Us* in our relationship!" Here one partner feels like they have insufficient contact with the other and are living too much apart. "You do your thing, I do my thing, and we hardly spend any time together anymore!"

Whenever a sharing complaint is expressed on either side of the relationship, how sharing with each other is being managed needs to be discussed and perhaps renegotiated. Usually, when sharing doesn't work for one party, the relationship is no longer working well for both.

## Mutuality

Mutuality is about both parties making sufficient effort to maintain equity of standing in their relationship. This means

- there is adequate *reciprocity*, so each party makes valued contributions to each other's and their joint well-being;

- there is adequate *consideration*, so each party is responsive to each other's sensitivities and welfare through those little acts of courtesy and tenderness that can signify so much;

- there is adequate *compromise* when wants diverge, so each party moves off immediate self-interest to find a common solution both can support.

Perhaps the most important parental guidance to give is a precautionary one. Since increased caring increases emotional vulnerability, the one you love the most can hurt you the worst, and hurts will happen. It's important to remember that love does not entitle the other person to harm you; does not obligate you to accept mistreatment; nor does it make it okay for you to unmindfully or willfully harm them. So when inevitable injuries are given or received, they must be discussed. On these painful occasions, expressing sorrow, apologizing, even making amends, are not enough unless accompanied by a commitment to reform: "I will never act this way again."

For sure, any sexual activity needs to be by mutual consent, and never manipulative or coercive or under the influence of substance use. Because sexual intimacy often generates feelings of emotional intimacy, the relationship between sex and love can become confusing. It's best for parents to remind the smitten young person that having sex does not signify love any more than feeling love requires having sex, and that having had sex one time in no way obligates a person to have it again.

Going forward from puberty, sexual attraction and arousal can become primal mood-altering experiences that, when excited, can seem to have a mind of their own. At such times it can be a challenge in older adolescent relationships, particularly during the more sexually active college age years, to keep sexual intimacy consensual. Self-centered and misguided thinking can force the situation and blame the victim. "If I'm turned on, you must be too." "Since you turned me on, you owe me satisfaction." "It's your fault for turning me on!" No, the person responsible for feeling turned on is oneself.

When, despite parental wishes to the contrary, the in-love relationship becomes sexually active, sexual mutuality in a caring relationship needs to be discussed. For sexual mutuality to be in place

- there needs to be adequate *reciprocity*, so the relationship is conducted in a way that brings pleasure to both parties;

- there needs to be adequate *consideration*, so the experience is observant of each other's sensitivities, comfort, and safety;

- there needs to be adequate *compromise*, so the experience is governed by joint agreement over what is done and not done.

Of course, once sexual consent is given, each person has a right to change their mind and have that change respected.

A young person might ask, "But how can I tell if my partner is truly consenting?" It's not complicated. First, make sure that at the moment the relationship is substance- and pressure-free. Next, stop action long enough to ask a direct question: "Is sexually getting together something you really want to do?" Wait for a reply before going ahead or stopping as the other person wishes, always respecting a change of mind after consent has first been given. When it comes to sexual consent, take the time to ask for what you need to know.

## Dating Variations

Variations in sexual orientation can make dating more socially challenging. At an age when young people are establishing their sexual identity, questioning or discovering that one is homosexual (attracted to one's own sex) or transgendered (feeling born in a non-fitting sexual body) exposes a young person to a host of negative stereotypes and pejorative names and attack humor about those who do not conform to the dominant form of heterosexual association—females attracted to males and males attracted to females. High school is usually a more homophobic place than not, so declaring that one is gay or transgendered can be scary, and perhaps unsafe, and often leads to keeping some degree of secrecy.

Because of this social jeopardy, in most cases a young person does not "come out" in high school, but usually delays until the last stage of adolescence. By this time he or she is graduated and away from home. Living in sexual hiding in high school, when hearing so much social hostility, denigrating terms, and attack humor toward homosexuality and transgendered identity, can create a lot of legitimate fears in a young person about discovery now and in the future. Some anxiety can become part of one's daily life.

The young person sees how four common acts of social mistreatment—prejudice, discrimination, harassment, and complicity—that oppress many other marginalized "social minorities" can be directed at them for being in a sexual minority.

- The power of prejudice is in the message of inferiority: "You are not as good as other people." The worst effect of prejudice is the poison of self-rejection: "There is something wrong with me."

- The power of discrimination is in limiting social mobility: "I am not allowed." The worst effect of discrimination is denial of equal opportunity: "If people knew about me, they wouldn't let me join and make my way."

- The power of harassment is in the threat of harm: "I better watch out." The worst effect of harassment is the ever-present sense of danger: "Some people are out to get people like me."

- The power of complicity is in how the majority, who are not directly affected, will ignore and accept unjust treatment, leaving the targeted sexual minority unprotected: "Witnesses will just look the other way."

The worst effect of complicity is how, through bystander inexpression and inaction, a conspiracy of silence tacitly supports the continuation of minority mistreatment. This is driven partly by limited caring ("We are not they") and by fear that prejudice, discrimination, and harassment might be directed toward bystanders for daring to speak up. In some ways times have changed for those in the gay or transgendered sexual minority, although in many ways they are still much the same.

Parents can let their adolescent know that they understand the kinds of oppressive social hurt from being in a sexual minority, and that they stand ready to offer support and advocacy should any of these harms occur. As for initially telling parents and receiving their emotional support (if these adults want to be told), the teenager needs to know that parental love is in no way dependent on her or his sexuality or anything else. "We will always love the person you are, we are here to help support and problem-solve with you, and we stand by you should mistreatment come your way." It can be hard to tell extremely rigid, intolerant, or judgmental parents. It is important for parents to remember that being gay or transgendered in high school can be a very isolating and vulnerable experience, carrying with it a high incidence of anxiety, loneliness, and despondency, and unhappily a higher risk of suicide as well. So if your teenager shares that he or she is gay or transgendered, or you suspect this might be so, an unconditionally loving connection to you can be a lifeline.

## Falling in Love

Falling in love feels accidental because it usually is not planned. While most adolescents do not experience in-love relationships in high school, a few do and when they do the desire for emotional and sexual intimacy tends to increase. In most cases falling in love takes time. Some occasion puts two young people in contact, some interest in each other is aroused, some attraction draws them together, a liking develops, infatuation strikes, and finally romantic feelings bloom as each becomes idealized in the other's loving eyes.

It's an intense awakening, alive with the mutual delight of each other's company and causing hunger for more. The initial sense is how much they share in common, how they are so compatible, how powerful the attraction is, and how much happiness depends on being together. Yet there are times of worry when something happens that gets in the way of their getting smoothly along. Now some unwelcome difference arises and threatens the harmony between them. "He didn't listen when we disagreed." "She didn't remember what she promised."

At this point there can be fear that the relationship is no longer perfectly wonderful and the love they felt is gone. That's the painful lesson that falling in love has to teach: perfectly wonderful relationships don't stay that way for long.

*In-love* can distort reality in two common ways. Each person can project upon the other how they ideally wish that person to be. "I've always wanted to be with someone who is happy all the time and looks on the bright side." And each person can strive to measure up to what it is the other person ideally wants. "I just want to act content and communicate the positive attitude that my love desires." These sentiments are not so much dishonesty as they are the playing out of wishful thinking to perpetuate the heightened pleasure in-love brings.

When in-love is lost for one or both parties and reality is revealed, a decision can be made to end the relationship. "She's not as great as I first believed." "He's not everything I thought he was."

In-love loses its luster. And falling out of love often occurs when the challenge of balancing common tensions in the relationship become too much.

- Desire for time together can contend with a need for time apart.

- Ever possessive, love can succumb to jealousy of other relationships and erode trust.

- Commitment can be violated if one party strays.

- Early openness of communication can become more guarded to honor the desire for a private life apart.

- Competing interests can get in the way of common interests.

- Freedoms given up for the sake of the relationship can become too burdensome to bear.

- Possessiveness can become too controlling.

- Conflict can cause injury.

- Disenchantment in one party can gradually grow.

Many are the causes for a breakup to occur.

Parents definitely need to monitor their teenager when a breakup of first love occurs, particularly when their daughter or son is the person brokenhearted. Parents must check for depressive or aggressive reactions. At issue is how the rejected party manages pain. For example, suffering from loss can lead a bereft young woman into depression when she feels that all that is worthwhile in her life has been taken away. Or, turning suffering to anger at rejection can cause a prideful young man to retaliate against his former love with degrees of serious aggression—from attacking reputation, to harassment, to physical assault. To prevent such outcomes, parents need to emotionally support recovery from rejection and set a watch over their late adolescent to ensure the breakup does not lead to further harm.

So should young people in high school avoid love because it is not likely to last forever? I think not. Although first love in adolescence is usually not lasting love, the conduct of that caring relationship can have lasting influence, particularly when positive treatment, adequate sharing, and basic mutuality are learned. Although the magic may wear off, good lessons from that good experience can linger on as adolescent love matures young people for later love experience to come.

CHAPTER FOURTEEN

# Social Substance Use

"Most everybody smokes and drinks and dopes;
it's no big deal!"

Come the high school years, parents should be prepared to confront the reality of more frequent substance use in the teenager's world. What follows outlines for parents What to Accept, What to Know, What to Watch Out For, What to Say, and When to Act when it comes to adolescent substance use.

## What to Accept

The bad news is that by the end of Late Adolescence (the high school years) most young people have had social exposure to, and probably experience with, some psychoactive (mood- and mind-altering) substance use—nicotine, alcohol, and marijuana being the most common. For example, the National Institute on Drug Abuse surveys student use each year. In 2016, over 60 percent of high school seniors reported ever using alcohol (a very common and dangerous drug). As you might predict, alcohol use, intoxication, and binge drinking only increase during the college-age years, the last stage of adolescence when a much wider array of illicit drugs appear on the social scene.

The good news is that "most" does not mean "all." A sizeable minority of high school students elect to abstain. So if parents are told that "everybody does it," that is not true. What may be true is that everybody in that teenager's social circle uses when they get together. Parents might want to suggest some substance-free gatherings, and maybe socializing with some non-using friends.

Parents should treat any substance use as a big deal, if for no other reason than that once a decision to start has been made, some pattern of use is likely to continue in a world with more available chemicals to help people manage their lives. There are recreational chemicals, health supplements, over-the-counter medications, prescription psychoactive drugs, and prescription medications that can have psychoactive effects, as well as illicitly available and an increasing variety of synthetic psychoactive substances. Some active "drug" use seems to be part of most everyone's daily life. It's not just smoking a cigarette to relax or drinking a jolt of morning caffeine to wake up, but even in what we eat, such as a sweet treat from the vending machine for a sugar "lift" to relieve afternoon fatigue. Substances are us. Huge legal and illegal industries traffic in these chemicals, are enormously profitable, and are not going away. So there is no good use in denying the drug-filled reality in which adolescents grow up.

## What to Know

During adolescence, substance use is alluring because it provides a shortcut to a psychological experience that is particularly powerful for the age—freedom. For example, there is freedom from normal conditions (escape), freedom *for* expansive activity (excitement), and freedom with other people (disinhibition) that can be liberating on all counts. Freedom is a powerful seducer for substance use in adolescence.

If your adolescent reports substance use, it's always worthwhile asking the motivation question: "Why do you use?" If the young person says to relax or to open up or to enjoy companionship, ask a follow-up question: "Is this just one way you reach these objectives, is it the usual way, or is it the only way?" If it's the only way, suggest how force of habit can lead to dependency. "So it's best to make use intentional, not automatic, and to have substance-free ways of experiencing escape, excitement, and disinhibition."

Underage drinking happens because it feels like a more grown-up way to behave when socializing with friends who are out for a good time together, and so there is often group pressure to go along. Alcohol consumption can be treated casually (light beer viewed as little more than a diet drink), while underage consumption of harder liquor in public can be *hidden in plain sight* by filling ordinary-looking plastic water bottles with clear liquors like vodka, gin, or tequila, leaving the adults, who are hosting a "drug-free" teenage gathering, none the wiser.

Most parents fail to address adolescent substance use in the beginning because they are not told. It's only by catching the young person with the evidence, or in dishonesty, or through other reports, or through making self-defeating or self-destructive choices for which no good explanation can be found, that they realize what they hoped they wouldn't have to consider. Wishful thinking by parents is no protection, because denial is "the enemy in hiding." The young person denies use and problems with use for fear of being found out, while parents deny that their adolescent could ever become seriously mixed up and messed up with drugs, hoping that something else must surely be the matter with their surly or errant teenager.

Why didn't the adolescent just forthrightly tell parents that some use was going on? I think the answer is that adolescents lead double lives—the one parents approve of and are told about and the one they would disapprove of and so are not. Come adolescence, parents will not be told everything, and all of what they are told will not always be the truth. Thus, when "first use" is reported or admitted, despite claims to the contrary, this is usually not first use, but first time caught using, and any promises not to use again are probably false since once substance use begins, it usually opens the door to some degree of continuation.

For starters, parents may want to open up a discussion of the experience, i.e., about the pressures and motivation to use, what the experience was like, and what was learned, and then restate their opposition by giving reasons why. They can repeat the risks of using involved at this young age that have been discussed previously and push for delay as the wisest and safest course. "'Not now' doesn't mean 'not ever,' because that is up to you. 'Not now' means we believe the longer you can delay beginning, the safer your decision to use is likely to be."

## What to Watch Out For

When it comes to detecting signs of substance use in their teenager, parents need to be watchful for signs of problem use. As I suggested in my 2013 book, *Surviving Your Child's Adolescence,* parents should keep an eye out for uncharacteristic changes in youthful behavior.

- When smart kids make stupid decisions.

- When good kids act bad.

- When truthful kids lie.

- When mindful kids can't remember.

- When conscientious kids become indifferent.

- When even-tempered kids develop mood swings.

- When kids with little money suddenly have a lot to spend.

- When capable kids fail.

- When dedicated kids lose interest.

- When communicative kids shut up.

- When open kids become secretive.

- When nice kids act mean.

- When responsible kids act irresponsibly.

- When reliable kids default on their agreements.

- When motivated kids start to not care.

- When careful kids act careless.

- When obedient kids break rules and laws.

- When focused kids have accidents.

- When honest kids steal.

- When healthy kids become run down.

None of these changes individually is a guarantee of problem substance use, but over time a pattern combining a number of these behaviors should be cause for parental concern.

If some degree of substance use is going on, parents can try to roughly assess the level of involvement from what they are told and what they can detect. Consider five levels of possible use, from least to most severe:

*Experimental use*: Trying a substance out of curiosity to see what it is like and, having tried it, not necessarily inclined to do it again. "I dropped acid and had a really scary experience. I won't do that one again!"

*Recreational use*: Expected repeated use in social situations that appears relatively safe. "Sometimes we smoke some weed on the weekends but it just lightens everyone up. It just adds to the fun."

*Excessive use*: Overdose can be accidental or intentional. Accidental overdose occurs when inadvertently taking too much too fast. "I was just taking one drink after another and the next thing I knew I woke up in the emergency room having my stomach pumped out." Intentional overdose occurs when deliberately going out to get drunk or wasted: "I drink to get bombed like my friends."

*Abusive use*: Taking substance use to the point of making self-defeating, self-destructive, or socially harmful choices, in all three ways doing harm to oneself, but the consequences do not deter ongoing use because they are discounted, because the person doesn't care. "The more I take the more amped up I get, even get into trouble, so what?"

*Addictive use*: Now there is a craving to use, a compulsive dependency on a self-destructive substance to cope and survive, and experiencing painful withdrawal when use is stopped. "No matter what, I keep using because I feel I have to, that's why."

Although an oversimplified way for parents to roughly assess a teenager's use, I believe level of use makes a difference. Every known episode of use should be talked out. Experimental, recreational, and accidental excess should all be subjects for discussion to help learn to safely self-manage substance use. Should parents suspect intentional excess, abusive, or addictive use, they should get a qualified substance treatment counselor to help evaluate what is going on and what might helpfully be done.

There is no safe substance use, because at every level of use the young person's perception, judgment, impulsivity, and/or reactivity is under chemical influence, leading to greater likelihood that damaging decisions can be made. In addition, freedom of choice is diminished with advancing levels of involvement. At the extremes, while the experimental user may be exercising free choice when deciding to try a substance, an addictive user feels trapped, consumed by the desire to use. Of course, not all experimentation is safe. At an age of early adolescent curiosity, innocently and ignorantly trying to get a high off sniffing household solvents can be life-endangering.

A final word to parents: in general, beware "empty home parties." These occur when the parent or parents are going away for a night and have entrusted home care to their high-school-age adolescent who assures them that she or he is responsible enough to take care of the place. Then the word gets out that there is an empty home space available to gather with no intrusive adult supervision present. Maybe the teenager just invited a couple friends over and that was it, except it wasn't—because the word got out and soon a lot of young people show up uninvited to the party and now the custodial teenager feels out of social control. As drinking and maybe other drug use gets heavier, more acting out is encouraged, leading to one or all of three unhappy outcomes: the home starts getting trashed; the gathering gets rowdy and neighbors call the police, or someone gets seriously hurt. So when parents return, the home they left and the teenager they trusted are in disarray, while they are feeling honestly betrayed. My advice is to just take this possibility off the table. Don't leave a high school teenager in overnight charge of an empty home.

## What to Say

As with other risky or illegal activities, responsible parents need to speak to delay, discouraging play with substances. With alcohol and other drug use, they often give a protective prohibition. "In this drug-filled world, at your age you do not have our blessing to use substances because when your mind is in an altered state you are more likely to make unwise decisions and get yourself hurt or in trouble." Parents can discuss some serious aspects of substance use, not to "scare young people straight," but to educate about recreational substance use and real life risks.

For openers they can itemize eight dire threats in adolescence—of serious accidents, social violence, school failure, emotional impulsivity, sexual misadventures, daring risk-taking, law-breaking, and suicidal despondency. And they can explain how all of these experiences are more likely to occur with substance use that alters mood, judgment, and reactivity. Many, if not most, first sexual experiences reported to me have been enabled by the use of alcohol and other drugs. *The safest path through adolescence is substance-free.*

As high school graduation approaches, so does moving out and away from family next fall, perhaps into a job and apartment-sharing arrangement, perhaps off to college; in both cases living away from the familiar comforts and security of home. At this time, the young person will encounter a dramatic increase in the extent and variety of substance use. Why so? Partly, I think, to indulge a degree of new freedom and independence, partly for the immediate physical and psychological pleasure that using can provide, partly to escape pressures of responsibility that growing older brings, partly because living away from home makes young people more of an open market for illicit sellers, and partly to cope with increased insecurity at social gatherings where young people self-medicate to disinhibit, fit in, act older, and give themselves chemical confidence to socially cope, kick back, let go, loosen up, and have fun.

Parents can suggest some strategies to the older adolescent who is likely to begin or continue use, to do so *mindfully*. By this term I mean *moderate* and *functional* use as measured by the kinds of self-management decisions young people make when choosing to put themselves under the influence of such casually viewed but very powerful drugs like alcohol and pot.

"Moderate" means knowing when one has had enough so that sober judgment is not significantly impaired or lost. "Functional" means maintaining essential operating priorities so that under the influence important responsibilities are not ignored and set aside. *Mindful consumption requires both moderate and functional use.*

The core issue of Moderation is Sufficiency. Consider the use of alcohol, for example. The more someone drinks, the easier it becomes to alter one's degree of sober caring. Sense of what matters can change from normal caring to caring less to acting careless to becoming carefree drunk where nothing may feel forbidden and everything may feel allowed. Now, to feel more disinhibited at the party, the nervous young person can become more freely expressive, permissive, submissive, or aggressive, more emotionally driven or explosive, more reactive and impulsive, depending on how much she or he drinks, and how that drug happens to take them. As feelings are freed to do one's thinking, there can be freedom from care about what happens now, what others may think, what risks are taken, what harm to self or others may be done, or what consequences might result. So a young man believes that driving drunk is not so hard to do.

If parents are moderate drinkers, they know when they have had "enough." They can share what "enough" means to them and how they learned to draw the line. "I've learned that two beers stretched over a couple of hours are enough for me."

The core issue of Functionality is Responsibility. Consider the use of marijuana for example. The more one smokes (or otherwise ingests), the easier it may become to absent oneself from dealing with pressing obligations of reality. It can feel tempting to delay and deny what needs to be done. Now there can be more forgetting and procrastination. Now there can be more inclination to escape daily demands like school or work or family or other commitments, rather than to engage in them. So the young person takes an extended lunch break with friends to smoke a joint before returning late to class, and pays less attention upon return.

With nonfunctional use, a young person may describe "spinning my wheels," by which they often mean the inability to get sufficient traction in their life to move themselves forward to meet significant goals or even smaller objectives. What can happen is a slippage of significant self-management responsibilities. If parents are *functional* users, they can describe when and how much they use. "I only smoke at the end of the day to relax, and not so much that it gets in the way of what I need to do."

Parents cannot control their older adolescent's determination to indulge in some degree of recreational substance use, but they can inform that choice. Parents might offer some additional guidelines for keeping substance use within a relatively safe range. Here are a number of suggestions to consider:

- Understand that any drug is just a poison with a purpose, always risky because intended good effects can have unintended negative side effects. Don't ignore a bad "use experience"; learn from it.

- Make the decision to use intentional, not automatic. Don't make use a regular habit because that can engender dependency.

- Make use a free personal choice, not a socially pressured choice. Don't let others determine your decision to use.

- Use in the company of friends. Don't use with people you don't know and trust.

- Use because you want to, not because you need to. Don't let emotions drive your use.

- Since the danger of the substance is partly in the dose, when using a substance start low and go slow. Don't use so fast you lose track of use or use in excess.

- When using, go at your own rate. Don't use to keep up with, show off, or compete with how other people are using.

- Know why you are using. If you believe it is the only way to relax or cope with a demanding situation, consider exploring some other ways.

- Know what you are using. Don't use when unsure about the nature of the substance being offered—what it is, what it's mixed with, what it interacts with.

- Stick to single substance use. Don't mix multiple psychoactive substances when you use, and if already taking prescription psychoactive medication like a stimulant or depressant, don't socially use.

- Use for enjoyment, not to medicate discomfort. Don't use to fortify resolve or escape from unhappiness.

- Use so that choices made when using are pleasing when looked back upon. Don't keep using if they are a source of regret or remorse.

- The longer you delay using until you are older, the less likely you will become a problem user. Don't feel you have to use to be "grown-up."

- Curfew your use. Don't use after midnight when all kinds of social risks start to rise.

- After use, evaluate your use. Don't ignore wise and unwise decisions made about using because both have something to teach.

- Learn from watching others. Don't ignore how some people use and get in trouble because that example can caution you against problem use.

- Use proactively. Don't begin use without a plan for how and how much you intend to use; stick to what you proposed.

## When to Act

I don't counsel young people for depression and/or substance abuse. I do try to refer them to more specialized help when these issues arise. The casualties from the interaction between the two are worthy of parental attention. Should signs of either or both occur, appropriate help should be immediately sought.

The relationship between feelings of depression and drug abuse is a two-way street. Feelings of depression can cause a young person to seek escape or relief through drugs. And drug use (particularly with a chemical depressant like alcohol) can intensify feelings of depression to self-destructive effect. It is important to get three definitions clear.

*Depressed*—as it is commonly, *not* clinically, used—refers to a normal, very sad emotional experience a person can experience in response to acute stress, painful adversity, or significant loss. Just because a teenager says he or she is "feeling depressed," this declaration, which should alert parents to keep an eye on their child, does not mean the young person is necessarily experiencing or heading for depression, particularly if he or she also shows other signs of positive resolve and constructive engagement with life.

*Depression,* as it is clinically used, which should cause parents to seek help for their child, refers to a severe state of despondency in which a person becomes emotionally stuck, typically suffering hurt, hopelessness, helplessness, anger, worthlessness, or sudden loss of appetite, without having energy or motivation available to make any positive change.

*Depressant* refers to a group of potentially addicting drugs (like alcohol) that "depress" or sedate symptoms of gloominess, nervousness, agitation, or insomnia, helping a person feel more calm, normal, relaxed, or able to sleep.

During the inevitable emotional ups and downs of adolescent growth, times of significant, persistent sadness in their child should be taken seriously by a parent because they may be either a precursor or consequence of substance use. What can a parent watch out for? A few common signs of feeling seriously depressed include:

- Withdrawal from friends

- Isolation and diminished communication within the family

- Through words and tears expressing significant unhappiness

- No longer liking, or even giving up activities previously enjoyed

- Acting more angry, provoking more conflict in the family

- Making statements reflecting low self-esteem

- Complaining about being bored all the time

- Having difficulty sleeping

- Experiencing a loss of traditional appetite

- Showing a drop in school achievement

- Having an unusual weight loss (too thin) or weight gain (too heavy)

- Expressing chronic fatigue

- Becoming increasingly pessimistic about life

If an adolescent appears unable or unwilling to talk about and work his or her way through depressed feelings after a couple of weeks, if an adolescent seems to be getting more despondent, or if an adolescent accidentally or intentionally begins to do damage to him- or herself (engaging in self-defeating or self-destructive behavior), then parents need to get the child evaluated for depression. To prevent harmful self-medication or acting out in destructive ways, get the child assessed and into counseling, where he or she can talk out whatever unhappiness is going on.

Drugs like alcohol are often chosen by people, both young and old, as a means to relieve feeling depressed or to escape from depression, but this substance may only increase the possibility of suicidal behavior when they are suffering from this despondent experience or this despondent state. Degrees of suicidal statements for parents to listen for are the following:

- "I feel so down and discouraged."

- "Sometimes I feel like just giving up."

- "Some days I wonder if life is worth living."

- "At times I wish I were dead."

- "I think about killing myself a lot."

- "Cutting myself makes other pain go away."

- "It would be so easy to just get blind drunk and drive the car off the road."

Although all the above statements should be taken seriously, the level of intention and planning increases and may warrant an immediate evaluation for a highly supervised time-out at home or protective hospitalization. Parents can speak to their child as follows:

"If you are so unhappy that considering suicide seems to be your best choice for dealing with the pain then we need to get you help to find other choices that will improve your life, not end it.

"We will act to make sure that you will receive the following:

- You will get to talk your unhappiness out with someone who understands how you feel.

- You will be adequately supervised for your protection.

- You will be kept free of any recreational substance use, and your past use will be evaluated.

- You will not have ready means for self-destruction available to you so long as you are at risk of this unhappy and impulsive state."

To keep the last commitment, parents either remove or secure any common suicidal means on the household premises including prescription and over-the-counter medications, household poisons, knives and razor blades, rope, guns and other weapons, and access to motor vehicles.

A scenario leading to a parent's worst fear, that of a young person committing suicide, might play out as follows:

1.  Getting into a depressed state from a performance failure or relationship loss. (Parents take significant failures or losses seriously and hear out hurt feelings.)

2.  Withdrawing into psychological *or* social isolation to conceal lowered self-esteem. (Parents increase support and expressions of personal affirmation.)

3.  Allowing distorted thinking to create an exaggerated picture of hopelessness and helplessness. (Parents provide a realistic perspective.)

4.  Resorting to substance use to self-medicate pain, thereby increasing the likelihood that impulse may rule. (Parents discourage resorting to drugs like alcohol, and encourage deliberately talking the suffering through.)

5. Having access to a ready means to end suffering by ending life. (Parents secure all household means for inflicting serious self-harm, including use of a car.)

The old adage truly applies: "It's better to be safe than sorry." Therefore, always evaluate the possible link between substance abuse and depression, because the connection can be suicidal. And, if an older adolescent away from home at college is reporting self-defeating behaviors like procrastinating and skipping classes, failing effort and failing grades, online escape at expense of academic engagement, feeling overwhelmed by demands, being socially isolating and painfully alone, and reports self-medicating with substances to manage the suffering, intervene if you can and seek some counseling onsite, or perhaps bring the young person safely home and get recovery help there.

CHAPTER FIFTEEN

# The Internet

"My parents only had my offline life to worry
about. Add the online world and today my
parenting has become twice as complicated!"

Adolescents are adventurers. They want to experiment and explore the larger world for more experience to grow. But today, in contrast to their parents' youth, the geography of that world is dramatically larger because of the internet revolution.

Even though parents have become acculturated to operating in the Virtual World of the internet as adults, most of them grew up in a Real World setting and have no historical frame of reference for parenting in both offline and online adolescent worlds of today. Parents must embrace this new complexity in guidance they provide. There are many aspects of this challenge, a few of which to be considered are: The New World, The Parental Role, Parental Guidelines and Goals, and Managing the Electronic Screen.

## The New World
Begin by honestly acknowledging how both parent and adolescent spend large amounts of non-work and non-study daily time online—checking and sending messages, making electronic arrangements, engaging with social media, gaming, information gathering, surfing for interest, making a purchase, or enjoying other forms of internet entertainment.

Both youth and adults have moments when it feels easier to get on the internet than it is to get off. Online life is designed to be extremely compelling this way.

While the two worlds interact, they are different. In the offline world, a teenager navigates by making direct choices over behaviors, often in face-to-face contact with others; in the online world, most of those choices are electronically mediated through mechanical clicks to make interaction happen. In the tangible offline world there is a sense of visible surroundings and social context; in the remote online world perception is focused through the window of an electronic screen. In the offline world, there is limited easy access to life experience and possibilities; in the online world, there is a "virtually" infinite mediated life exposure at hand. In the offline world, parents had some say over what information a young person was given and when; in the online world, a young person is only a curious click away from whatever information catches their interest.

Gone are the days when parents could say, "We will wait to tell you about that when you are older." Parents no longer control access to information.

To consider this new reality, start with the occurrence of older internet exposures. Parents cannot stop this exposure. They can only try to keep up with it by talking about it and by trying to place it in a perspective that they believe is healthy. Suppose parents find out their shy high school freshman has registered herself on an online dating site. Perhaps they might say, "Of course you think about dating. You want to find ways for comfortably meeting people to make that happen. But posting information about yourself on an adult internet dating site can put you at risk of predatory attention from unknown older responders who may be out to do you no good. So let's talk about dating possibilities within your circle of friends at school, in social circles outside of school, about safe and enjoyable ways that you might start the process, and even ways we might be of social help."

Consider what they might say when a sixth grader entering puberty has his first exposure to internet pornography—something parents alert to because of the sudden surge of sex site invitations that suddenly flood their home computer. Perhaps, after listening to the young person describe what he was curious about, what he saw, and what he learned, they begin by putting the experience into perspective through matter-of-fact communication. Of course, every parent has his or her own values and individual perspective to offer. Here is what they might want (or not want) to say to their young adolescent:

"It is normal for you to become more interested in the sexual part of yourself and relationships as you get older. However, compelling as it may feel to watch, pornography—pictures of nude people having sex for spectator stimulation—can give you some unrealistic ideas for managing sexual activity as you grow older. For starters, pornography makes it seem like everything you see these couples do in a sexual relationship is what you should want to do. It makes relationships seem all about having impersonal sex, with no other interest in social or emotional connection. It makes casual sex look free of serious harm, with no dangers to beware, with no sexual protection necessary. Pornography gives you a lot of fantasy without much reality. It's made for entertainment, not education. It's not a good instructor. So we want to offer what we think is important for you to consider when it comes to sex, answer any questions you have now, and give you our commitment to talk with you about sexual matters that develop, as they will. We can also share what we remember not knowing at your age, and what we believed we knew that wasn't so. Sexual curiosity is healthy and so is our discussing any topic or questions you may have."

Sometimes parents wonder why the virtual world holds so much power for the adolescent. Why isn't the real world, with all it has to offer, interesting and challenging enough? The answer is in the freedom to grow through online experiences without physically going anywhere. It used to be when the teenager was at home parents knew where the young person was located. Now when the adolescent is at home, parents may have no idea where on the World Wide Web he or she may be travelling, talking, or trading.

Consider just some of what is offered online: a destination meeting place, a ready means of electronic verbal and visual communication, participation in social networks, a constantly changing marketplace, an endless encyclopedia of information, an entertainment palace for immediate escape, a place to lead and conceal a double life, a studio for creative expression, a game-playing arcade, a trove of adult information, a programming and problem-solving laboratory, an ever-ready antidote to being bored. And the list goes on. All that is needed is a computing device at one's fingertips. Like other adolescent freedoms, access to online freedom can be a cause worth pushing and fighting for.

## The Parental Role

Parents falter in addressing online experience because they have no precedent for what to say and what to do. They often ask, "What's our role parenting an adolescent when in this virtual world?" I believe the role is basically the same as parenting in the real world. Consider parental responsibility in this manner: today they are putting an adolescent in the seat of two different freedom machines.

Most parents have a pretty clear set of rules when it comes to operating the great offline freedom machine, the automobile. They don't simply hand the keys to the family car over to the newly licensed teenager and say, "Go where you want, with who you want, doing what you want with no guidance and oversight from us, with no words of caution from us, without having to tell us anything about what's going on." Few parents would give this blanket unaccountable permission.

But compare regulating use of this offline freedom machine with use of its unlicensed online counterpart, the computer. This great online freedom machine comes in an increasing variety of technical guises with a multiplicity of screens and a seemingly limitless array of applications to activate. The virtual world to which the adolescent has ready access is much larger than the real world of face-to-face daily interactions. So what permissions are parents prepared to give, and what manner of accountability do they expect?

If, in the online world, the teenager can be "safely" at home and yet parents can have no idea where in the internet the young person is, how are they going to set and supervise rules of operation and reporting requirements? At most, they can try to limit the travel capacity of home devices. They might explain travel restrictions that come with using the home computer based on their family values. "We don't want certain kinds of information coming into our home, such as those promoting social violence, drugging, gambling, easy money, stranger dating, pornographic sex, and hate sites." However, such prohibitions don't prevent exposures that young people can have through the electronic devices of friends. And, of course, prohibition provides no preparation; it only plays for delay.

A real world automobile caution about emotion might be: "Don't take exciting dares from your friends while driving." A virtual world computer caution about emotion might be: "Don't accept any free offers or invitations, or open any attachments, that sound too good to be true." In both cases, ignoring these cautions can lead to trouble and perhaps harm. Then there are the interactive possibilities between the two worlds to be concerned about.

*Online experience can affect offline perception and maybe behavior.* Think about how the simulating influence of some adventure gaming can encourage insensitivity to violence, or how the stimulating influence of watching pornography can shape sexual expectations. A young person's approach to aggressive or sexual behavior can be influenced. "This is okay to happen; this is how I'm supposed to act; this is what the other person wants."

Parents need to communicate so that the young person knows how fantasy simulation is meant only for entertainment and is not a healthy model for offline behavior or an accurate representation of actual reality.

*Offline needs can seek online satisfaction.* Think about how a student's need for answers might lead to plagiarizing unverified and un-credited information for a school paper because "what the internet knows is there for the taking!" Or think about how real world boredom with offline demands leads to entertainment escape to online destinations so frequently that a habit of self-defeating procrastination is encouraged, the young person doing internet fun now and routinely putting off real world tasks until later. Parents need to communicate how meeting offline responsibilities must come before enjoying online escape.

*Online contact can interfere with offline communication.* Then there are issues about mixing online contact with offline communication at home. Parent and adolescent can get in the habit of automatically interrupting direct communication with each other when one person immediately answers an online text message or call, thus breaking off the offline conversation that was going on. The online connection takes priority over the offline connection. "I have to get this now!"

## Parental Guidance and Goals

Parents wrestle with the issue of guidelines and goals for adolescent internet use and the devices that enable that use. What follows are just a few I have heard from parents over the years.

"The primary condition for our supporting your online activity is accurate and adequate communication about what you are doing on the internet daily, and faithfully observing some of the limits we agree upon."

"We will have regular offline family time where there is no online interruption or distraction."

"Just as we routinely ask and expect you to share about what has happened in your offline day, we will do the same about the goings-on in your online day as well."

"Your online activities will not interfere with your offline responsibilities for home and school."

"You do not frequent any online sites from which we are password-protected out."

"You don't convey personal and family life information to strangers."

"You don't sleep with your smartphone just in case you get a text."

"You understand that online activities through your various devices will be randomly monitored by us to check and see that you are sticking to our conditions."

"You observe the 'five year rule' and don't post or send any information about yourself that you might regret other people seeing five years from now."

"If you ever encounter any danger or get into any kind of trouble on the internet, you will come to us for help."

"You will be self-aware that the internet is the greatest mass social surveillance system, collector of personal data, and invader of personal privacy yet invented. Knowing that, with every click you make identifying where you go, what you do, what interests you, and who you are; you will proceed online with responsible care."

"You don't message or text when feeling upset or angry, at risk of emotionally posting something you later regret but cannot retract."

"You don't use immediate access to the internet as an electronic mood management system to salve emotional discomforts and to escape problems."

One common parental concern regarding adolescent preoccupation with the internet is: "With all this time spent on screen-mediated communication, our teenager will lack or lose fluency with face-to-face communication," The answer to this objection is that it can be both false and true. On the false side, I think the data generally suggests otherwise. With the new technology, young people have more ways to communicate than ever before—short-burst messaging and sending photographs and video over their phones, for example. Besides, when parents first began to use landline phones, that technological advance usually didn't appreciably diminish their capacity to traditionally communicate face-to-face. On the truth side, however, at home it can be harder for parents to beat the electronic competition and get screen-free time to communicate with their adolescent. Parents often tell teens, "I want to talk to you face-to-face, not just to the side of your head!" And sometimes the adolescent can make the same complaint about the parent.

An important parental job is educating their adolescent in how to intelligently process this readily available universe of online information. Consider three filtering questions to help when accessing and assessing this endless trove of information, evaluating what the content may have to offer.

There is the Purpose Question (and the matter of Agenda), the Trust Question (and the matter of Truth), and the Application Question (and the matter of Use.)

The Purpose Question is "Why is this data being posted?" All data on the internet is posted for a purpose, hung out there like bait to hook visitor interest. So whatever website you are viewing, ask yourself, "What is the agenda? Is it to entertain me, to educate me, to locate me, to motivate me, to profit off me?" Ask yourself, "Why would someone want me to be interested in this?"

The Trust Question is "Should this information be treated as valid?" Is it worth considering, crediting, and given convincing value? How can you tell if the reporting, examples, opinions, testimonies, promises, pictures, offers, or claims are to be believed and trusted? You don't want to admit into your core of working knowledge what is mistaken, misleading, or false—useless shortcuts, quick fixes, illusions, outrageous claims, and/or magical solutions. You don't want to be led to believe and behave as though fantasy is reality. Ask yourself: "On balance, is this too unlikely, too simple, too seductive, too sensational, or too good to be true?"

The Application Question is "Should I act on, interact with, or put this information to personal use?" Assuming the agenda seems legitimate and the content valid, do you want to place personal welfare on it by utilizing whatever the information is supposed to be good for, be it for education, guidance, membership, or for purchase? Because the outcome is always to some degree a gamble, encourage the young person to take Predictive Responsibility by asking themselves what could possibly go wrong if they used this information, and what plan do they have in mind should this eventuality occur. Ask yourself: "Does the use justify the risk?"

The internet is a fabulous human invention, and the traffic of endless data is a wonder to behold. In response, the new parental job is to provide perspective when internet exposures give adolescents worldly knowledge at a much younger age, and to help them learn to sort out the huge amount of information that comes their way for what is valuable and safe, and what is not.

In general, parents might consider three possible internet goals for their adolescent:

*Competence.* Learn good technical and navigational skills. Educationally, occupationally, and socially, fluency on the internet is now a requirement for making one's way in the world.

*Safety.* Exercise adequate risk awareness about online dangers. It's not only easy to be seduced by online activity into forgetting personal vulnerability; it's also easy to believe that there is anonymity, un-traceability, protection, and security on the internet, all of which is not true.

*Balance.* Prevent online presence from eroding healthy offline skills. Internet appeal can encourage habitual entertainment escape at the expense of offline engagement meeting real-life concerns, demands, and responsibilities.

Finally, there is the increasing consumer fixation on the electronic screen to be electronically connected at all times to seek pleasure, to socially connect, to get information, to keep current, to create diversion, and to relieve boredom.

## The Electronic Screen

What is it with all the electronic screens in our lives? We rely on these visual monitors for information about our world, for mediating our relationship to the world, for interacting with others in the world, and for escaping the world's demands. In doing so, an enormous amount of our daily hours are spent staring at screens.

Times have certainly changed. In my parent's generation came the movie screen, in my generation came the television screen, in my children's generation came the computer screen, and in my grandchildren's generation came the modern multiplicity of screens. Today, when you add up some of the screens people can watch— game station screens, DVD player screens, TV screens, computer screens, movie screens, reader screens, cell phone screens, pad screens, just to name a few—the electronic screen consumes huge amounts of our attention. Outside of occupational hours spent in front of a computer aside, just think about how many recreational hours per week the "average American" of all ages, and the "average American adolescent" in particular, spends viewing these screens. It adds up to so much that most people would rather not know, so they don't record the hours spent and downplay the investment.

I do hear parents become concerned about the amount of screen time their adolescent is putting in on a regular basis. "It's not just that my teenager has to have her screen on all the time; it's how the screen has a constant claim on her!" "He spends so much time playing computer games." "She spends so much time social networking." "He spends so much time streaming video." "She spends so much time texting." "He and his friends are into endless computer games." "She's forever checking her email." "He can't go anywhere without his electronic brain." "She lives in a world of full-time entertainment." "They act like they must maintain internet availability at all times!"

For me, it's hard to tell if the increasing amount of leisure screen time adolescents and adults put in each week is an emerging problem or simply a social and cultural adjustment to major technological change that is here to stay. Certainly the electronic screen is a vast platform or window or stage on which young people can act out a wide variety of roles—as audience, as spectator, as creator, as player, as communicator, as networker, as shopper, as seller, as trader, as researcher, as searcher, as performer, as student, as helper, as teacher, and as entertainer, to name a few. The possibilities are mind-boggling. The electronic screen is now a means to so many ends.

At worst, some voices cry "addiction!" as though a self-defeating or self-destructive degree of "screen dependence" has developed. Applying the addiction notion to compellingly absorbing internet involvement (for example, "video game addiction") can feel scary to parents. I'm not sure it is physiologically applicable. However, if the young person becomes—by craving and compulsion—driven to be constantly screen-connected and experiences painful withdrawal when he or she is not, at least metaphorically, the concept might fit.

To a degree, such dependence can be commercially encouraged. As it was once cynically explained to me, "When you have something to sell, you want to encourage repeat use. That's why addicts are the best customers. Once hooked, they keep coming back." In the case of screen dependence, the marketplace can be seen as a powerful and unprincipled pusher that has only one goal: to consume more consumer lifetime and attention and resources. All screen time makes money for someone, and all screen time is at the expense of screen-free activity elsewhere.

Of course, before parents treat leisure screen time as an adolescent problem, they need to factor in their own screen time. In most cases I have seen, they are at least as "dependent" as their teenagers. They only differ in their viewing, surfing, communicating, networking, game playing, escape, and other entertainment habits and tastes. Interestingly, it is very common for parents to interrupt their counseling session to pull out their commandingly vibrating or ringing cell phone in order to see who is calling now, but to date I have never had an adolescent do such a thing. So if parents want to examine their adolescent's screen time, they would do well to examine their own and the example they set.

Where parents seem to have immediate concern is when adolescent attachment to the electronic screen preempts direct real-life relationship with them. For starters, during family time, do they spend more recreational time attending and interacting with a screen or attending and interacting directly with each other? Do they communicate in constant competition with screen time going on? Is talking to the side of someone's head and split attention the best listening they can give and get? If so, at least when there is something important to discuss, they may want to opt for clear channel communication: face-to-face talking with all electronic screens turned off. Best to teach the adolescent to treat the internet as a useful servant and not a commanding master.

**5**

## ISSUES IN TRIAL INDEPENDENCE
## (AGES EIGHTEEN TO TWENTY-THREE)

# STEPPING OFF MORE
# ON ONE'S OWN

At this final stage of adolescence, fantasies about freedom of functioning and the realities of independent self-management collide. No young person is entirely prepared for the increased degree of responsibility, ignorance, complexity of choice, accountability, disorganization, and distraction that has arrived. The multiplicity of demands can at times feel overwhelming. There is so much to do.

Common contributors to lifestyle stress at this vulnerable age include: anxiety from not keeping everything together, sleep deprivation from late night activity, procrastination with work, indebtedness from overspending, loneliness at being away from home, social insecurity in a new situation, poor nutrition and health care neglect, uncertainty of future direction, substance and internet use for escape, breaking commitments to self and others, and loss of esteem from feeling incompetent when stable footing is momentarily lost.

All of the above is partly why the last stage of adolescence is the most challenging of all.

# CHAPTER SIXTEEN

# Graduation Separations

"I feel like I'm leaving my whole life behind!"

Graduation from high school is an affirming accomplishment, but at the same time it sets in motion several separations from the past—from family, friendships, and often from romantic attachments—that may make moving on more difficult to do. If one is not finishing high school but is graduating from parental care to live apart from family at this age, many of the challenges are the same.

Why *challenges*? Because the price of departure is some degree of loss. There is usually a financial lifestyle drop that comes with moving out on one's own. "No more full refrigerator to snack from anymore!" Not only that, the future someone envisions often proves something of a letdown in reality. One confronts the stark demands of functional independence. So what follows describes hard separations and common disillusionment that can complicate the final stage of adolescence.

## Hard Separations

Consider three possibly painful separations that a young person can experience when graduating from high school or from parental care.

There is loss of daily residence and membership that comes with leaving the structure, support, and supervision of the family home.

There is loss of companionship and hanging out with friends as their social community disperses and friends go their separate ways.

There can be loss of romantic attachment and intimacy when loving partners in high school pursue different and more distant paths.

In each case of graduation separation something of historical value must be let go and may be missed. Take these one at a time.

## Separation from Family

Sometimes, when a young person graduates from high school and enters into military service, into a shared apartment with a job, or takes up residence at college sharing a dorm room with a roommate, parents will look at the empty room left behind and decide to repurpose it for another family use. So they box up for storage what was left behind and reassign the space. Changing the status of the old bedroom specifically, however, they forgot that for the absent adolescent it still has enormous symbolic value.

"You did what to my room? How could you do that? Just because I'm not staying at home doesn't mean I don't still live here anymore! You can't erase my place!" The room, vacated but remaining filled with old belongings, was how the young person marked active membership in the family; a belonging place to which they could always return. Parents need to remember that it will be many years before the young person has an independent home and family as powerful as the one they grew up in. In addition, there is a need to be kept in the loop about changes in family member lives and have routine access to current family communication. "Just because I'm not living at home anymore doesn't mean I don't want to know what's going on!"

To be out more on one's own can be adventurous and exciting; but it can also be lonely and scary. For this reason the family tether needs to remain intact. Having a sense that there is a secure and welcome home to visit should want or need arise is a comforting bulwark against sense of family loss. The young person needs to know that out of sight is not out of mind. She or he needs to know that missing home, even feeling homesick, testifies to the loving connection that separation from home is not empowered to break. So the message parents need to give is: "You are not alone, you are always in our thoughts and hearts, you can call anytime, and you always have your family place to come home to."

## Separation from Friends

Spend your high school years and more with the same set of friends you knew growing up and that community becomes a social world that can feel hard to leave. Hence there can be the "long goodbye" of senior year, when parting (going away) parties become more frequent and important. Everybody promises to keep in touch.

However, when the post-graduation diaspora occurs and friends move off in new directions to start separate lives, the old sense of group affiliation starts falling apart. "Graduation is breaking up that old gang of mine." Social networking while away, and staging reunions when returning home for holidays and vacations, become strategies for reconstituting and holding on to what has been lost.

Some young people suffer "the curse of the happy high school," and for them the separation from friends can feel hardest of all. It's one thing if high school was just okay or even not that great and you felt eager and ready to leave, but suppose it was a socially triumphant experience? Suppose you were extremely popular, a superior student, held leadership positions, and were a person everyone wanted to know? Now graduation can create a loss that the young person fully appreciates when they go from being "Mr. Somebody" in high school to "Mr. Nobody" on a college campus. "No one knows my name or even seems to want to. What a letdown!" In the larger world beyond high school, the son or daughter may say, "It's like socially starting over. I'll never stand out and do that relatively well again. Suppose those were the best years of my life and it's all going to be downhill from here?"

The parental message at this time might be: "The high school years were good because you made them so. Use that as evidence that you can do well for yourself again. Just because in the larger world you are not likely to experience the same relative level of performance and social prominence, that doesn't mean that you won't do just fine."

## Separation of Romantic Attachment

Perhaps the hardest graduation separation is from a romantic one, when a couple who are in-love attached are physically separating, one leaving and one staying behind or both leaving for different destinations. In either case, the custom of daily contact and socializing as a couple is going to be disrupted. "In high school, a big part of who we each were was being together."

Graduation brings about complicated questions. What is going to happen to their relationship now? Is there enough mutual missing to make in-love feelings last? Should they separate the relationship? Should they try to keep romance together through a long-distance relationship? Should they feel free to socialize and date in their new locations?

From what I've seen, honoring the caring they share with honesty is how to treat each other. As physical distance grows between them, so do social and emotional distance. It is natural to question the relationship now that the high school context has been lost. In most cases, high school romances don't last, although a few young people do manage to marry their high school sweetheart.

If asked what to do, parents might suggest the separating couple honor the caring they shared in this extremely important relationship. To do so, they agree to let the other person know if either starts falling out of love; if either wants more freedom to socialize; if either wants to begin serious dating; or if either finds another relationship of greater value.

Living apart from family, whether graduating from high school or not is a big change, and change creates loss of the valued familiar. That said, the other side of loss is always freedom. Freedom from old restraints and freedom for new opportunities create room to redefine as one grows. Enrollment in a life of independent choices begins. And to some degree the young person painfully learns that the alluring concept independence is not all that is was idealistically cracked up to be.

## Disillusionment

Life is full of disillusionment. Beliefs one develops or is taught become sources of great disappointment, even betrayal, when they turn out not to be true. Think of when one discovers how the Tooth Fairy and the Easter Bunny and Santa Claus are actually fictions created by trusted adults to inspire innocent imagination. Now the child learns that parents can tell a deliberate lie. Or there is a more powerful disillusionment with the power of parents and a promise that children want their parents to make: to always keep the child safe.

The child wants parents to say the following:

"We will always be there when you have need."

"We will always protect you from harm."

"We will always make good decisions for you."

"We will always know what to do."

However, by the young person's adolescence, their experience with parents falls short of this expectation. So the adolescent makes some jarring discoveries.

"They won't always be there when I have need. I am on my own."

"They can't always protect me from harm. Bad things will happen to me."

"They won't always make right decisions. I will sometimes pay for their mistakes."

"They won't always know what to do. I must figure life out for myself."

One painful part of growing up is giving up believing parents can provide security.

Now consider a great disillusionment that comes at the end of adolescence: "When I reach independence I can run my life!" After all, isn't that the goal of the whole turbulent adolescent process, to be able to operate on one's own grown-up terms? But now, in counseling sessions with young people in their midtwenties, what I hear is not a cry of triumph—"*Free at last!*"—but rather a moan of despair: "Now my life is all up to me!" What happened?

The sad reality is that when parental authority lets go and steps aside, "the system" takes over. What the young person discovers is that parental protection provided a measure of shelter in which direct exposure to the more complex and arbitrary demands of social authority were kept at bay. This awareness makes for a rude awakening. By comparison to these impersonal forces of social conformity and social compliance, parental attitudes were more caring, parental demands were far fewer, and parental rules were more flexible and forgiving.

Now having to pay bills, having to hold a job, or having to make one's way through the world all revise some ideas about basic freedoms the adolescent was looking forward to, but which the young adult now discovers are really fraudulent ideals.

When it comes to freedom of action, "I am not free to totally do what I want."

When it comes to freedom of individuality, "I am not free to be totally myself."

When it comes to freedom of speech, "I am not free to totally speak my mind."

When it comes to freedom of future, "I am not free to achieve anything I want."

These can be hard realities to accept. And yet valuable lessons are learned.

To get along, sometimes one has to go along. To fit in, sometimes one has to accommodate. To communicate, sometimes one has to shut up. To make one's way, sometimes one has to take what one can get.

As one young man concluded, "About the only real freedom I have now is dealing with any troubles I get into by myself!" In so many words, what the young man wistfully concluded was that "I'll never be as free as an adult as I was as a teenager. Back then, I could rebel, I could question authority, I could ignore some home rules, I could stand out from the crowd, and I didn't have to worry about being on my own. What I wanted, I already had, but I didn't know it at the time—the freedom to have parents who supported and took care of me."

His anger is understandable. He really felt betrayed by what he was led to believe over the course of his adolescence. Somebody had sold him a bill of goods about the freedom of independence, and that someone turned out to be himself.

# CHAPTER SEVENTEEN

# Over-Demand and Stress

"Independence is harder than I ever
thought it would be!"

It's the job of parents to prepare young people to meet the rigors of young adult life. During Trial Independence (age eighteen to twenty-three), the increasing demands required to support independent functioning can feel excessive. The young person isn't lying when they say, "There's too much to learn and keep up with all the time!" The last stage of adolescence is often the most stressful of all. This is why it can be helpful for parents to talk with and coach young people at this age about the nature and management of stress. Parents can explain how, typically, the high-stress times in people's lives are when there are excessive changes. There are four types of life-change demands that come with Trial Independence.

There are demands from starting something new (like moving out from home and in with friends); demands from stopping something old (like doing without parental supervisory support); demands from increasing the frequency of what one must do (undertaking more self-management responsibilities); and there are demands from decreasing the frequency of what one was used to (cutting back on spending to live within more limited means). Trial Independence is so demandingly stressful because of all the grown-up changes there are to manage.

What follows are four aspects of stress that parents might discuss with their last-stage adolescent. These are The Major Source of Stress, The Warning Signs of Stress, Three Gatekeepers of Stress, and Maintaining Wellness during Stress.

## The Major Source of Stress

A parent can talk to their teenager about those times in life when the adult has created or been given more to do than she can realistically or comfortably accomplish with the personal resources available or within the time allotted. On these occasions, two threatening questions typically arise: "Can I get it all done? If I can't get it all done, what will happen to me then?" The dominant emotion of stress is anxiety because extreme demand can feel overwhelming.

Parents can explain how most, but not all, stress results from this experience of over demand. Why? Because meeting demands takes energy, and everyone's supply of energy (one's potential for doing and action) is limited. When demand exceeds readily available energy, people rely on stress to force their system to generate emergency energy to meet dire circumstance. Stress is a functional survival response.

So, behind in his work after being sick, and with the emergency assistance of stress, a college freshman forces himself to stay up all night to finish a class project he wasn't sure he could get done. And the next day he is very tired. That's the consequence of occasional stress. After that emergency effort, he feels drained and worn out. When, however, he relies on stress continually and not just occasionally to meet the demands of life, significant physical and psychological costs can be incurred. This is why parents want to encourage their teenager not to make stress a habit.

A common stress habit young people can carry away from high school and get in the habit of is procrastination—postponing what needs doing now until later, or until so much later that only anxious last-minute effort or negotiating an emergency extension will save the day. In either case, delay increases stress that a more prompt response would have spared. When the young person gets accustomed to playing the put-it-off/pull-it-off game in response to work, inducing stress can become a habit. They can become stress dependent. One helpful parenting goal in high school can be graduating a young person from their care with a habit of getting work done in a timely way. Parents can warn how constant, chronic stress can wear the human system down.

## The Warning Signs of Stress

Because the costs of stress from constant over demand can have serious consequences, the teenager needs to know the major warning signs to look for. Parents from experience can suggest four possible signs, in descending order of severity.

1. Beware of constant fatigue: "I feel tired all the time." Fatigue is like a mind- and mood-altering drug that causes a person to become increasingly discouraged and negative over time. Ongoing stress can wear down one's positive outlook.

2. Beware of nagging discomfort: "I worry and ache all the time." Medically check it out, but factor in that body and mind can register stress in painful ways. Ongoing stress can actually hurt.

3. Beware of emotional burnout: "I have lost caring for what I usually care about." When what traditionally matters ceases to matter, that loss is worth attending to. Ongoing stress can be depressing.

4. Beware of physical breakdowns: "I can't seem to get myself going anymore." When less than normal functioning feels beyond the reach of effort to correct, then attention must be paid to demands of life. Ongoing stress can become debilitating.

Unfortunately, because these levels of stress are frequently cumulative, by the time someone reaches breakdown, he or she is usually burdened by some degree of fatigue, pain, and burnout. Parents can tell the teenager that because the effects of continual stress from over-demand can be serious, she must constantly monitor her well-being. Continuing stress can erode resilience and harm health. Parents can advise the young adult to not just ignore the experience or pop a pill to self-medicate away the message, but attend to what the warning signs are saying. Parents can then suggest practical ways to moderate demand.

## Three Gatekeepers of Stress

It is by keeping demands from oneself, from others, and from the world—within reasonable energy expenditures—that stress can be moderated. Parents can tell their teenager that there are three gatekeepers for controlling major sources of demand: goals, standards, and limits. Each regulates a different source of demand. Consider some high school examples of how a young person might encounter these gatekeepers of stress:

*Goals* have to do with how much a teenager wants to accomplish for herself. This is the problem of ambition. If she is committed to becoming a student leader, working extra hours at her job, dropping fifteen pounds, and trying out for the lead in the school play, she is creating a very high demand life for herself, one that has a high likelihood of stress. "I have to do a lot to do enough."

*Standards* have to do with how well he must operate all the time. This is the problem of perfection. If he is determined to maintain a 4.0 grade average, to win all competitions, and perform error-free, stress is more likely to come his way. "I won't tolerate making mistakes."

*Limits* have to do with refusal, with the capacity to turn down wants from others or from self in service of not undertaking too much. If she believes she can't say "no" to others for fear of displeasing them, or can't say "no" to herself for fear of disappointing herself, then she lacks a major defense against over-demand and the stress it can bring. "I can't stand turning down requests or opportunities."

Simply put, the higher a young person's goals, standards, and limits, the more demand one builds into life, and the more one is at risk of stress from over-demand. The only way to reduce this stress is to reset goals, standards, and limits to moderate demand. Goals, standards, and limits are not genetically ordained; they are chosen. Parents set these for children, but over the course of adolescence they increasingly turn those decisions over to adolescents so that by the end of high school the young person begins setting personal goals, standards, and limits for themselves. Parents can encourage adolescents to take on this responsibility.

For the older adolescent to continue to set goals, standards, and limits that are unrealistically high is to invite over-demand. A thoughtful parent may ask, "Out of high school and now more on your own, how high do you want to strive, how consistently well do you want to perform, how much do you want to undertake? When it comes to placing these demands on yourself and what is enough; that is now up to you to determine."

## Maintaining Wellness during Stress

If one cause of stress in the late-stage adolescent's life is over-demand; the other cause is *self-neglect*. In the first case, energy is overspent; in the second it is undernourished. The general rule is: without adequately sustaining oneself, energy runs down. And with lowering energy, less gets accomplished. Keeping energy in good supply is an ongoing challenge in Trial Independence. Here is one way to think about how this might be done:

How is personal energy (one's potential for doing and acting) to be kept up? Consider two ways energy is spent by the young person. The first is on maintenance activities. Maintenance means fulfilling recurring needs and wants that are essential for people to be able to move from one day to the next feeling good about themselves, with a full complement of energy at their disposal. Maintenance is routine self-care. It includes a multitude of basic life support activities such as eating regularly and well, sleeping enough, earning money, adequate hygiene, housekeeping, provisioning, relaxing, exercising, tending significant relationships, and many other activities. There are so many of these essential regular activities, in fact, that if they were all enumerated, perhaps as much as 90 percent of what one needs to accomplish each day could be considered part of basic self-maintenance.

Because it takes such an enormous outlay of energy just to self-maintain, one would think most young people would place a high priority on investing in energy sufficiency, yet they often do not. Why so? Consider how often anyone says to the young person (or the young person says to themselves), "Congratulations, you've just covered the basics and made it through another day!" The usual answer is not very frequently. Why? In general, maintenance is expected and taken for granted and is much less honored than the more glamorous way of investing energy—in change.

Consider contrasting value sets that are associated with these two different ways of spending energy. Change values emphasize doing new, more, different, better, and faster. Change is stimulating and exciting, and by following change values, goals can be accomplished, improvement gained, progress made, and success achieved. Concerned about the future, a young person can become focused on fulfilling an agenda of positive changes they want to make in their lives—be it educational, occupational, monetary, or relational.

By comparison, maintenance values can feel downright dull, having more modest and less glamorous objectives. They emphasize repeating the old, keeping up the same, continuing to do as well, perhaps doing less, and even creating times for slowing down. Maintenance is associated with sustaining and support, relaxation, and renewal. Thus while younger people may be drawn more to the excitement of change, older people (like their parents) can become more preoccupied with matters of maintenance. There is often a generation gap.

The dilemma found in Trial Independence can be that unless maintenance is recognized and rewarded for the vital contribution it makes to well-being, a young person is in danger of discounting and ignoring basic self-care. Investing in change is at the expense of maintenance, and can cause younger people to run themselves physically and emotionally down. "I have so much I want to do that I've had to cut out much of what I need to do like getting a full night's sleep and exercising regularly and eating well, and spending quality time with the person I love. Sometimes I think I'm sacrificing too much of myself to get myself ahead!"

The most common maintenance deficit I see at this last adolescent stage is young people shorting themselves on sleep. "Because I've got so much I have to do and want to do, rest is not that important." Except it is, because inadequate sleep can result in ongoing fatigue, moodiness, irritability, inattentiveness, and forgetfulness, all of which make it harder to effectively cope. Better to practice getting sufficient sleep. And remember, extreme sleep deprivation can be torturous.

Both change and maintenance are important to the last-stage adolescent's well-being, on the one hand creating new growth and on the other sustaining ongoing functioning; but they must be kept in balance. If about 90 percent of the young person's daily energy is required for maintenance, then that leaves maybe 10 percent to engage in change. While working for future objectives matters, working to sustain the present needs must not be neglected.

Managing a healthy mix of maintenance and change is a life-long challenge for everyone; but that education begins in earnest during the last stage of adolescent growth. So when it comes to stress from over-demand, the parental advice might be:

- "Respect that personal energy is a limited, easily exhausted, vital resource, so spend it mindfully.

- "Take responsibility for the personal gatekeepers of change—setting goals, standards, and limits to operate under demands that feel realistic.

- Avoid the temptation of excessively investing in change and ignoring basic maintenance, because that can lead you into lifestyle stress."

CHAPTER EIGHTEEN

# The Need for Self-Discipline

"Sometimes I miss being told what to do!"

There's no getting around it. For young people, the effective management of independence takes a lot of self-discipline. One way to think of self-discipline is this: the capacity to motivate oneself to accomplish necessary tasks in life that are dull or hard or unwelcome to do. Self-discipline has a lot to do with work ethic, with mobilizing the initiative to accomplish what needs to be done.

To appreciate the challenge of self-discipline, consider this comparison. At the outset of adolescence the youthful outcry against discipline often was "You can't make me!" because parents wielded ruling authority to which the young person objected. However, at the end of adolescence, the outcry often is "I can't make me!" because now the young person has become their own governing authority, and they must struggle to motivate and direct themselves. Witnessing this painful self-encounter always reminds me of the words of cartoonist Walt Kelly, "We have met the enemy and they are us!"

In the last stage of adolescence, Trial Independence, being on the losing end of this internal conflict can contribute to a lot of failure as partly exemplified in the average college retention rate of around 50 percent (see *Journal of College Retention*). I believe one significant factor for this high attrition rate is a lack of adequate self-discipline.

So, what self-disciplinary skills might parents encourage that adolescents can rely on to support functional independence when they graduate parental care? Consider these five: Concentration, Completion, Consistency, Commitment, and Cooperation. The important thing to remember about all five skills is that they are learned and can be maintained and strengthened through practice. Take them one at a time.

## Concentration

Concentration is expensive because it requires paying attention to the task at hand and resisting distraction and escape. Thus the amount of time it takes different young people to accomplish the same amount of homework can vary widely. An adolescent who can pay sustained attention and not be diverted by other distraction, or lured away by the temptation of entertainment escape, can get assignments done quickly and efficiently. Another teenager, however, who is easily distracted and vulnerable to entertainment escape, can stretch the work out over a much longer time due to frequent interruptions and a need for relief and diversion.

It is far easier to concentrate on what one likes or loves doing than what one dislikes. Thus you can have a teenager who can comfortably spend hours absorbed in playing computer games or social messaging for fun, but who can't stand attending to what feels unenjoyable or non-rewarding, like assigned work, for more than a very short length of time.

Concentration focuses attention. Parents can suggest: "To improve concentration, practice staying on task for longer periods of time, and positively recognizing gains in your increased attention span."

## Completion

Completion is expensive because it requires follow-through from beginning to end. It can require pursuing the objective when it becomes hard or harder to reach. Completion requires persistence in the face of fatigue and frustration. A lot depends on the power of the goal and the dedication of the young person. Some young people with a low tolerance for frustration give up easily when the going gets tough. Maybe they meant to reach a goal, but ran out of determination along the way. As execution feels more arduous, it can feel easier to leave a job half-done than fully accomplished. Other young people, when faced with a setback, may buckle down harder than ever to fulfill their original plan.

Completion finishes what was begun. Parents can suggest: "To improve completion, practice breaking the job or task down into manageable steps, recognizing progress as you incrementally proceed."

## Consistency

Consistency is expensive because it requires continuity of effort for the ongoing effect to be achieved. Repetition can maintain a level of conduct or performance that matters—turning schoolwork in on time or regularly studying for tests. Routine can become habit-forming; productive work habits are one result. Like the ambitious young musician says, "The only way to keep up my skills and get better is to practice every day." So one adolescent enjoys feeling physically fit, exercising regularly to keep this regimen in place. A friend, however, who would like "to be in shape," but can't adhere to a regular workout schedule.

It is far easier to engage in intermittent effort when someone feels like it than to make it an automatic habit. Consistency requires repetition of what one doesn't always feel like doing and so can require tolerance for boredom because repetition for its own sake can feel tiresome and dull. Effort in the moment is often less rewarding than the cumulative outcome. "I always like being in condition, but I don't always like working out."

Consistency sustains repetitive effort. Parents can suggest: "To improve consistency, after meeting a routine need, schedule another act of repetition as a reminder when it must next be done."

## Commitment

Commitment is expensive because it makes a promise. Commitment is like contracting, where one agrees to be as good as one's word. An adolescent who keeps commitments can be counted on to mean what is said, and can count on themselves. An adolescent who breaks agreements to self and others not only doesn't deliver on getting something done, but also becomes untrustworthy. "People don't believe I'll do what I say, and neither do I." And when failing to do as promised, the young person becomes a victim of his or her own default. It is far easier to *make* a commitment than to *keep* it. Like New Year's resolutions, a promise is no substitute for performance.

Commitment keeps agreements made. Parents can suggest: "To improve commitment, notice how good it feels to act like a promise-keeper, and resolve to treat yourself in this esteem-filling way."

## Cooperation

Cooperation is expensive because one must sacrifice some self-interest for the sake of accomplishment and getting along. The more independent one grows, the more collaborative relationships come to matter. It's very hard to make one's way through the world in isolation, going it alone. To work and play with others, one has to find common ground, joining forces, sometimes compromising, sometimes making concessions. If a young person has a history of playing a team sport, or being part of a student organization, knowing how to depend on others and contribute to others' success provides a great benefit. In this sense, being a joiner is better preparation than being a loner. Although it can feel easier to fly solo at the older age, focused only on fulfilling a personal agenda, in caring relationships and in the workplace giving in and going along are increasingly required for getting ahead.

Cooperation requires managing a common interest. Combining the understandings of two can be wiser than one, and giving for the sake of getting along builds relationships. Parents can suggest: "Improve cooperation by seeing how working together can accomplish more than working alone."

Since these five skills that support self-discipline are mostly learned through experience, it is never too late for a young person to get this practice underway. Resulting self-discipline can make a significant difference in the older adolescent's life: "I'm finally getting traction," "I'm no longer spinning my wheels," "I'm finding my footing," "I'm part of a team," "I'm making headway at last!" All of which can come as a relief for concerned parents: "We wondered if she'd ever put her life together, but she finally has!"

Self-discipline can support self-esteem as it sustains independent functioning. So, if possible, don't graduate a young person from your care who *can't* do the following:

- Pay attention to what needs doing.

- Finish what is begun.

- Maintain continuity of important effort.

- Keep promises to self and others.

- Sacrifice some self-interest to work with others.

Self-discipline helps the older adolescent catch independent hold.

# CHAPTER NINETEEN

# The Struggle for Independence

"I'm glad I have family to come back to;
but I wish I'd found my footing first time out."

In the final and most complicated stage of adolescence the young person must forsake dependency they have grown used to and must dare to act autonomously beyond their accustomed and comfortable limits. Between preparation that is missed and new demands that must be faced it can feel like a dual threat period of growth. I wrote more fully about this complexity in my 2011 book, *Boomerang Kids*.

Consider three aspects of this challenging time: When Life Can Feel Overwhelming, When Mentorship from Parents Helps, and When an Adolescent Boomerangs Home.

## When Life Can Feel Overwhelming

The last-stage adolescent must contend with a complicated mix in life. There's more worldly experience, but there is also more worldly challenge. There's more independence, but there's also being left more on your own. There's more to get to do, but there's also more of past value to relinquish. There's more freedom anticipated, but there's also more responsibility to be assumed. There's more autonomy to enjoy, but there's also more self-management to learn. No wonder a young person, missing the familiar and frightened of the future, feels unready and reluctant to further grow up. Just as the early adolescent had mixed feelings about separating from childhood, there are a lot of grounds for ambivalence and anxiety during Trial Independence. So the young person can be honorably conflicted between wanting the new and missing the old.

For example, consider how a young person may elect to cling to the holding pattern of being a "student"—a person who is not yet ready to assume adult responsibility and who is still in a stage of educational preparation, not wanting to move on and commit. The young person is pushing for another year in community college by accumulating some incompletes and changing majors a couple of times. The student designation may also justify a continuation of parental support. Because of the stubborn pattern of chronic incompletes, parents may offer to continue to pay for college schooling, but in a different way. Instead of paying tuition up front, they leave that to the adolescent. Maybe the young person can work and save money for a year to cover the next registration, with the agreement that they will reimburse all tuition on the back end for any classes completed.

The multiplicity and magnitude of life demands at this stage can feel overwhelming. As mentioned in the last chapter, the low average college retention rate (around 50 percent, according to the *Journal of College Retention*) offers painful testimony to the number of ill-prepared high school graduates that flounder as college freshmen. If parents have an older adolescent in college who is still having a hard time, recommend he get help. Short of being in emotional crisis, if feeling significantly stressed, recommend he contact the College or University Counseling Center for sensitive support and educational guidance before going to the Health Center, where medication is more likely to be initially prescribed. When parents send a young person off to college they should commit to regularly check in with the young person to monitor how well or badly this significant adjustment is going. This is not "helicopter parenting"; it is simply communicating to see that engagement with this next step in growing up is generally, not perfectly, being accomplished. What parents don't want is for the young person to encounter significant difficulty, with attendant anxiety or despondency, and not tell them or anyone what is going on. "I got into emotional trouble because I thought I should be old enough to go it alone, should keep unhappiness to myself, and when I did my life got a lot worse."

While freedom during most of adolescence was often alluring and exciting, adolescence on the threshold of young adulthood can be scary and dispiriting. Most young people are not fully prepared to meet all the expectations needed to support a more functional independence, which is why this last stage is a "trial" effort, when some degree of parental support is often still in place. It is a "trial" in the sense of having to endure missteps and failures as an "adult-in-training," and learn from the errors of one's ways in a struggle to catch independent hold. Because mistake-based education is the order of the day, it can be hard to sustain self-esteem: "I keep messing up!"

At this juncture, there is no parental criticism allowed because the young person is already self-critical in her or his own eyes. And parents need to restrain expression of their worry because it can be perceived as a vote of no confidence when the young person has worries enough of her or his own. Parents just need to encourage learning from past missteps, recognize progress, and support planning next steps forward.

At this age, it's very easy to feel *rootless,* helpless, useless, aimless, worthless, and even hopeless. The "-less" is significant because it means "less than" what one felt "more of" in high school—more connected, competent, directed, useful, valued, and hopeful. During the trials of this last stage, "I feel stuck" is a common counseling complaint I hear. Or, "I'm not getting anywhere!" But in most cases the young person only *feels* "stuck." Closer examination suggests they are growing and learning hard life lessons of great value. They are developing mental toughness and resilience from recovering and continuing to try, they are showing courage in the face of challenge, and they are gaining more worldly knowledge and experience. So in fact they are making progress; frustration and discouragement just makes it hard to see. Parents might point out this hard progress. "By how you acted you've figured out how *not* to act that way again, a painful but important lesson to learn."

Young people who are still comfortable during this time of life may be in some denial. In truth, they can feel riddled with self-doubt, contending with a host of urgent and troubling Adequacy Questions for which reassuring answers are hard to find. Consider the following eleven questions:

1. "Can I find my way?"

2. "Can I keep it all together?"

3. "Can I motivate myself to work?"

4. "Can I manage living more independently?"

5. "Can I prepare myself for a successful future?"

6. "Can I deal with the fallout from bad choices?"

7. "Can I figure out the solutions to my problems?"

8. "Can I depend on myself to do what I know is right?"

9. "Can I stay healthy and happy living apart from family?"

10. "Can I get by on less or earn some more money?"

11. "Can I cope with feeling stressed and overwhelmed?"

Negative responses to these questions sow the seeds of self-doubt in the face of much uncertainty. Most importantly, they undermine the self-confidence needed to carry on. Adolescents at this age are at a very important self-management choice point—whether to doubt themselves or express confidence in themselves. Attitude has much to do with actions they take.

Doubt is disabling; confidence is empowering. So parents can encourage the young person to shun the first and embrace the second. "True, there are some things that need attention in your life at the moment; but take time to credit all the things that are going well." Doubt pre-maturely forecloses on positive possibility and creates its own sad self-fulfilling prophecy. Doubt is a defeater. Doubt thinks, *I can't.* Confidence thinks, *I can.* Of course confidence doesn't guarantee success, but by making the effort the young person continues his or her pursuit of positive possibilities. This is why the antidote to doubting questions is asking the affirmative action question instead: "If I was not filled with doubt, but confidence, what would I choose to do to advance my best interests?" Then encourage the adolescent to consider trying that initiative.

Prompted by this question, the young person, instead of letting a job application languish because a callback was not received, decides to call up the employer to check on the status of the application. Such actions help keep hope alive and initiative in place.

In addition, it helps to accept the reality that one is dealing with an honorably challenging change—the transition from older adolescent to young adult. It's normal and okay to occasionally feel overwhelmed at the end of adolescence. What is not okay is letting "feeling overwhelmed" lead to delay or avoidance or escape from what is best to do. At this age, internet entertainment, social partying, and substance use can lead to giving up, which is the enemy of growing up. As mentioned previously and worth repeating: if significant anxiety or despondency start the young person thinking and talking in self-defeating terms ("I'm such a failure!") or in self-destructive terms ("It's not worth living!"), get the young person some counseling help. Parents need to maintain enough contact to monitor the away-from-home transition. Out of sight should not mean out of mind. They should stay in enough communication to monitor the adjustment going on.

Finally, respect how the last stage of adolescence is the most courageous stage—the time to brave low confidence and high uncertainty and find a point of entry into young adulthood. Of course, life won't get any easier from here forward, but by engaging with the demands of more independence, increased strength and self-assurance will be available for whatever major challenges come next. And be mindful that at this age, contrary to parental expectation, the adolescent needs access to parents more than before.

## When Mentorship from Parents Helps

Some parents think that when their son or daughter graduates from high school, adolescence comes to an end, adult independence begins, and their parenting is mostly done. Better for parents to tell themselves, "It's not over yet." There's a lot of the parenting game yet to play.

What parents need to understand is that in most cases the hardest stage of adolescence comes last. At this age young people are faced with a daunting task of having to live apart from family, to scramble to catch a responsible hold on life, and to begin to chart a path into the unknown future.

Now they must keep a firm footing while they spread their wings; they must watch where they're going while they are not sure where they are headed; and they must act more maturely while they are making more mistakes. There is a lot to learn. To adolescent regret and parental dismay, this final lap around the adolescent track is when setbacks and mishaps often occur.

That their older adolescent must rely more on themselves (or at least try to) doesn't mean they don't still need parents to be involved in their lives. In fact, because of the challenges that come with trial independence, parents are needed more than ever before. However, they are needed in a different way. At this last stage of adolescence, the ground rules for effective parenting significantly change. The age of managerial parenting is over and the time for parental mentoring has arrived. At this last stage of adolescence it is essential that parents change their vertical role from being managers (imposing supervision and regulation as an authority) to a horizontal role, becoming mentors (offering personal sharing, consultation, and advice from more of a peer perspective.)

Fortunately, come their son or daughter's trial independence, parents have an opening for involvement they didn't have before. While still at home, high school students may not have been inclined to ask for parental advice because that would admit to ignorance or incapacity at a time when they wanted parents to think all was firmly under adolescent control, and so leave them alone.

Then, parents can experience a surprise. Once they have moved out in late adolescence, young people suddenly encounter a host of practical challenges from living on their own for which they were not fully prepared. Suddenly they encounter the impact of their inexperience coping with more complicated demands, and as they do, their perception of their parents tends to alter. These adults who were not credited with much knowledge worth offering in high school suddenly become people valued for the worldly advice they have to share. In trial independence, as a young person's confidence about practical knowledge starts going down, appreciation of what parents know starts going up. Writer Mark Twain had it right when he said, "When I was a boy of fourteen, my father was so ignorant I could hardly stand to have the old man around. But when I got to be twenty-one, I was astonished at how much the old man had learned in seven years."

Now, if they haven't before, the last-stage adolescent needs to have open access to the parental brain trust—all the hard-earned wisdom from longer life experience from which the young person can practically benefit—whether it's how to be a smart consumer, finance a major purchase, figure out a contract, consult on solving a tough life problem, or how to avoid or recover from a host of pitfalls into which parents painfully fell at the young person's age. In trial independence young people can really welcome the life management knowledge of parents, assuming it is offered in a collaborative way, and not given in a commanding, corrective, or critical one. "I really appreciate how my parents share what they've learned when there's so much I need to know. They were ignorant and made mistakes at my age too!"

From many more years of life experience, and from knowing the young person since birth, parents have a wealth of knowledge to offer through remembering, informing, instructing, advising, preparing, predicting, problem-solving, helping, coaching, personal sharing, and the like. So, what kinds of mentoring knowledge does the parental brain trust have to offer?

## Historical Memory

Having known the young person longer than anyone else, parents have this growth record in mind. "I know you feel that this college breakup is too painful to survive, but we remember how you struggled and recovered when your neighborhood best friend from early childhood moved away in fifth grade. You had what it took to deal with hard loss back then and recover yourself, and we believe you have what it takes to deal with hard loss now. Let's talk about how."

## Similarity Connections

Different parents have different similarity connections with different children, and those connections can be mined to useful effect. "I'm not saying you are me, but I believe we are alike in this. Like me, you love being very busy and there is a great deal you enjoy getting involved in. This is why you did so much in high school, sometimes wearing yourself out in the process. So, just to share, let me tell you how I've come to deal with my temptation to take on too much. Over the years I've learned to prioritize and strategize for efficiency. And I've learned to say 'no' to the hardest person to refuse of all—myself! Here is some of what I do to keep myself in check and on track."

## Worldly Information

Because parents have so many more years of experience, they have seen more of life than their adolescent, some of which can be helpful for the growing young person to know, particularly to counter or counter-balance what they have been told by peers that may not be so. "I'm not saying what you've heard from friends is all wrong, but sometimes it may not be entirely right. So you've heard that defaulting on your health club contract won't trigger debt collection, that taking a stimulant when your tired won't do you harm, and as for ignoring parking tickets, well police have bigger offenses to keep after so don't worry. Just to let you know, my personal experience doesn't square with any of that."

## Self-Management Strategies

All parents have had to deal with reversals and adversities in life and from that experience have derived ways of managing themselves that can be helpful for their adolescent to know. "I know you're upset because of the mistake you made. All I can tell you is that dealing with my mistakes has always been a challenge for me. It's easy to get down on myself and beat up on myself for what I should have known better not to do. I can punish myself afterward, which just makes things worse and moving on harder to do. So, for what it's worth, from my experience, after you've learned from the consequences, it's best to let the bad decision go, start afresh, and carry on. Just like the seasoned athlete, you need to be able to let a bad shot go so it doesn't get in the way of carrying on your best game."

## Cautionary Tales

It can be valuable for parents to share some of the errors of their ways while growing up so that, through this vicarious learning, their adolescent is spared committing the same unhappy experience. "Seeing you go off to college makes me mindful of one unhappy episode freshman year I hope you can avoid. It took me a lot of help to come to terms with what I did that was my responsibility, and with what happened to me that was not my fault. I'd never been to a college party before. Because I was nervous I drank too much too fast, and before I knew it I couldn't think clearly about what was being done to me until too late. The one thing I can tell you about college drinking is that while it may help you feel more socially secure in the moment, it can definitely make you more socially unsafe at the same time."

## Problem-Solving

It's in the last stage of adolescence that having the parental brain trust comfortably accessible is most important because young people are away from home with more life management responsibility than ever before. At this time, most of them do not find their independent footing right away, but make all manner of miscalculations, causing significant life problems. Feeling overwhelmed, having access to the parental brain trust only a phone call away, the young person can describe the trouble they have chosen their way into and can begin getting seasoned counsel about how they might choose their way out. "I used my charge card without thinking, and now I've got debt I never had before. What can I do to get out?"

There are so many ways a last-stage adolescent can get in over their head, get behind in their obligations, get tempted by freedom-loving peers, get crossways with adult requirements and laws, and get lost in all the demands that come with functional independence. At a time when they expect and are expected to be more self-reliant and less dependent on parents, they often need a second head on their shoulders; they need the benefit of parental thinking more than ever.

Although parents are doing more letting go as the adolescent detaches and does more letting go of them, when growing up draws to a close and brings active daily parenting to an end, they are not abandoning the relationship or cutting off communication to the young person. Rather, they are affirming that the parental brain trust will always be available for the asking.

However, if as a managing parent the adult barges in and tries to control the adolescent's troubled life at this late stage, they may risk rescuing their child from learning life lessons. They may undercut the growth of self-reliance. Help out too much and they risk protracting dependency. If they are quick to fault failures and to blame shortcomings, they may estrange the relationship and reduce communication with a young person who refuses to be censured by them anymore.

"I would rather have nothing to do with them than to hear their complaints!"

To maintain a workable connection at this time, when this connection is sorely needed, parents need to establish a collaborative *mentoring* relationship where there is more equity between them, where they are living alongside each other in terms of mutual respect. The mentoring contract is based on mutual respect. It states that the parents will respect the young person's right to make independent decisions and to take responsibility for dealing with consequences, and the young person will respect the wisdom of longer life experience the parents may have to offer, if asked.

Mentoring needs to be a consensual, consultative, and collaborative relationship where parents help with problem-solving, sharing what experiences and ideas they have to offer. "Based on the difficulty you describe, here is how you might want to choose your way out of this problem. Of course, this is your life, you know it best, and the decision is entirely up to you."

What parents have to offer are lessons that were often learned the hard way—from painful misadventures and mistakes. So they can say, "From reflecting on how it was for me, here is a possibility you might want to consider . . . to manage your money . . . to resolve your conflicts . . . to organize your responsibilities . . . to remember your obligations . . . to maintain your health . . . to keep up your spirits . . . to motivate your efforts . . . to reduce your stress . . . that has worked for me and that might work for you."

Mentoring allows last-stage adolescents the chance to profit from their parents' longer life experience. To effectively discharge this new parenting role, they must let go of all corrective discipline and positional superiority. If they want the young person to come to them and maybe learn from them, they must forsake all expressions of frustration and disapproval, disappointment and worry, impatience, and anger. The relationship must be emotionally safe for the young person to risk the exposure and vulnerability of asking. They must respect the young person's right to make her own decisions, even when they do not agree with those decisions. They are no longer in the business of trying to bend the conduct of her life to their will. Facing real world consequences will provide discipline enough. Their job is to empathize, encourage, and advise.

There are three principles for providing mentoring that parents might want to consider.

*Acceptance before advising.* If parents cannot accept the young person's right to independent choice without giving the respect conveyed by that acceptance, their son or daughter, feeling disapproved, may "wall off" from parents for self-protection during a hard and vulnerable time. Parental acceptance opens the door for parental advice to get in.

*By invitation only.* Mentoring needs to be at the young person's request. He or she needs to take the initiative by asking, thereby creating the opportunity for parental consultation to occur.

*Be operational not evaluative.* To ensure that advice given is considered and not rejected out of hand, it needs to be judgment-free. No criticism allowed. And the focus needs to be mostly operational, objectively focused on specific behaviors, happenings, and events, on what the young person might helpfully choose to do or not to do.

Finally, mentoring takes patience because young people can be so ambivalent about independence. They really want to be responsibly self-sufficient and operate on their own, and at the same time they really don't. They want to take care of themselves, and they still want to be taken care of. So, paraphrasing the words of Paul Simon, the closer last-stage adolescents get to their destination of independence, the more they may start "slip sliding away." This is why, when respectfully done, parental mentoring can help them move through this ambivalence and claim young adult standing at last.

## When an Adolescent Boomerangs Home

After the young person actually leaves the family nest and parents are expecting their daughter or son to fly solo from then on, it's very common for the young woman or man to encounter some difficulty getting started. For example, the young person could encounter an array of problems like homesickness, substance abuse, stress, too much freedom, educational failure, job loss, romantic breakups, roommate troubles, emotional duress, future fear, and financial mismanagement.

And so for many parents, just when they think the nest is finally empty and their son or daughter successfully launched, that old bedroom is re-occupied by a returning older child coming home not just to visit, but to stay. Precise estimates are hard to come by, but the *New York Times* cited that 40 percent of young people in their twenties move back and in with parents ("boomerang home") at least once. ("What Is It About 20-somethings?" *The New York Times,* August 18, 2010.)

It may be that they need a place to carry them over a break in their work or educational lives. It may be that they have lost their independent footing, encountered some life crisis, and need a safe place to recover before stepping out on their own again. They need home as sanctuary should need arise. Whatever the case, this return can create an awkward homecoming. How are parents and adolescent to define this new stage of their relationship? It can be an awkward dance.

Having become accustomed to living separately (without exposure to each other's daily presence and influence), moving back in together is an adjustment because both parent and adolescent must give up some freedom in the process. The parent has to give up freedom from ignorance about the young person's conduct, and the adolescent has to give up freedom from parental scrutiny. While the parent struggles with how much parenting responsibility to reassert, the adolescent struggles with how much autonomy to surrender.

Both usually agree that since the young person has been functioning independently and is older, their relationship should now be more grown-up. But here is where the return home can start to get abrasive. The adolescent thinks, *I'm now too grown-up to report my comings and goings to my parents.* However, parents want to know how late he or she will be home at night so they don't have to worry. The parents think, *Our adolescent is now sufficiently grown-up to live in the neat and orderly way we like.* However, the adolescent wants home to be relaxed enough to not have to worry about picking up after himself all the time.

What's going on? Usually, the answer is regression. The frame of reference that each imposes on the return relationship tends to resemble the one that described how it was when they last lived together. So they each revert to those past expectations. Parents remember insisting that the adolescent adequately inform them when going out at night. The adolescent remembers ignoring, or at least delaying, some compliance with housekeeping needs of parents. The return home typically revives some old habits of behaviors in them all; parents act invasive in adolescent eyes, and the adolescent acts neglectful in the opinion of parents.

Clarification of expectations and committing to conditions of exchange need to happen. For adequate clarification, the basic terms of return must be specified and agreed upon. For adequate exchange, cooperative efforts must be made by both sides to help make the relationship work.

## Clarification of Expectations

From what I have seen of these boomerang situations, the return home goes best when parents are proactive about declaring what they need in the relationship. Play "wait and see how it's going to be" with the returning young person, and parents risk living on returnee-terms they don't like. They need to come up with a set of conditions that will minimally structure the young person's stay so that it works well for them, and also for her. Because the young person needs welcoming parents, not complaining ones, he or she needs to know the basics of what they expect. The three necessary conditions are: purpose, limits, and demands of the stay.

Start with purpose. What is the objective of coming home? If the young person says, "To take a break, hang out here for a while, and forget my troubles," this answer is insufficient to justify parental permission to return. A better answer might be, "To use the time to take a couple community college courses to test my interests, to hold a job, to save my earnings, and so at the end of a year I have enough money to move out and to live independently again." Always specify objectives for coming home that, when achieved, result in increased readiness to leave when growth is gained, or at least lead to a re-contracting discussion, say in six months.

Next there are limits. What limits do parents want to set on the adolescent's freedom while at home? For example, what limits do they want to set on the young person's socializing at home, determining what is watched on the family room TV, use of the computer, driving a family car, eating whatever is in the kitchen, borrowing parental belongings, sleeping in during weekdays? Of course, the first limit to set is how long the stay is to last. An open-ended stay can drag on for a long unproductive time.

Finally, consider demands. What demands on the adolescent's time and energy do they want to make? For example, what demands do they want to make about contributing household responsibilities, helping around the home, making his or her own spending money, shopping for and cooking family meals, looking after younger children? Such demands are not intrusive, but they are supportive. They give the young person a constructive role to play in the family.

Having mentioned these suggestions to some parents, they shook their heads and objected. "That's no way to treat a guest!"

"That's right," I agreed. "You need to treat your returning adolescent not as a guest, but as a returning member of the family coming home for a *working stay* designed to turn out well enough (not perfectly) for everyone.

## Conditions of Exchange
A major cause for a return home to work out badly is when the adolescent proceeds to live in a one-way (all his way) relationship to parents and they accept this inequity to their hurt and angry cost. Instead, they must insist on an adequate exchange. She must live

with them on two-way, not one-way terms. Simply put, this means practicing contribution, collaboration, and courtesy.

*Contribution* in the relationship is achieved when each party actively supports the well-being of the other. Just as parents provide a home base for the adolescent, the adolescent provides some housekeeping services to help maintain that base.

*Collaboration* is achieved when each gives some to get some of what the other wants. Thus when parents want to know the adolescent's nightlife plans and the young person wants those arrangements kept private, they reach agreement so parents are at least told a time to expect the young person home, and the adolescent has a social life that feels independent.

*Courtesy* is achieved when each party in the relationship makes an effort not to tread on each other's sensitivities. Thus the adolescent keeps personal space picked up enough for parents to tolerate, and parents do not keep bugging the adolescent about her or his future plans.

If the young person is simply unwilling to meet their minimal conditions and live on a two-way exchange with parents, then they should not criticize or get angry. They should respect the young person's choice, and say something like this, "We understand that you have reached an age when living only on your own terms is what you need to do. Since this will not work for us, let's talk about how you can make other living arrangements. Of course, while you are still in town we would love to get to see you as always."

Being allowed to return home after having lost independent footing is an essential support to have on offer. Young people with no home to return to may have to make emergency arrangements that can be to their disadvantage, perhaps berthing where they are not safe or where they are at-risk of being exploited. Returning home is a not a luxury available to everyone.

Some refer to this boomerang return as a "failure to launch," but I believe that is a harmful view to take and an injurious term to use. The young person just needs time to learn from what went amiss, practice any lagging self-management skills, do some more growing up in the shelter of family, and then get ready to try independence again. It does the young person no motivating good to label himself as a "failure" for not being fully prepared any more than it helps parents to take on that label for somehow not providing all necessary preparation.

For parents, whether with a reluctant-to-leave or a returning last-stage adolescent, parents do need to be mindful that there is no fixed schedule for growing up. Some take independence early, while others take it late, and that is usually fine. What parents have to determine is whether there are some signs of acting older or taking actions that advance independent responsibility. A slower effort is still an effort, and that is usually okay. Every young person proceeds at her or his own developmental rate.

Because the last stage of adolescence is often the hardest of all, parents need to provide monitoring of how the adjustment is going in case it becomes emotionally endangering. They need to provide mentoring on request where lessons and wisdom from the personal life experience of parents can be helpful, And they need to provide sanctuary should a young person lose footing and need a short term return home to gather himself before stepping off to try independence again.

Of course, on the positive side when it works out well, parents and boomerang adolescents are given a kind of bonus time—additional family time together that both can truly enjoy and value.

# FACTORS THAT CAN INTENSIFY ADOLESCENCE

Of course, every adolescent passage is unique. All I have tried to do in this book is place a series of diverse growth experiences in rough developmental sequence so parents can anticipate common changes and challenges as they typically unfold. This said, besides major hardships from abuse, neglect, privation, abandonment, and loss that create formative survival issues, there are lesser factors that I believe are powerful enough to intensify adolescent growth, and what follows is a brief description of four of these.

Parental Divorce tends to cause adolescents to take more independence early; Rate of Growth (whether delayed or accelerated) can precipitate a push for rapid change; a Strong-Willed Child makes for a stronger-willed adolescent; and a closely attached Adolescent Only Child and parents can have a painful time letting each other go.

CHAPTER TWENTY

# Parental Divorce

---

*"My parents' divorcing is not the end of the world,*
*but it is the end of the single family I grew up in.*
*And that really hurts."*

Although parental divorce with children and adolescents is common, that doesn't mean this parental decision should be treated as a casual family change. In the life of a child and adolescent, parental divorce is an adverse event, a watershed event, and a formative event. Parental divorce is an adverse event because it creates the profound and permanent loss of the unified family into which children were born or adopted. It is a watershed event because it historically separates the time when family was all together from when a dual family life began. It is a formative event that shapes the growth of children and adolescents.

What follows discusses Why Divorce Is Impactful, Differing Responses by Child Age, Restoring Trust in Parents, and "Getting Over" Parental Divorce.

## Why Divorce Is Impactful

For many girls and boys, divorce is a heartbreaking change: now children must redefine their loving relationship with parents by factoring in the anguish that they feel over the marital breakup. Family will not be the same again.

There is interpersonal loss, social dislocation, lifestyle adjustment, increased family complexity, and emotional upheaval, as well as lasting lessons about the risks of hurt when love proves not to be forever. Divorce introduces a massive change into the life of a boy or girl no matter what the age. Witnessing loss of love between parents, having parents break their marriage commitment, adjusting to going back and forth between two different households, and the daily absence of one parent while living with the other, all create a challenging new family circumstance in which to live. In the personal history of the boy or girl, life that follows divorce is significantly changed from how life was before. Simply put, divorce with children, young or older, upsets and resets the terms of their family lives. It unmoors them from the trusted dependence on family with which they began, and to some degree casts them socially adrift, now resolved to increasingly steer life on their own.

At worst, when ex-partners cannot come to emotional acceptance of whatever differences drove them apart and cannot move forward, jointly committed to working together for the children's welfare, you can get an unreconciled divorce. In these unhappy cases, embittered feelings and embattled behaviors create ongoing parental divisiveness with which the adolescent must painfully contend. "They get along worse now than they did before! Sometimes I think they love to hate each other more they love us kids!" To the degree they can, divorced parents need to let grief and grievances go and recommit to jointly raising their children.

## Differing Responses by Age

Consider one way to distinguish how children often react to parental divorce in contrast to how adolescents often respond, and then consider some adjustments that may intensify adolescent lives. Understand that I am talking here about tendencies, not certainties.

I believe there can be somewhat different responses to divorce depending on whether the boy or girl is still in childhood, up to about eight or nine, or has entered adolescence. Basically, divorce often tends to intensify the child's dependence and it often tends to accelerate the adolescent's independence. It tends to grieve the child and create grievance in the adolescent. It tends to elicit a more regressive response in the child and a more aggressive response in the adolescent. Consider why this variation might be so.

## Divorce and the Child

The child's world is a dependent one, closely connected to parents who are one's favored companions, heavily reliant on parental care, with family being the major locus of one's social life. The adolescent world is a more independent one, more separated and distant from parents, more self-sufficient, where friends have become favored companions, and where the major locus of one's social life now extends outside of family into a larger world of life experience.

For the attached young child, divorce shakes trust in dependency on parents who now behave in an extremely self-absorbed way. They divide the family unit into two different households between which the child must learn to transit back and forth, for a while creating unfamiliarity, instability, and insecurity, and never being able to be with one parent without having to be apart from the other. Convincing a young child of the permanence of divorce can be hard when his intense longing fantasizes that somehow, some way, Mom and Dad will be living back together again someday. He relies on wishful thinking to help allay the pain of loss, holding onto hope for a parental reunion much longer than does the adolescent, who is quicker to accept the finality of this unwelcome family change. Thus, guilty or well intentioned divorced parents, who put in a joint presence at special family celebrations and holiday events to recreate family unity for the child, may only feed the child's fantasy and delay his adjustment.

The dependent child's short-term reaction to divorce can be an anxious one. So much is different, new, unpredictable, and unknown that life becomes filled with scary questions. "What is going to happen to me next?" "Who will take care of me?" "If my parents can lose love for each other, can they lose love for me?" "With one parent moving out, what if I lose the other too?" Answering such worrisome questions with worst fears, the child's response can be regressive. By reverting to a more childish way of functioning, more parental caretaking may be forthcoming. There can be separation anxieties, crying at bedtimes, breaking toilet training, bed-wetting, clinging, whining, tantrums, and temporary loss of established self-care skills.

The child wants to feel more connected in a family situation when a major disconnection has occurred. Regression to earlier dependency can also be an effort to attract parental attention and concern, bringing them close when divorce has pulled each of them further away—the resident parent, now busier and more preoccupied, the absent parent, less available because of being less around.

For the parent who divorces, the priority is establishing a sense of family order and security for the child. This means observing the three R's required to restore a child's trust in security, familiarity, and dependency: Routines, Rituals, and Reassurance. Thus parents establish household and visitation Routines so the child knows what contact to expect. They allow the child to create Rituals to feel more in control of her life, like when saying goodbye to one parent and when greeting another. And they provide continual Reassurance that the parents are as lovingly connected to the child as ever, and for the child's sake are jointly committed to making this new family arrangement work.

## Divorce and the Adolescent

The detaching, differentiating, more independent-minded and individually expressive adolescent tends to deal more aggressively with divorce, often reacting in a mad, rebellious way, more resolved to disregard family demands and take care of himself since parents have failed to keep commitments to family. Where the child may have tried to get parents back, the adolescent may try to get back at parents, perhaps communicating with them less, to give them less access. Where the child felt grief, the adolescent has a grievance, and that grievance can intensify hurt and resentment. The adolescent only child can take parental divorce particularly hard because the history of attachment is so strong, standing in family so important, one is so used to self-needs being given parental priority, and so the only child has much of her or his family world to lose to divorce.

Even witnessing marital discord and unhappiness, most adolescents don't want parents to divorce, and don't agree with that decision when it is made. Often they take injury and offense, feeling and possibly saying, "It's not fair. Nobody asked me whether I wanted them to divorce and split the family, but I'm family, aren't I? I feel so sad and angry and yanked around! They think that doing what feels right for them should feel all right to me. But they are wrong!" For some adolescents who are very closely attached to parents, parental divorce can be an unforgivable offense, producing an abiding sense of grievance that can linger long after the event has passed.

Now the adolescent can act aggressively to take control of his life by behaving even more distantly and defiantly, more determined to live his life his way, more dedicated to his self-interest than before. He feels increasingly autonomous in a family situation that feels disconnected. He now feels more impelled and entitled to act on his own.

Adolescents often feel betrayed by the broken parental commitment to family and thus become angrier and less communicative. For the child still embedded in the family circle, divorce tends to increase dependence and holding on. For the adolescent who is more concerned with her community of friends, divorce tends to energize more independence and pulling away from family and letting go.

Although not in these exact words, I hear adolescents justifying their more independent ways in the wake of divorce. "If my parents can put their interests ahead of mine, then I can put mine ahead of theirs." "Since I can't count on my parents to be there the way they were, I need to count on myself more." "Since my parents can abandon their old commitment to family, then so can I." "Since my parents are now more caught up in themselves, it's okay for me to act the same." "Since they didn't consult me on this decision, I don't need to consult them on my decisions." At a more disaffected age with parents, divorce can often intensify this disaffection.

Three major dynamics that drive the adolescent transformation—separation, experimentation, and opposition—tend to become more intensified in the wake of parental divorce.

Separation from family tends to increase by more reliance on one's group of friends for social belonging.

Experimentation tends to become more pronounced in the search for his or her changing expression of individuality.

Opposition to parental authority tends to increase when the young person becomes more determined to get and go his or her way.

By late adolescence teenagers are awakening to romantic infatuations, in-love attachments, and even love relationships. At this vulnerable time, the significance of the broken parental vow and the loss of parental love for each other can have enormous impact. If commitment is not firm, if love is not lasting, and if loss of love is so painful, then what is the adolescent supposed to do when he or she comes to significantly care for a social partner?

Reluctance to trust committed love can be hard to shake. In their love relationships, older adolescent and adult children of divorce honorably manage issues with commitment that they can encounter in a number of self-protective ways:

- Afraid of choosing (or choosing wrong), they can be very cautious and delay commitment for a long time in order to be "sure."

- They can keep relationships casual and superficial to avoid the necessity for commitment.

- They can feel very conflicted in caring relationships, ready to commit at one moment, ready to break it off the next.

- They can be controlling to ensure the other person will not leave.

- They can enter a committed relationship armed with the belief that if it doesn't work out they can always break it off and "divorce."

Adolescence also makes visitation arrangements more difficult to manage. The increased social needs of adolescence can complicate visitation when time with the other parent competes with priority time with friends. So parents usually have to be more flexible about visitation with adolescents than with younger children. This is an age when bringing a peer along on visitation can create a good compromise. The young person can be with the other parent and still not totally sacrifice precious time spent with friends.

Adolescence is also an age when young people may desire to take up primary residence with the same sex parent to spend more time around that gender model. This is usually less a matter of greater love for one parent over another than it reflects a need for gender identification at this formative age.

## Restoring Trust in Parents
To some degree, divorce is usually a breach of trust in parents. That said, what restores adolescent trust in divorcing parents more than anything else is the adult capacity to create two kinds of commitments to each other.

The first is emotionally reconciling whatever differences drove them apart so that the adolescent does not feel caught up in the unfinished emotional business of the adults' former marriage after the divorce.

The second is forming a working alliance in which ex-partners are dedicated to cooperate and collaborate for the teenager's welfare. In many, but not all cases, it is possible to have disliked life with the old marriage partner but still come to value the ex-wife or ex-husband as co-parent with who you still share concern for your common children. I described this alliance in my 2006 book, *The Everything Parent's Guide to Children and Divorce*, in what I called being able to sign "The Ten Articles of Consideration" in their relationship as parents. Here are the articles:

1. "I will be *reliable*." I will keep the social arrangements I make with you and the children. You can count on my word.

2. "I will be *responsible*." I will honor my obligations to provide for the children. As agreed, I will provide my share of their support.

3. "I will be *appreciative*." I will let you know ways in which I see you doing good for the children. And I will thank you for being helpful to me.

4. "I will be *respectful*." I will always talk positively about you to the children. If I have a disagreement or concern, I will talk directly to you.

5. "I will be *flexible*." I will make an effort to modify childcare arrangements when you have conflicting commitments. I will try to work with unexpected change.

6. "I will be *tolerant*." I will accept the increasing lifestyle differences between us. I will accept how the children live with us in somewhat different circumstances and on somewhat different terms.

7. "I will be *supportive*." I will back you up with the children when you have disciplinary need. I will not allow them to play one of us against the other.

8. "I will be *involved*." I will problem-solve with you when the children get in difficulty. I will work with you to help them.

9. "I will be *responsive*." I will be available to help cope with the children's emergencies. I will be on call in times of crisis.

10. "I will be *reasonable*." I will talk through our inevitable differences in a calm and constructive manner. I will keep communicating until we work out a resolution that is acceptable to us both.

When adolescents sense there are no lingering hard feelings between parents and when they see this parental alliance in action, they come to realize that although the adult commitment to the marriage has been broken, the joint commitment to parental partnership is as strong as ever.

Sometimes parents will ask at what age a child can make an easier adjustment to parental divorce, often assuming the older the better, because of increased maturity. But I disagree. The more years of personal history there are with married parents heading the same household, the more challenging the adjustment becomes because the girl or boy has more years of historical investment and familiarity to modify when family life is split asunder.

I believe a five-year-old can often make an easier adjustment to parental divorce than a fifteen-year-old, although neither can do so without some pain. The same goes for adjustment to parental remarriage (which happens more often than not) because the five-year-old is capable of accepting and bonding with a stepparent in ways that the fifteen-year-old usually cannot. And just because the parent is now "emotionally" used to the divorce is no reason to expect the adolescent to have the same rate of recovery and "get over" the divorce as quickly as the adult who is ready to get on with a new and better life.

## "Getting Over" Parental Divorce

I believe the notion of "getting over" parental divorce misses the mark. "Getting used" to parental divorce is a more realistic expectation. "Getting over" implies putting the experience behind you and carrying on, like it was nothing more than another bump in the road of growing up. Getting used to parental divorce means learning to live in a divided family, integrating the challenges and consequences for one's growing up, and living with some lasting influences ever after. From what I have seen, it can take up to a couple years for a young person to make enough adjustment before they can freely move on with their lives.

Finally, sometimes parents can get impatient and frustrated with an adolescent who is still struggling with the impact of divorce when they just want the young person to get over the event, engage with the new family program, and move on. For example, consider these words of painful reflection by an older adolescent:

"My parents divorced when I was eleven. After that day I lost stability in my life, traveling to and from both households on a regular basis, seeing the family torn in two. Not knowing which parent's house I would be staying in for the day drove me crazy to the point that I would secretly cry in my room hoping that one day my parents would unite once again. Strange enough, my mum used to tell me I was lucky to have double houses, bedrooms, etc. I never bought that argument. After a few years my mum was annoyed hearing that I'm still hurting about the divorce and she wanted me to sort of like just get over it. I guess she always assumed that divorce affects the parents more than the children. Over the years I managed to console myself, but now being twenty and looking back I do still wish they hadn't divorced."

From what I have seen, the most developmentally vulnerable time to have parents get divorced is when the young person is in the first stage of adolescence, around ages nine to thirteen. Adolescence is an act of courage. To bravely start separating from childhood and parents requires a secure connection to family to push off from. When divorce coincides with the early adolescent need to start detaching for more independence and differentiation for more individuality, pursuing these goals of growing up can become more urgent to do. Now it's easy for the process of growth to become intensified as the push for independence and individuality becomes stronger, as social distance created from parents becomes more pronounced, as grievance at parental betrayal breeds more resentment, as resistance to parental authority becomes more common, and as social belonging to a competing family of peers comes to matter more.

Parents need to appreciate the magnitude of an adolescent's adjustment when coming to terms of acceptance and learning to live with parental divorce. Briefly, consider this adjustment in terms of ten common losses that parental divorce can factor into adolescent lives.

1. *Loss of Happiness*. Most young people mourn the loss of the intact family. They miss some of how life used to be when they lived as an original unit.

2. *Loss of Stability*. Particularly early on, parental divorce can feel chaotic as parental separation, sometimes litigation, and establishing twin residences and maybe changing living places and schools can create a lot of confusion.

3. *Loss of Faith*. Probably the most disturbing lesson for an adolescent about parental divorce is that love can be lost, that love does not necessarily last forever, that the commitment of love can be broken.

4. *Loss of Connection*. Parental divorce tends to reduce old accessibility to parents; a custodial or primary parent can be much busier and a noncustodial parent can be harder to frequently see.

5. *Loss of Confidence.* Parental divorce brings a complex of simultaneous changes. Ended is celebrating full family occasions together; begun is getting used to a visitation schedule. More household help responsibilities are expected, and there is less time with each parent. This multiplicity of change demands can erode confidence to cope for a while.

6. *Loss of Understanding.* Parental divorce takes the adolescent from a known experience of family life into one where the present can feel inexplicable and the future unpredictable. "What's going to happen now?" Plus there is the question: "Why did my parents divorce?" Often each parent will give a somewhat different explanation.

7. *Loss of Power.* Most adolescents feel disenfranchised by parental divorce: "I have no say about how divorce is turning my life upside down!" It's easy to feel helpless and angry as parents undo marriage and alter the adolescent's family life.

8. *Loss of Familiarity.* When a parent divorces, both by necessity and desire, they begin to make a host of personal changes as well that can alter the adult in adolescent eyes. A single parent picks up responsibilities the other parent used to do and can initiate new interests, while the other parent may be using new freedom to create a different definition.

9. *Loss of Trust.* When parents, for their own self-interest, divorce and divide the family, the adolescent tends to lose some trust in their leadership, particularly when it comes to parents directing the young person's life.

10. *Loss of Compatibility.* Parents decide to divorce because they cannot get along. For the adolescent, the hope is that they will relate better living apart than married. This is not always so.

Adolescents do not get over parental divorce so much as they get used to it by rising to the challenge of meeting a host of difficult adjustment demands, a few of which, those associated with loss, have been listed above. In the process of making these adjustments, there can be some lasting burdens and some lasting gifts from the adversity. Some burdens on later life can be doubting the lasting value of love, fear of making a loving commitment, and avoidance of conflict. Some gifts in later life can be strengthened resilience, power of determination, and capacity for responsible independence.

But what parents need to remember is that although parental divorce is meant to change adult lives for the better, it changes the personal lives of adolescents just as much, in some ways for the worse.

# CHAPTER TWENTY-ONE

# Rate of Growth

"One of our teenagers we had to push out the door while the other was early to leave."

Adolescence in high school can be intensified by rate of growth—catching up when there has been developmental delay or rushing ahead when there is early maturity. In the first instance, the young person can experience a compressed adolescence. In the second instance, a young person can experience aging out of high school early. In both cases, parents can have a lot to deal with in response.

## A Compressed Adolescence

Consider this conversation with parents of an adolescent. With their daughter about to enter the transforming passage of middle school, the parents were feeling anxious about the abrasive adolescent changes soon to come.

"We know this isn't elementary school, but we wish we could just delay adolescence a while longer and enjoy the easier times of her childhood a few years more."

"Be careful you don't get what you wish for," I replied. "The longer adolescence is delayed, the more intense it is likely to be when it arrives."

Why did I say that? Because with highly attached children, highly sheltered children, slow maturing children or, often, with an only child—all children who are reluctant to break with childhood—

the onset of adolescence can be delayed beyond its usual starting date, around ages nine to thirteen. In these cases it may not begin until the early high school years, and when it does it can proceed to unfold faster than parents and adolescent are comfortable with or anticipate.

What results from this developmental delay is what I call a compressed adolescence, when the first three stages of growth unfold in overlapping succession as the young person appears to be in a desperate hurry to catch up to her age. Now the drives for separation, differentiation, and opposition that empower more independence seem to fire off all at once, and parents are usually caught off guard by the sudden, massive change.

"We can't understand it. Up to the end of sophomore year in high school she was the same motivated, focused, fun-to-be-with child we had always known. Then it's like a bomb exploded inside her and all that caring and concentration, all those good times, were blasted away. That's when she started treating us like we were against her and not for her the way we've always been. And we did disagree with her more often because of the new choices she was making. Now she wanted less to do with us. And time we did have together was spoiled by her complaints about what we didn't understand and arguments about what we did and didn't want her to do. All that seemed to matter to her was freedom to be left alone and to be with friends! What happened?"

What happens in a compressed adolescence is that the first three stages of adolescence, instead of being spaced out from late elementary into high school, are *compressed* into a couple of very intense high school years. Now the negative attitude, active and passive resistance, and limit testing that are the hallmarks of early adolescence have no sooner begun when the conflicts over more worldly freedom, need to be with peers, and tyranny of now in mid-adolescence kick in. This is almost immediately followed by the late adolescence desire to act more grown-up, experience older adventures, and act more socially independent. For both teenager and parents, this time frame can be a wild ride.

Sometimes parents wonder if the young person's dramatically altered behavior is the result of alcohol or other drugs. While substance use can certainly add to the confusion, the major culprit is usually rapid developmental change.

During their teenager's compressed adolescence, what the young person needs from parents most is stability from the consistency and constancy of their steadfast care. They must hold to the guidance, supervision, and family structure they have traditionally provided, empathizing with the teenager's plight while continually insisting on responsibility—all of which are very hard to do. And they need to expect that the young person is not going to appreciate their loyal support during this frenzied time, a time that will calm and subside after development has caught up and sufficient individuality and independence has at last been gained.

## Aging Out of High School Early

Most parents know that the kindergarten through grade twelve (K–12) organization of education in the United States is not scientifically justified but is socially arbitrary. Children progress through this system year by year, each year occupying a different grade. Sometimes parents will see that their child is developmentally out of step with the usual progression; their child may skip a grade due to being academically advanced for her age, or they may hold their child back a year to allow more time for his physical and social growth. In either case, parents adjust placement in the K–12 system to fit their child's needs.

Now consider what can happen when along about late sophomore or the start of junior year a young person feels like she is aging out of high school early. Most commonly this feeling is described as not belonging there anymore, not fitting in, being out of step with peers; the sense that she is socially "done" with high school and is ready to move on, to graduate early and get a job or maybe go to college. In any case, she is looking toward a next step in life and sees a final year of high school for its own sake as just getting in the way of the greater independence she feels ready for. She is in a hurry to get going with her life, and feels impatient with being held back by a twelve-grade convention that makes no developmental sense.

An older teenager may have reached this place of discomfort from socially maturing faster than her age mates; she may have formed close friendships with upper classmen who are now graduated and gone. She may have academically accelerated her course of study so that college now feels like the logical next step. She may want to enter the world of work and get started operating on her own. She may be truly tired of being parented. She may feel that completing a fourth year of high school will only hold her back, rather than move her forward in life.

When a young person starts talking to parents in these terms, they need to take the discussion seriously. To graduate high school early requires accumulating sufficient academic credits in a shorter period of time. It takes a lot of additional initiative, effort, and responsibility; working with the high school counselor on early graduation planning; and coming to terms with missing out on a lot of the social fellowship with old friends that is celebrated senior year.

Specifically, how can a high school student gain the required credit hours to accomplish early graduation? Consider a few possible ways:

- The student may be able to earn additional credits by attending summer school.

- The student may be able to take a "zero hour" class offered before the standard school day begins.

- The student may be able to take an accredited correspondence or online course in addition to those taken at school.

- The student may be able to take an outside class at a local community college and perhaps receive dual credit for high school and college.

- The student may be able to get credit by exam, passing a state-approved exit exam for a course not actually taken.

- The student may be able to get into a college that has an early admission program that accepts students not yet graduated from high school.

For parents, this push for early graduation can be difficult because the young person will be taking independence earlier than they anticipated. However, just because the school system is designed K–12 doesn't mean that progress through the system cannot be accelerated where appropriate. After all, young people develop in adolescence at different rates and thus the timing of leaving the shelter of family often varies from one child to another.

To treat a teenager strictly according to her age at home and grade at school, when she has demonstrated maturity beyond her years, makes no good sense. If she is ready to move on with her life because she has aged out of high school early, if she is willing to do the extra work to make early graduation happen, and if she has a specific plan for what she wants to do next, then the time has probably come to let her go.

In high school, at either end of the developmental extreme, whether growing slow or fast, an adolescent's life can be intensified.

# CHAPTER TWENTY-TWO

# The Strong-Willed Adolescent

*"When he wants something badly enough,
he acts entitled to get his way."*

Consider three possible antecedents to having a strong-willed adolescent. There is the Willfulness of Adolescent Growth; there is the case of having been a Strong-willed Child; and there is the case of having a Strong-willed Parent.

## Willfulness from Adolescent Growth

In general, adolescence is a more willful age than childhood because self-determination begins driving growth toward individuality and independence in predictably powerful ways. Through words and actions, the young person says and shows new assertiveness by statements like the following:

"I will want more freedom to grow."

"I will question rules and authority."

"I will do things my way."

"I will dress as I like."

"I will not like being told what to do."

"I will choose my own friends."

"I will be more private from parents."

"I will want more money."

"I will decide how much truth to tell."

"I will try older experiences as desired."

Increased willfulness creates more disagreements and arguing with parents, so they need to anticipate more push and pushback during adolescence.

## Having Been a Strong-Willed Child

If their adolescent was a strong-willed child, that conflict is likely to be more frequent and intense. There is a distinction to draw.

Deny a non-willful child what he wants, and some degree of sadness may follow before he lets go of the disappointment and moves onto other things. For a strong-willed child, however, there is usually a different emotional response such as anger and holding on to what was wanted. Why?

One characteristic that identifies a strong-willed child is the tendency to make a *conditional shift* when deciding on what is wanted, and when that want is refused. This is the sequence of thinking that seems to take place:

*If I want something, I want it a lot.*

*If I want it a lot, I must have it.*

(Now the conditional shift occurs)

*If I must have it then I SHOULD get it.*

*If I don't get what I should, that is unfair so I will be angry.*

*Mad at this unfairness, I will keep after what I feel entitled to.*

Feeling wronged by the injustice of refusal to perceived personal entitlement can energize angry pursuit of what has been denied.

A strong-willed child is one who has great strength of want. To the "good" this can mean he is highly directed, motivated to achieve what he desires, is persistent in pursuit of personal goals, and does not give up easily when resisted, rejected, or refused. It's a mixed blessing. To the good, he won't take "no" for answer; to the "bad," he won't take "no" for an answer. To the "bad" this can mean demanding control, never easily relenting or backing down, refusing to compromise, needing to be "right" all the time, fighting to win at all costs, being wed to getting one's way. Since willfulness is a double-edged sword, the difficult task for parents is to maximize the good side and moderate the bad.

If you happen to have a strong-willed child (up to ages eight or nine), he or she is likely to be an even stronger-willed adolescent. Therefore, while still in childhood it is worthwhile to help the boy or girl channel willfulness toward challenging interests, learn to become more tolerant of delay and denial of gratification, reduce conditional thinking by separating desire from entitlement, and understand the damage to relationships that extreme willfulness can insensitively do. The parent continually tries to explain this difference.

"It can be good to know what you want and to go after what you want and not give up until you get what you want; but it may not be good when you do so at other people's expense or oppose reasonable limits that others in responsibility have set. What can be hard to manage is the frustration you feel when you know what you want and what you feel is your right, and other people disagree. When we deny what you want, we are always willing to hear you talk your frustration out."

So what are some possible parental guidelines for managing a strong-willed adolescent? Consider the following:

- Do not ignore conduct with a willful adolescent that you don't agree with in order to stay out of conflict. Parental avoidance empowers willfulness.

- Do not grant requests you do not agree with to keep the peace. Giving in to placate only encourages more willfulness.

- Do treat disagreement primarily as a chance to communicate to improve understanding, not as a competitive challenge to prevail. Turning conflicts into power struggles over who will win only encourages willfulness.

- Do give adolescent arguments a full hearing, but having stated and explained your final position clearly, do not keep arguing back. Continuing to argue keeps open the possibility that you will change your mind if the adolescent argues harder.

- Do not engage in any disagreement that is not conducted safely and respectfully. Allow abusive or manipulative arguing and the parent can encourage that behavior in their relationship and in other relationships to come.

- Do be firm and consistent and follow through in high-priority parental rules and requests. Inconsistency in supervision sends an irresistible double message to the strong-willed adolescent—"sometimes my parents mean and keep after what they say and sometimes they give up and don't." (The willful teenager will usually vote for "don't.")

- Do be non-evaluative when correcting. Specifically, take issue only with the teenager's decision: "We disagree with the choice you have made, this is why, and this is what we need to have happen in consequence." Attacking a strong-willed adolescent's character, conduct, or capacity with criticism is usually inflammatory.

- Do recognize and appreciate willfulness when the adolescent carries an ambition to conclusion or keeps a hard commitment. Affirming the positives of willfulness encourages that side to grow.

- Do stick to the "golden rule" in all interactions. Treat your strong-willed adolescent as you want that young person to learn to treat you.

- Do remember that acting willfully is not something she or he is doing to you; it is a characteristic the young person is struggling to learn to manage. So don't take the willfulness personally.

- Do declare the responsible reality of parenting: "When it comes to what you want or do not want to have happen, we will be firm when we have to, and flexible when we can; we will let you know where we stand and will listen to all you have to say."

## Willfulness from Having a Strong-Willed Parent

I define a strong-willed parent as one who is determined to direct, correct, persist, and to prevail in matters of control over what their child is allowed and expected to do.

Come the child's adolescence, this parental willfulness is put to the test as the teenager becomes more self-determined and pushes against, pulls away from, and more frequently evades their authority to gather freedom to grow. At this more individual and independent stage of development, I believe how the parent exercises their strong will, and how the teenager responds to it, can have formative effect on the adolescent, shaping how the young person manages significant social relationships later on.

Before considering some problems that can be caused when one is a strong-willed parent of adolescents, it is well to remember some of the benefits, because like many aspects of parenting, willfulness is double-edged. On the positive side, the teenager knows where the strong-willed parent stands and what she wants, knows the parent won't back down or give up in the face of protest or resistance, knows the parent will speak up when concerned, knows that the parent means what she says and will follow through on her word, knows that the parent provides a secure family structure with consistent rules and demands, and knows that the parent cares enough to insist on what she believes is for the best, even when she may be wrong.

On the problematic side, the risk of being a strong-willed parent of a more self-determined adolescent is asserting authority at all costs and becoming overbearing to live with. Now the need for control takes precedence over the expression of concern, being right reduces readiness for discussion, and personal conviction rejects the teenager's point of view. In consequence, the parent can become domineering and dictatorial to the cost of how they relate to their teenager, and how the teenager, often in imitation during conflict, relates back to them.

Overbearing how? Consider the following examples: "I don't take 'no' for an answer," "I don't back down to anyone," "I make more demands than requests," "I hate losing an argument," "I resent changing to suit other people," "Once I make up my mind I stick with it no matter what," "I say what I expect and I expect to get it," "I won't have my decisions questioned," "When others disagree with me they are usually wrong," "The right way is my way," "I can't tolerate mistakes by others," "I don't like admitting mistakes myself," "I don't like to apologize," "I need other people to do things my way," "I expect other people to live up to my standards," "I don't give up," "I don't give in," "I will win at all costs," "I want to know everything that is going on," "I don't trust other people to take care of my business," "I never admit defeat," "I want other people to play by my rules," "I'd rather give help than ask for help," "I don't like being told I'm wrong," "I don't like listening to what I disagree with," or "I don't like being told what to do."

If ten or more of these statements seem to fit, then you might qualify as a strong-willed parent. Possible traps exist that entangle parents, but also formatively affect the teenager's growth.

First, when the adolescent is inclined to follow the older example and identify with the adult, the outcome can be a strong-willed teenager with whom power struggles over control can become extremely intense. In this case, conflict creates resemblance as more conflicts cause them to become more similar over time, the adolescent learning to become as stubborn as the parent, neither one backing down. Now conflict becomes a training ground for growing opposition. The parent is no more inclined to sacrifice authority than the teenager is to submit to it. The more the adolescent contests rules and pushes for independence, the more out of control the strong-willed parent feels, the more aggressively they may reassert control. As the parent resorts to more extreme measures, the teenager digs in and becomes more actively and passively resistant. By losing the individual contest with the more powerful parent, the teenager comes out ahead because practice taking on the dominant adult only strengthens the young person's willfulness over time. It is this willful determination to direct, correct, persist, and prevail that the adolescent is likely to bring to future significant adult partnerships. This resistance can often be to his or her cost.

Second, when the adolescent is inclined to get around the rules set by the dominant adult, the outcome can be a manipulative, deceptive teenager, resulting in less reliable communication and trust issues. In this case, the teenager tends to cope with the strong-willed parent by keeping the adult at arm's length as direct confrontation and conflict are studiously avoided. The young person learns to take evasive action with parental authority, acting agreeable but often finding ways to slip out of agreements. She becomes expert in saying what the parent wants to hear, disclosing minimal specific information, concealing or stretching or lying about the truth when it is hard to verify, and making good excuses to escape accountability. The manipulative teenager can be a slippery customer for the strong-willed parent to deal with. The parent acts in charge but often feels subtly managed, denied full or honest disclosure that would come with a more forthright relationship.

If you notice signs in your teenager of coping with an overbearing parent, there are two adjustments you might consider making. First, review the strong-willed characteristics listed earlier and consider moderating some of those that apply to you. Change the example you set and you can change the influence you have on your teen. Second, encourage healthier behaviors in your teenager. Teach a strong-willed adolescent to be more collaborative with you by being more collaborative with him. Teach a manipulative adolescent to be more straightforward and direct with you by being less oppressive with her.

CHAPTER TWENTY-THREE

# The Adolescent Only Child

"She's our precious only child, so we keep her
close to keep her safe."

Because parents and an only child are so strongly attached and claim so much in common, the differentiation and detachment of normal adolescence can be scary and painful for the child to do and for the parent to see. As I wrote in my book, *The Future of Your Only Child*, growing apart and growing different can be hard for the only child in adolescence partly because the adjustment and acceptance can also be hard for the parents. "Our relationships changed; she's not the same child she was!"

Being the beloved beneficiary of all that parents have to give can be a lot to give up when the adolescent only child starts disrupting, or at least adjusting, the comfortable status quo. The process can be deferred and delayed, and, sometimes, rate of growth slowed down, creating a compressed adolescence during the high school years as discussed in Chapter Twenty-One. Letting go of control and accepting the growth of independent initiative and individual diversity can be hard for parents to do. They have a lot to lose; their adoring and adorable child. Having multiple children often makes the adolescent push for independence and the expression of individuality easier for parents to accept because they are more flexible and less fixated than with a single child. So the adolescent process can be intense for parents and only child.

Now think of three distinctive characteristics that contrast only-child families from those with multiple children, each characteristic capable of ramping up the pressure of performance in a different way:

1. Because the only child is the first and last child in one and so is the only chance at parenting the parents get, they want to get it "right." Thus they take this charge very seriously. Because they want to do right by their son or daughter, parenting an only child can be high-pressure parenting. They don't want to make mistakes at the child's expense and so are very conscientious and deliberative (not casual) in their parenting. Usually the only child feels a comparable obligation to do right by the parents, to please the adults providing such dedicated care, to turn out well for all they have provided. This is not a laid back family because everyone is trying extremely hard to do right by each other, striving to please and not let each other down. Mutual dedication of parents and only child to do their best by each other can contribute to higher intensity of life.

2. Because the only child gets the entire social, emotional, and material resources those parents have to provide, he or she is the sole beneficiary of all they have to give. Because parents typically make a high investment in nurturing and providing for the only child, they often have a high expectation of return. Giving one's all to someone, it's easy to want that someone to give a lot back. They may expect the child to do as well by them as they do by the child. And they may expect the child to turn out "well" by meeting the agenda of their ambitions in ways they approve and that do not disappoint. As a parent once memorably told me, "No one who has an only child is content to have an average child, or at least to believe they do." Striving to live up to this parental agenda can contribute to the only child's higher intensity of life.

3. Because the only child has only parents for immediate family company, it's easy for the child to become

"adultized" (socially and verbally precocious) from identifying with and interacting with these grown-up family companions. Putting oneself on an equal standing with these adults ("I should have an equal say"), it's easy for the only child to apply equal performance standards ("I should be able to perform equally well.") But the only child is only a child, not an adult. Having unrealistically elevated personal performance standards can contribute to a higher intensity of life.

None of this is to discredit only-child family composition as providing added pressure only. From what I have seen, only children tend to be powerfully and positively parented. Let me suggest just five of the beneficial outcomes that often come with growing up "only":

1.  Well esteemed by parents, the only child tends to esteem themselves highly.

2.  Used to alone time, the only child tends to keep themselves good company.

3.  Focused on what she or he wants, the only child tends to be directed and persistent.

4.  Accustomed to discussions with parents, the only child tends to be confident and comfortable talking with and relating to adults.

5.  Self-invested, the only child tends to want to do well for themselves, and is often less susceptible to peer pressure.

Well attached to parents and well nurtured by them, the only child receives a lot of parental attention, affection, and acceptance. However, for the only child who is struggling for and against separation in adolescence, growing up can be scary.

• Will he or she pull so far away that the attachment to parents will be broken?

• Will he or she become so different that acceptance from parents will be denied?

- Will he or she push so hard against their authority that their affection will be alienated?

Now the challenge for parents is to stay connected to their son or daughter while adolescence is growing them apart. They must not take adolescence personally, as if it is something their teenager is deliberately doing to offend or injure them. Adolescence is a hard process of growth toward individuality and independence that the only child is daring to do for him- or herself. With this understanding, parents must then give the following assurance to their one and only: "No matter how far you pull away from us, no matter how different from us you become, no matter how hard you push against us, you need to know this. Come what may, we will continue to hold you in our loving hearts as we always have and always will."

# Parenting Your Adult Child

"But I thought my parenting was done!"

Before parenting an adult child can begin, letting go of the adolescent must be accomplished, and this is no simple task. At each stage of growing up, parents find themselves under pressure to loosen their hold as the adolescent pushes for more expression of individuality and more assertion of independence, bent on becoming her own unique person and charting her own way in the larger world. Letting go is often the agony of parenting because it always entails risk and loss.

Consider the parent who stated her loss at this last letting go in very human terms. "Is this the return I get for all I've invested in my teenager? Now she sets me aside, pays less attention to our relationship, and leaves home to focus on her own life after all I've done?"

"Yes," I replied, "that's the reward parents have been working for all these hard adolescent years. It's called 'independence.' Holding on, guiding, and providing support to their growing child was a great labor of love; but at the end of adolescence, the greater loving is to let the loved one go."

Thus after their child's adolescence has concluded around the end of the college-age years, a functional independence and a fitting identity gained, not only do the major problems in life lay ahead and not behind, but for mothers and fathers the parental role in relation to the adult child continues over the rest of their lives.

The challenges of parenting do not subside at the end of adolescence because the two tracks of growth—toward independence and identity—keep evolving and expressing as freedom of action and definition continue to develop. Further detachment takes place, for example, as the young adult moves geographically further away from home and becomes more preoccupied with the busyness of their own life. And further differentiation takes place, for example, as the young adult starts pursuing a chosen occupation and falls under the compelling influence of a significant partner. The life changes roll on, and as they do, parents are called upon to do more letting go and to be more accepting, to roll with these changes.

But what happens when parents intervene in or criticize the young adult's decisions? Suppose they prohibit or censure life changes to which they take offense? Suppose they pull rank of traditional parental authority. The outcome can often strain the caring connection they want to maintain with the grown daughter or son who decides it is time to draw the line about who is in charge of running their life.

About independence, the adult child replies, "I know you are feeling disappointed that I'm not returning home for the holiday as I always have in the past. I am not doing this to hurt you, but I have other plans, intend to direct my life as I think best, and don't need your permission to do so."

About identity, the adult child replies, "I know converting to a different denomination to marry my intended spouse is hard for you to accept, but that is what I have chosen to do. My personal beliefs are up to me, I don't appreciate you objecting to my decision, and I don't need your approval to make this choice."

Often the biggest parenting adjustment parents have when their adolescent assumes young adult standing is the changing of terms in their relationship. Up through adolescence, the young person still clung to the notion that in many ways they had to live on parental terms regarding what they wanted, allowed, and valued. As a young adult, however, now a *growth* reversal takes place. Parents have to start living more on the adult child's terms by adjusting to young adult availability and definition. Parents who insist on their old standing in the face of this changing reality can find that efforts at influence and expressions of intolerance can jam the relationship. Their refusal to let go of control and to accept normal redefinition can make independence for the adult child painful to accomplish.

Of course, change is not all one-sided. Parents are changing too; in their preferences, in their paths, and even in their partners. Because of growth going on in both sides of the relationship, it can be hard to tell just who is doing the significant changing, each often blaming the other for becoming harder to adjust to.

Like poet T. S. Eliot said, "In a world of fugitives, the person taking the opposite direction can appear to run away." So, who has become more distant, more difficult in the relationship, and who needs to be more understanding? Before blaming the adult child for some estrangement or rift, parents need to inventory their own role in whatever is going on. "Maybe we could have been more accepting of his breakup and more welcoming of his new romance."

Come young adulthood, the adult child and parent relationship must continue to redefine. As the young adult becomes more focused on personal life than family life, parents find themselves living at more of a social and emotional distance. Now parents become more of a peripheral concern for a young person who is focused on building an independent life. And when a significant partnership develops or results in marriage, parents become further demoted in the adult child's personal priorities of caring and attention, even more so when that adult child becomes a parent with a family of her or his own. In the face of this reality, it's important for parents to remember that becoming less of a priority in the adult child's life does not betoken a loss of love. New caring connections simply take more time and precedence.

Change keeps reinvigorating life, upsetting and resetting the terms of everyone's existence, and their relationships. On each side, the transitional demands created by change require constant accommodation: from old to new, from same to different, from familiar to unfamiliar, from known to unknown, from welcome to unwelcome. Parents must continue to be able to dance with the adult child's changes as they did with the adolescent's changes. They must remember: Parenting an adolescent is not about getting the adult child they ideally want so much as loving the grown person they actually get; just as the grown child is tasked with loving the actual parents she or he has been given and not the perfect parents that were wanted. Each side must settle with and accept reality.

When parents won't grow with changes made in their adult child's life, refusing to adjust to, and accept, what can feel difficult at first, hurt and estrangement can often result. As the young person's alterations do not fit important expectations such as predictions, ambitions, or conditions to which parents hold steadfastly, even loss of the relationship can follow.

At such times, it can be worth it for parents to remember that many unexpected changes in the adult child's life must be encompassed in the unforeseen years ahead. The rule seems to be that once a parent, always a parent. As one's adult child grows through life, parents can grow with them, learning from the next generation of human experience and cheering them on. And at the end, life can come full circle: first the old care-take the young, then the young care-take the old.

The question that prompted this book was "Who stole my child?" By now, hopefully the reader's answer is "Nobody did." The process of growth is responsible because it begins with the separation from childhood and ends with the empty nest. Adolescence necessarily entails loss. This is the price that must be paid for rearing a young person to independence. In parenting, life seems to proceed evenly, at first giving a child into their care with one hand, at last taking the young adult from their care with the other.

## ALSO BY CARL PICKHARDT, PHD

*Surviving Your Child's Adolescence: How to Understand, and Even Enjoy, the Rocky Road to Independence.* San Francisco: Jossey-Bass/Wiley, 2013.

*Boomerang Kids: Why Our Children Are Failing on Their Own.* Naperville, IL: Sourcebooks, 2011.

*Why Good Kids Act Cruel: The Hidden Truth about the Pre-Teen Years.* Naperville, IL: Sourcebooks, 2010.

*Stop the Screaming: Turning Conflict into Positive Communication.* London: Palgrave Macmillan, 2009.

*The Future of Your Only Child: How to Guide Your Child to a Happy and Successful Life.* London: Palgrave Macmillan, 2008.

*The Connected Father: Fathering Adolescents.* London: Palgrave Macmillan, 2007.

*The Everything Parent's Guide to Children and Divorce: Reassuring Advice to Help Your Family Adjust.* Avon, MA: Adams Media, 2005.

*The Everything Parent's Guide to the Strong-Willed Child: An Authoritative Guide to Raising a Respectful, Cooperative, and Positive Child.* Avon, MA: Adams Media, 2005.

*The Everything Parent's Guide to Positive Discipline: Professional Advice for Raising a Well-behaved Child.* Avon, MA: Adams Media: 2004.

*Keys to Developing Your Child's Self-Esteem*. Hauppauge, NY: Barron's, 2000.

*Keys to Raising a Drug-Free Child*. Hauppauge, NY: Barron's, 1999.

*Keys to Parenting the Only Child*. Hauppauge, NY: Barron's, 1997.

*Keys to Successful Step-Fathering*. Hauppauge, NY: Barron's, 1997, revised 2010.

*The Case of the Scary Divorce* (children's novel): Washington DC: Magination Press, The American Psychological Association, 1997.

*Keys to Single Parenting*. Hauppauge, NY: Barron's, 1996.

*Parenting the Teenager* (Austin American Statesman columns). Self-published, 1983.

A complete list of Dr. Pickhardt's books, including works of fiction and illustrated psychology, may be found on his website, www.carlpickhardt.com.

* Some books in translation in the following languages: Chinese, French, Arabic, Spanish, and Korean.